Rhys, Stead, Lessing,
and the
Politics of Empathy

EVERYWOMAN
Studies in History,
Literature, and Culture

Susan Gubar and Joan Hoff-Wilson
General Editors

RHYS, STEAD, LESSING, AND THE POLITICS OF EMPATHY

JUDITH KEGAN GARDINER

INDIANA UNIVERSITY PRESS
Bloomington and Indianapolis

Manufactured in the United States of America

Library of Congress Cataloging-in-Publication Data

Gardiner, Judith Kegan.
Rhys, Stead, Lessing and the politics of empathy.

(Everywoman : studies in history, literature, and culture)
Bibliography: p.
Includes index.
1. English fiction—Women authors—History and criticism.   2. English fiction—20th century—History and criticism.   3. Women and literature—Great Britain—History—20th century.   4. Rhys, Jean, 1890–1979—Criticism and interpretation.   5. Stead, Christina, 1902–1983 —Criticism and interpretation.   6. Lessing, Doris May, 1919–   —Criticism and interpretation.   7. Empathy in literature.   I. Title.   II. Series: Everywoman.

Library of Congress Cataloging-in-Publication Data

PR116.G37   1989   820'.9'9287   88–45460
ISBN 0–253–35010–7
ISBN 0–253–20498–4 (pbk.)

1 2 3 4 5 93 92 91 90 89

*For my daughters, Viveca and Carita Gardiner
and my mother, Esther O. Kegan*

CONTENTS

ACKNOWLEDGMENTS

For acts of good will, criticism, and support, I thank Jonathan Arac, Noel Barker, Lynda Boose, Susan Gubar, John Edward Hardy, Marianne Hirsch, and Leah Marcus.

For tough and helpful readings over many years, I am especially grateful to Elizabeth Abel, John Huntington, and Linda Williams, exemplary friends and scholars.

I thank the Humanities Institute of the University of Illinois at Chicago for research time, the Newberry Library in Chicago for carrel space, and two anonymous sources for information about Christina Stead in California.

For permission to quote brief passages from the unpublished works of Jean Rhys, I thank Sidney F. Huttner, Curator, Special Collections, McFarlin Library, University of Tulsa. For permission to use passages from my previously-published essays, I thank the editors of John Hopkins University Press, *Studies in Short Fiction*, *Tulsa Studies in Women's Literature*, and the University of North Carolina Press.

Rhys, Stead, Lessing,
and the
Politics of Empathy

I

INTRODUCTION

This book began with the question of what characterizes writing by women. As an American feminist critic and a mother of daughters, I was attracted to theories of female bonding as a source for female creativity, and my first answer to that question was in the form of a metaphor: the hero is her author's daughter. This metaphor locates the distinctive aspect of women's writing in the author's relationships with her characters, relationships analogous to those that women form with other important women in their lives. It suggests that literary "identifications" between a woman writer, her autobiographical heroes, and her readers are analogous to psychological identifications between mothers and daughters, and, because it is a cross-generational analogy, it also implies a temporal dynamic: if the literary hero is not merely some aspect of a writer's self, but resembles a daughter, then literary relationships are necessarily historical ones.

Once I began to study the interrelations among women writers, their characters, and their readers, however, I realized that my original question was too broad and my original answer, too narrow. The category of "writing by women" implies a false universal, unmodified by history, culture, or differences among women, and the metaphoric answer related only to women's psychology, and only to one aspect of that. I decided to focus on three twentieth-century authors—Jean Rhys (1890–1979), Christina Stead (1902–1983), and Doris Lessing (1919–). These three writers, all remarkably long-lived and productive, are idiosyncratic originals. Each has a powerful and distinctive literary voice, and the three together represent a wide range of modern English fiction by women. I thought that all three were undervalued and their works worthy of sustained attention. In the course of surveying these three authors' works, my "maternal metaphor" sometimes proved useful, a "heuristic tool for reworking images and meanings" or an "enabling mythology," but sometimes limiting and inadequate (Stanton 174). My interest in psychology then led me to the concept of empathy, a concept often associated with women, yet one denoting that bridging of differences between self and other, including gender differences, that makes fictional representation possible. The most distinctive characteristics of women's literature, I found, lay not in specialized content, style, or images in women's writing but in the entire ensemble of gendered relationships among a writer, her texts, and her readers, a model for which is empathetic engagement. Analyzing these three writers' works in some detail led me once again to theorize about women's relations to literary works, in comparison with other women's and with men's. These theories conclude the study.

Like all interpretive choices, mine are political as well as esthetic. The concepts I return to are empathy, history, and identity or the self. These concepts may be roughly associated with three disparate approaches to literature—those of American feminist psychoanalysis, of English materialism, and of the French poststructuralist attack on identity. In trying to put these concepts into fruitful juxtaposition, I am also attempting to forge a critical technique that can use the insights of these approaches without parochialisms, though my attitude to the first two is more cooperative and to the third, more contentious. The "politics of empathy" extends from my model of literary relationships to my goals as a critic, hoping to engage my readers, too, in a process of critical collaboration.

The concept of empathy has come to prominence in contemporary "mothering theory," a reformulation of object relations psychoanalysis that purports to be truer to women's experience than orthodox Freudian psychoanalysis. This theory deduces female personality structure from the relationship between mothers and daughters (Chodorow, Dinnerstein, Gilligan). Nancy Chodorow argues that women's personalities develop in identification with their mothers through strong early bonds whose pleasures are so compelling that women throughout their lives yearn for maternal nurturance and learn to give it to children, men, and other women. Comfortably intimate with others, women are so profoundly interdependent with one another, especially their mothers and daughters, that their identities may seem to merge into one another. In this theory the fluid nature of female personality arises specifically from the mother's relationship with her daughter, a relationship that is fundamentally empathic and one that fosters the development of empathy. Contending against traditionally negative psychoanalytic assessements of female personality, contemporary mothering theorists may instead idealize women's traits, and they thus tend to sentimentalize empathy as loving and nurturant understanding.

A more balanced and workable definition is that employed by self psychologists: empathy "is a value-neutral tool of observation. . . . We define it as 'vicarious introspection' or, more simply, as one person's (attempt to) experience the inner life of another while simultaneously retaining the stance of an objective observer" (Kohut *How Does Analysis Cure* 174–75). Empathy in twentieth-century Western culture has become a specially marked female trait, cognitive as well as affective, and potentially either good or ill, compassionate or manipulative and intrusive. It is not an intuitive natural capacity but one formed through experience and capable of training and development, a training currently more common among women than men. I hypothesize that contemporary women's literary relationships, too, are likely to be characterized by empathizing as expressed through various configurations of narrative voice, narrative structure, and literary identifications, although modern women's ambivalence about autonomy also leads to ambivalent but powerful responses to mergers with other women's writing.

There is a danger, however, in separating empathy from history and allocating the former to women, the latter to men, as some "mothering" theorists seem to do (Chodorow, Dinnerstein). These theorists imply that women become their mothers, endlessly duplicating the same natural cycles, while men make changes and dominate the earth. History includes both the sum of past human experiences and our changing constructions of the past, constructions that may vary according to the interpreter's gender, culture, and other circumstances. Judith Newton and Deborah Rosenfelt caution us not to see history as "an assortment of facts in a linear arrangement, not as a static tale of the unrelieved oppression of women or of their unalleviated triumphs, but as a process of transformation" in which cultural productions are contradictory and in which "ideological struggle and social change" are possible (xxiii).

The concept of the "self" is even more slippery than the concepts of empathy or history. Its usages sometimes overlap those of the person as a whole material being, or the subject of a discourse, or a person's self-image or "identity," where identity refers to both a core configuration of personal character and one's consciousness of that configuration (Erikson *Identity and the Life Cycle* 116). Although antihumanist critics consider identity a bourgeois illusion, Elaine Showalter sees "a search for identity" as the main theme of women's literature since 1920 (*Literature of Their Own* 13), and Barbara Christian asserts that a desire "to change our societies" sent her on "a search for the development of the self" in Afro-American women's literature (171). According to self psychologists, "The self is not a thing or an entity; it is a concept; a symbolic abstraction from the developmental process. The self refers to the uniqueness that separates the experiences of an individual from those of all others while at the same time conferring a sense of cohesion and continuity on the disparate experiences of that individual throughout . . . life" (Basch 53). Depending on a person's developmental experiences, the sense of a cohesive self may or may not develop, and many twentieth-century people experience themselves as split, fragmented, or alienated. Polly Young-Eisendrath and James Hall highlight the provisional, even literary aspects of the concept of self in calling it "a representational unity," "a pretext" through which we "construct life histories and pose questions of meaning." "The self as pretext can then be seen as shared reality, founded on linguisticality and desire for continuity, rather than primarily on experiences of integrity, intentionality, or agency." This "pretextual account of self" "relies primarily on a particular telling of self" and is therefore allied with narrative (6–7). Thus the concept of the self, like that of gender, need not imply "essentialism": there are no fixed essences in persons or in gender unmediated by historical factors.

I chose three writers as the subjects of this study because one or two seemed too few to establish any meaningful generalizations or sense of variety. I chose no more because three is the most I could handle while attending to their full chronological development, and these three because they are major authors whom I admire. Although two of the three have died, this approach assumes that the concept of the woman writer is not yet dead. "How we sign or designate ourselves," Mary Ann Caws reminds us, "comes sooner or later to bear on whatever it is we think of ourselves as bringing forth"; "what we look like and write like and speak like depends on how we know," and "not always, but often, male and female knowledge differ in kind and result" (44). Moreover, the dangers attributed to the patriarchal idea of authority diminish in the case of female authors who have been historically undervalued. Nancy K. Miller argues, "the post-modernist decision that the Author is dead . . . does not necessarily work for women and prematurely forecloses the question of identity for them" (106). I invite my readers to join me in attending to these authors, rather than, as some contemporary critics do, disabling them so that the only human authority in the critical text becomes the critic's own authority.

By studying three authors' canons, I try to overcome the current dichotomy in literary studies. This exists between life-and-works monographs with their rich but narrow particularity and global theoretical essays that may ignore history altogether or replace it with allegorized textual fragments, with tomograms computed from intersecting discourses, or with the generalized accomplishments of generations. Instead, I chart the histories through which three authors differently interpret their particular twentieth-century contexts. These contexts include the pressures that the authors' lives, political theories, and past works place on works in progress. To see the author's life and former works as part of each fiction's context, however, does not mean accepting these self-consciously self-presenting women as the sole authorities about their fictions.

The body of this book studies the fiction of three authors, devoting a chapter to each writer. Because they track development, these chapters highlight first and last works and authorial revisions. Rhys describes feminine consciousness in an elegant style, but her work appears static and claustrophobic to those who deplore her repeated portraits of female victims. I argue, however, that the texts vary in the relationships they establish among the narrator, the characters, and the reader. Taking gender as a fundamental category in the construction of her fictional world, Rhys opposes empathy to exclusion, and the history of her short fiction lies in its own development of empathy.

In contrast, Stead criticizes modern capitalism in loose, unwieldly polemics, positing class as her primary social category and opposing narcissism to empathy. She uses many male protagonists, and her female heroes often seem male-identified. Thus a critique involving theories about female psychology would seem to fit Rhys neatly but balk at Stead. Whereas feminist critics have simply avoided much of Stead's work, concentrating on a few autobiographical fictions, I explicate the full range of her writing. That a woman writer in patriarchal culture would develop strategies for becoming "male identified" is understandable, but such strategies can be understood fully only through the interactions between her known femaleness and cultural constructions of identity. The utopian fantasy of male bonding in her brilliant satire on banking, *House of All Nations*, for example, is a woman's fantasy completely untroubled by the psychology of male homophobia. To appreciate Stead's work, it is necessary to empathize with her politics, revealing the emotional dynamics that public institutions and ideologies create in people of differing social classes.

Lessing's prolific and diverse short stories follow what she called her "masculine" and "feminine" lines, yet race, not gender or class, is her basic category for understanding otherness as she opposes empathy to domination. Although she is hardly a neglected writer, her short fiction has received surprisingly little critical attention, and it includes some of her most accomplished work. Problems arise when she estranges empathy from history; on the other hand, her fiction sometimes implies that empathy is necessary to change history and that fiction is the means by which we can be changed so that we are capable of changing the world.

After separate analyses of the three authors, I turn to explicit comparison in a chapter devoted to their "masterpieces," the novels by which each writer is likely to be best known—Rhys's *Wide Sargasso Sea*, Stead's *The Man Who Loved Children*, and Lessing's *The Golden Notebook*. Virginia Woolf initiated feminist rethinking of the "masterpiece" in stating that "masterpieces are not single and solitary births; they are the outcome of many years of thinking in common" (68). In this chapter I suggest that these three mid-century novels take varying strategies with reference to literary traditions, adopting, respectively, the position of mother's daughter, father's son, and self-originating child, in order to resolve a common conundrum about female identity in the period between the second and third waves of Western feminism.

In conclusion, I return to the question of what characterizes writing by twentieth-century women, offering a model that adapts concepts from Heinz Kohut's historically-sensitive self psychology. This model uses the multiple positions of "narcissistic transferences" as analogies for the many kinds of relationships people establish with literary texts and suggests how these relationships are likely to be gender-inflected for contemporary English-speaking writers and readers. Sandra Gilbert and Susan Gubar describe Virginia Woolf's *"fantasy* about a utopian linguistic structure—a woman's sentence" as a disguised effort "to revise not woman's language but woman's relation to language" (*No Man's Land* 230). On such gendered relationships to literature my speculations focus. In this scheme, empathetic engagement becomes one possibility among others, typical of but not exclusive to women.

The politics of empathy favor multiple possibilities rather than binary polarizations. One such exaggerated polarization sees writing practices as completely retrogressive if they appeal to feminist humanism's aspirations for freedom and fulfillment within community and only revolutionary if they discard our entire current mental and linguistic apparatus. Hélène Cixous inspires women by claiming that "a feminine text cannot fail to be more than subversive. It is volcanic" and aims "to smash everything"; "writing is precisely *the very possibility of change* . . . the space that can serve as a spring board for subversive thought, the precursory movement of a transformation of social and cultural structures" (888, 879). Not only writers but also readers, I contend, may open spaces for "subversive thought," and not only avant-garde writers but also relatively conventional twentieth-century women writers like Rhys, Stead, and Lessing, who, in partial and exploratory ways that should not be dismissed simply because they are so, expose social injustices and encourage social and cultural transformations. Thus a politics of empathy points to strategies for engagement across difference, accessible to men as well as to women and hopeful of bridging the gaps between reading and writing, teaching and criticism, and representation and action.

Jean Rhys is often considered the paradigmatic portrayer of "feminine consciousness" (Staley 19). Her short short story "On Not Shooting Sitting Birds" may be read as a parable about female creativity as it is shaped in a patriarchal culture, that is, as a parable about the sexual, and therefore gendered, core of female fiction making. It exemplifies women's muted representation within the dominant culture and the late Victorian "female aesthetic" characterized by psychological polarization between the sexes (Showalter "*Feminist Criticism in the Wilderness* " 262; *Literature of Their Own* 240–42). The story can also be read in terms of women's relation to history and of the woman writer's relation to her characters and her audience; my analysis will open out from close explication to the story's historical and psychological contexts. The subsequent investigation of twentieth-century women's writing will expand from this one short story to other fiction by Rhys and also by Stead and Lessing, looking at chronological changes within each writer's work.

In "On Not Shooting Sitting Birds," 1976, a first person narrator recounts an incident in which she picks up a young man who interested her; looking forward to their date, she buys some new silk underwear. They have dinner in a restaurant "with a bedroom very obvious in the background" (*Sleep It Off, Lady*, cited hereafter as *Sleep* 94). The atmosphere is strained; the young man can't figure her out. She distracts him by telling him a story about hunting while she remembers the real event set in her West Indian childhood. A *faux pas* in the story shocks him, and he takes her home barely speaking to her. Although under nine hundred words long, Rhys's story is a rich meditation on the differences between men's and women's experiences, values, stories, and ways of story-telling.

The story's title is awkward, dichotomous, and negative. It prepares us for a story that polarizes male and female language and desire. Like many essays in the Western tradition of authoritative male discourse, it begins with "on," though "not" immediately reverses the sound and the conviction of certainty. The action of "shooting" in our culture connotes man the hunter, the he-man, perhaps the sexual predator as well, since the Freudian equation of gun and phallus is so widely accepted. Thus the words "on not shooting" might introduce a feminist protest against male sexuality as male violence, even though no shooting is actually described in the story, which explores the meanings of holding fire with regard to both sex and narrative. "Shooting" implies representation as well as killing, as in shooting a photograph, a connotation enhanced by the word "sitting," since one sits for portraits. "Sitting birds, " like sitting ducks, are easy victims, passive prey, and in British slang "birds" are women, so that the story's title might be read as an instruction not to take advantage of women.

The central incident of the story is ambiguous about who is taking advantage of whom, although it is clear that women and men live under different sets of rules that it is to men's advantage to enforce. The stiff young man grows colder and stiffer when he can't categorize the woman's social and therefore her moral status. By assenting to the compromising tryst, she appears to be sexually available; however, he can't decide the value that this availability has to him unless he knows her social placement: "But you're a lady, aren't you?" he asks in confusion (94).

The young man can't place the woman; the woman doesn't know much about the young man. A colonial, she has formed her ideas about English tastes and values by reading novels, which lead her to believe that hunting always interests Englishmen. Therefore she decides to fill in the awkward silences by telling the young man a story about hunting in the tropics. She does not reveal to us readers the fiction that she invents to distract or seduce him. Instead, she recounts "the real thing," "the genuine shooting party," which presumably underlies the version she elaborates for him (95). She remembers that when she was a girl, she straggled through the forest behind her brothers. She says she joined their expedition because she "couldn't bear to be left out of anything," but she was afraid of the gun's noise and therefore hid before the actual kill (96). Nevertheless, she apparently describes a kill for the young man, since he interrupts her story: " 'Do you mean to say that your brothers shot sitting birds?' His voice was cold and shocked" (96). The honor of the sporting kill is at stake. If her brothers did not follow the hunting code of English gentlemen, presumably they are not themselves gentlemen, and then their sister is no lady. If she is not a lady, she becomes merely a sitting bird, no longer a desirable quarry. His snobbish discomfort with her indecorous story extinguishes her desire and thus silences her. "But by this time I wasn't sure that I liked him at all so I was silent. . . . " The dinner ends without a seduction and with almost no further conversation:

> It was a most uncomfortable dinner. We both avoided looking at the bedroom and when the last mouthful was swallowed he announced that he was going to take me home. . . . Neither of us spoke in the taxi except to say, "Well, good-night." "Good-night" (96–97).

The narrator describes herself as sensuous, spontaneous, fluent, and cowardly. She describes the young man as stiff and snobbish, tied to a male code of honor that values killing for sport and properly conducted seductions. He plays by the rules and rejects her when she does not know what they are, and these rules seem to exclude and oppress her as a colonial and as a woman. She characterizes the fiction she tells him as lies, and these lies mediate between the uncontrollable, autonomous forces of female memory and desire and the patriarchal social conventions that seek to control them. At the end of the incident, the sex remains unconsummated, the shooting unheard, and her story, untold: "I felt regretful when it came to taking off my lovely pink chemise, but I could still think: some other night perhaps, another sort of man. I slept at once (97)." The hero ends asleep and alone, yet her retreat is strategic, not final. From memory she moves to hope, and she refuses to refuse to desire. Rhys encourages us to share that desire by a final narrative tease in which a young woman removes her underwear to reveal, not a female body, but instead a woman thinking about her future.

As a parable about female creativity, the story illustrates wider possibilities for the female artist than those available to its hero. In telling her story through the narrator as she does, Rhys does not expose women's secrets. Rather, she splits the story's audience between a conventional male within the frame, who can be distracted if not seduced with lies based upon the tradition of male literature, and us readers. In the central incident, the narrator tells the man the lie we don't hear and us the "true" story that he interrupts.

The story's awkward, negative title fits the frustration and incompletion throughout the narrative, which seems to be about how not to do something—how not to hunt, how not to seduce a young man. On the other hand, we might read the tale as the successful story of how a woman can avoid seduction and of how she can preserve herself from lethal male codes by telling stories. By both telling and withholding her story, Rhys solves a paradox created by the polarizing female esthetic, and she does not reveal the secret sources of female creativity to the dominant culture. Nonetheless, she manages to tell the truth about female experience; it is this truth, she implies, that renders a woman's text valuable (Gardiner "The Grave").

We can read this story as a demonstration of a specific, late Victorian esthetic based on polarized assumptions about female superiority to male values and also, more generally, as an artistic expression of female desire muted by the dominant male culture. These readings generalize from one historical interpretation of the text, but ignore others. For example, we might see in the story the class and gender conflicts of British Imperialism around the start of World War I, the "rules of the game" that the war will disrupt, and the psychological conflicts engendered by the Victorian patriarchal family, for example the split between desirable, debased women and beloved, respectable women that Freud describes men experiencing as a result of oedipal conflicts ("Special type" 1910).

Time and memory are introduced as themes in the story from the first paragraph, though it has few overt historical markers. It begins in an unspecified present and looks back.

> There is no control over memory. Quite soon you find yourself being vague about an event which seemed so important at the time that you thought you'd never forget it. Or unable to recall the face of someone whom you could have sworn was there for ever. On the other hand, trivial and meaningless memories may stay with you for life (93).

What is so important at the time turns out not to be so important judged by this uncontrollable, irrational faculty of memory; we often remember trivial rather than significant things. The central incident of the story concerns the control of desire rather than the insubordination of memory, but the frame tends to conflate memory and desire, so that we see the way that sexual and class relations affect both. Moreover, our conventions about reading forbid us to find anything "meaningless" or "trivial" in a story this brief. We assume that every detail has a significance that will reverberate throughout the story. What the narrator says about memory, then, and what we expect from stories like the one we are reading set up a friction. The narrator gives us exemplary "trivial and meaningless" memories, which lead to the anecdote about the young man and in which we are teased to find the meaning and importance:

> I can still shut my eyes and see Victoria grinding coffee on the pantry steps, the glass bookcase and the books in it, my father's pipe-rack, the leaves of the sandbox tree, the wallpaper of the bedroom in some shabby hotel, the hairdresser in Antibes. It's in this way that I remember buying the pink milanese silk underclothes. . . . (93)

The narrator shuts her eyes, like a child, to recall these scenes apparently from her childhood, a bourgeois, colonial, and comfortable time. The woman on the pantry steps, probably a servant, is eponymous with an age. The household is not only well off, but it is also cultured; at least its glass bookcase contains books, and the father's pipe rack connotes middle-class male leisure. From the house, the narrator's chain of memories moves to the sandbox tree, with its associations with childhood play and exotic climates, then away from the comforts of home to a shabby hotel and resort town where the narrator is no longer servanted and well off. Thus these "meaningless" memories in free association unfold the story of the narrator's life as one of exile and downward class mobility.

The central anecdote expands our sense of the historical forces at play as this woman meets this man: capitalism, colonialism, and perhaps war and the sexual revolution as well; the years preceding World War I saw increased suffrage militancy and the beginning of new attitudes toward sexuality that would appear in the work of Lawrence, Joyce, and other modernists. The narrator's desirability to the man depends on her class status: is she a lady or a whore? She may be either one, and the man will know how to treat her, but at the same time he insists that the question "are you a lady" has a simple yes or no answer that will categorize her completely. However, as a colonial, her class value is uncertain; West Indian hunting may not follow English codes. Her sexual conduct is also anomalous to him.

The narrator's memory begins, it seems, in Freud's time in a secure bourgeois patriarchal household, then moves to the disconcerting world of the twentieth-century sexual revolution. The narrator is a "sitting bird" in a sexual transaction, agreeing to a tryst whose conclusion seems fore-known and complicitly making herself a commodity or fetish for the affair by packaging herself in new silk underwear. Yet she does not see herself as a passive object of male desire, but rather as a desiring subject. She represents her psychology, too, not as that of a prostitute or sexual pro-letarian but as that of an enterprising individual. "I had few acquaintances and no close friends," she explains. "It was perhaps in reaction against the inevitable loneliness of my life that I'd find myself doing bold, risky, even outrageous things without hestitation or surprise" (94). She is not enmeshed in a family, not a housewife or mother. From this position of personal isolation, she becomes a bold risk-taker, acquiring the kind of personality appropriate for a capitalist entrepreneur. She is a woman with limited capital: the only asset she owns to speculate with is her sexuality, yet it is speculation, not forced sale. She is not a public woman, a prostitute who must sell her body to live. By taking her to the sort of establishment he does, the young man implies that if he pays for her dinner, she should repay him in the bed. But the narrator, her desire, and her underwear are hers to spend or reserve as she wishes.

This historical reading offers some additional insights on the story over the prior reading in terms of the female esthetic, but it, too, has its limi-tations. The story contains few direct historical allusions: the restaurant-hotel resembles a similar establishment in Rhys's story "Till September Petronella," which takes place in 1914. The vignettes of the narrator's West Indian childhood, with their paper-loaded guns, hark back to the Victorian era. Yet the story, one of Rhys's latest, most condensed efforts, was written in the 1970s and published in 1976. Thus the tale is set over sixty years before its time of composition. In reading the story in its historical context, then, we need to think not only of the colonialism, imperialism, and sexism of the era between 1890 and 1914, but also of the possibilities made available to the author because she wrote the story in the 1970s rather than earlier. For one thing, the narrator expects her readers to accept her as a woman who picks up men and who buys underwear so that she will be well dressed to undress, not to reject her categorically on the basis of a sexual double standard. But the relationship between the reader and the narrator is more complex than one of acceptance or rejection based on the narrator's implied morals. Like the young man, we wonder if the narrator is a "lady." We are even more likely to wonder what are the sexual conventions that are supposed to apply in the situation described to us. The story may have the effect, then, on its 1970s or later readers of causing us to speculate on the nature of the "sexual revolution" and what it meant for whom. Retrospectively, the story might encourage one to read the sexual revolution as not so revolutionary after all, but instead as merely a minor readjustment of patriarchal Victorian conventions.

Besides the historical placement of the text in terms of its setting and its date of composition, the text also has its own history. An earlier draft of the story is more explicit about the narrator's sexual initiative:

> "This happened," she said, "during my reckless period when I was ready for anything that seemed at all exciting. I would allow myself to be picked up, sometimes in the street, sometimes in a park. I decided very quickly who I'd allow to speak to me. I had only one qualification. Did he, by his voice, his clothes, his walk, in any way whatsoever remind me of the one I thought I loved so much?" (Tulsa typescript Oct. 20, 1974)

Rhys's revision of this passage is perhaps designed to make the narrator more sympathetic, less aggressive, and less the compulsive or sentimental repeater of another sexual story. The earlier version does not include the narrator's framing memories but instead plunges right into the anecdote about her encounter with the young man. That anecdote elegantly allegorizes women's creative if muted responses to male dominance; however, it says nothing about female bonding or mother-daughter relations. These themes do glimmer, at least, through the frame that Rhys later drew around the story.

The first words of the published story are, "there is no control over memory." If "control" names a typical male issue, memory recalls the maternal, originating in and returning back to the reign of the childhood mother. Presumably one memory of an earlier, better time is the memory of the preoedipal mother, of early feeding and fusion, the environment in which the child's identity first forms. Although the narrator's mother is not mentioned in the story, it does whisper a nostalgia for lost origins and better times, for a maternal home. A sign of memory's deviousness, the narrator says, is that one can't "recall the face of someone you could have sworn was there for ever." Our first memory, our first act of recognition, presumably, centers on the mother's face. Here the narrator says that face cannot be named or called back; one's own words, even sworn ones, are powerless against this absence. Moreover, the sense of danger and loss to a maternal figure is perhaps compounded by the connotations of the story's title, since the "sitting birds" that may not be shot sound like brooding hens.

Although the narrator's mother is absent, her place is filled by a warm maternal presence in the narrator's first memory, the servant Victoria grinding coffee on the pantry steps, starting the day with a comfortable and nurturing routine that evokes childhood sights, smells, and sounds. The narrator expresses both her original security and its loss in claiming, "I had started out in life trusting everyone and now I trusted no one" (93). Basic trust, according to Erikson, is the necessary prerequisite to the formation of a self; it is the first goal of the infant's development, and it depends— in societies in which women rear children—on a supportive maternal atmosphere (Erikson *Childhood and Society*). The narrator has achieved that first stage of inner security, and though her life later degenerates, this trust stands her in good stead. At the end of the story, she can still look forward to "some other night perhaps, another sort of man" (97).

This reading is congruent with current French-based theories that see the feminine as the silent suppressed childhood memory of maternal plenitude that cannot be fully expressed in the paternal realm of symbolic discourse (see Garner, Kahane, Sprengnether 22–23). Although the overtly maternal is absent from the story, one might say its hero acts like her author's daughter, not merely because she is more than a generation younger but rather because the narrator steps into the vacant maternal position to instruct us daughterly readers in catching men and in avoiding harm. She encourages us to treat her young hero as she does, with compassionate empathy and also with detachment.

Any one text offers pools of possibilities to stare into, but if we do so, like all narcissists, we face the danger of looking only at our own reflections, no matter what the nature of the pond. Thus it is necessary to move beyond a paradigmatic case, to anchor women's texts in full and various contexts— the contexts of the women's lives and works, their ideologies, and their historical cultures.

Rhys, Stead, and Lessing offer enough points of similarity to be comparable, yet are diverse enough to force our theories to acknowledge them in their distinct and changing specificities. Besides their writing longevity and esthetic merit, these three writers have in common being colonials, more particularly being born at the periphery of the English empire—Rhys in Dominica, the West Indies; Stead in Australia; and Lessing in Persia, now Iran, from which her family moved five years later to Rhodesia, now Zimbabwe. As young women, each of the three left a colonial home traditional in its sex roles for England, which promised a freer personal life and the chance to be an artist—Rhys at age sixteen in 1907; Stead at twenty-six in 1928; Lessing at thirty in 1949; Stead and Lessing arrived in London wanting to be writers; Rhys trained as an actor first.

For the colonial woman writer of the colonizing race and class, the exile that sends her from the colony to the cultural center must always be profoundly ambiguous. The three writers are shaped by parallel and paradoxical forces that may be represented by the words "home" and "exile." These words signify the writers' ambivalence because they grew up in contexts in which "home," for some purposes, meant England, not the nation in which they were raised. Because England was unknown to them and alien to their immediate experiences, these writers were able to see English culture critically and to feel its domination as arbitrary, unjust, and foreign. At the same time that they grew up with adults who thought of "home" as elsewhere, their own family homes were places of confinement and restraint for them as girls; they were expected to grow up as lady-like participants in white English culture. "Home" was therefore a trap from which they had to escape as well as an implied goal. Like the conventional hero of the *bildungsroman*, each woman travelled from her provincial backwater to the more appreciative, more cosmopolitan, more diverse center, to London (see Abel, Hirsch, Langland 7–8). To be exiled from the periphery to the center of one's culture is not the traditional meaning of exile, yet these writers do not define this center as "home" either: neither place is home; each is alternatively desirable and oppressive. This situation heightens their resistance to the sentimental claims of the home canon, country, and culture. As admiring and resentful foreigners, as colonials, they can see English culture as a dominating discourse imposed upon their creativity, at the same time that it enables that creativity by freeing them from psychological entrapment within home as the family of origin. In short, what being a colonial-in-exile does for these three women is put into play an oscillation whereby no place is home; home is ambiguous and ambivalent, here and elsewhere, and so there remains always a missing point of origin in their works, a fruitful unsettledness that makes the three women simultaneously inheritors and antagonists to imperialism rather than self-sufficient local colonists or comfortable, controlling citizens of a global village. For all three, the English literary tradition is the reassuring heritage of a mother tongue, but it is also somewhat alien, shadowy, and duplicitous. Moreover, and more simply, their situation between cultures helps them recognize that personal circumstances are inevitably politically charged and that the family is a political institution (see Heilbrun 49). They record their cultural circumstances in psychologically-specific ways and read their individual psychological dramas as part of larger cultural forces. They perceive home—in both directions—as periphery and center, as individual colonial family and as dominant culture—as a site of oppression in which they learn to articulate that oppression.

Lessing's parents were English, her father an eager, her mother a reluctant exile from English middle class work and social codes. Rhys's father was Welsh although her mother's Creole family dated back in the West Indies for generations, for enough generations, in fact, to have been prominent slaveholders. Stead's grandfather had emigrated from England, and the family preserved his myth about his travels, in which Dickens's *Great Expectations*, with its suddenly wealthy transported convict, inspired him to set out young and alone to make his fortune in Australia. Thus all three women grew up in homes that paid homage to the "home" of the dominant culture and literary canon, and they therefore did not identify the familial home that they wanted to escape with the physical place that they lived, but instead with their families' internalization of the values of the home-country, values that seemed meretricious to them because they were incongruent with their direct experiences of the resident country, a locale which they could romanticize but which they could not assimilate as truly "home," as truly their own.

A Lessing short story vividly illustrates these ambiguities of "home" and "exile" and the psychological tensions created for the white colonial girl by living within these ambiguities. Adolescence is the time in which girls confront society's expectations for them and its confusions about female sexuality, and often the time at which girls rebel against their mothers as the enforcers of these patriarchal social expectations (see O'Rourke). The narrator of "Flavours of Exile," 1957, is an unnamed twelve-year-old girl who is unimpressed with the English tinned foods her parents eat "with a truly religious emotion" and a shared "nostalgia" (*African Stories*, cited hereafter as *African*, 576). The adults "agreed that the soil of Africa was unable to grow food that had any taste at all" (576), whereas the narrator finds just the reverse. "Brussels sprouts, cherries, English gooseberries— they were my mother's; they recurred in her talk as often as 'a real London pea-souper,' or 'chestnuts by the fire,' or 'cherry blossom at Kew' " (577). The mother's exile is the child's home; the parent's tastes alien, and their love for things English a lie, as the supposed flavorlessness of the local food is a lie that carries over from fruits and flowers to the parents' other judgements. "I no longer grudged these to her," Lessing's narrator says of her mother's English enthusiasms, not quite accurately, if we judge from the grudging tone of the story; "I listened and was careful not to show that my thoughts were on my own inheritance of veld and sun" (577).

The story associates England or "home" with an inauthentic, nostalgic clinging to dominant values that is inappropriate to the colonial setting, and this "home" is superimposed on the girl's own patriarchal family. The oppressive imposition of adult values on children parallels the impositions of the master culture on the colonial one and is complicated by the imposition of male authority on women. The narrator's active, angry mother resents having moved to accommodate her husband's desire for adventure. She regrets being on an African farm rather than in England or in Persia, where her husband had been "a minor official" and they had lived "among roses and jasmine, walnut trees and pomegranates. But, unfortunately, for too short a time" (577). Therefore she clings to memories of her English garden, her English vegetables and ways of cooking them, even to "the large china vegetable dishes brought from that old house in London." In contrast, she feels her African garden is, like her unwilling life in Africa, a "defeat" (575).

Although the parents' marriage is bitter, the story champions heterosexuality, at least insofar as it poses an adolescent girl's crush on a boy as a liberating stage of growing up. Insofar as identification with her parents' culturally dominant values represents "home" for the narrator, then her heterosexual desire propels her away from home and its values, and the story thus redefines heterosexuality as itself a kind of exile, breaking the dominant culture of home, encouraging motion away from its closed circuit, and therefore enabling art.

The girl enjoys an innocent sensuality with her friend William MacGregor. Under the cape gooseberry bushes, "intoxicated" by the smell, she says, "we would laugh and shout, then quarrel; and William, to make up, shelled a double handful of the fruit and poured it into my skirt and we ate together, pressing the biggest berries on each other" (576). Three years older than she is, William humors the adults by pretending that their bitter brussels sprouts are delicious, and the narrator then emulates this "beautiful lesson in courtesy" by pretending that she, too, likes English foods (577). Suddenly the narrator becomes infatuated with her childhood chum, feeling that he is the answer to all the emotional deficits of her adolescence. She sees "a promise of warmth and understanding I had never known" in his eyes. "It hurt to be shut out from the world of simple kindness he lived in," she thinks, and she daydreams about him until she dwells perpetually in a "marvellous feverish world" (578–79).

This sudden infatuation takes place at the same time that she is trying to identify with her mother's tastes by fostering her mother's sickly pomegranate tree. It not only represents the narrator's effort to unite with her mother but also her adolescent self on the verge of sexual awakening: the tree, she says, "was about my height, a tough, obstinate-looking thing" (578). As its fruit matures, its sexual connotations become more pressing, and she wants her friend William to be present when the fruit bursts: "It seemed as if my whole life was concentrated and ripening with that single fruit" (579). At the same time, the pomegranate becomes associated with the mother, with maternity, and with female sexuality: "the fruit looked lumpy and veined, like a nursing breast" (580). The fruit cracks while it is still on the stalk, and black ants invade the oozing red flesh. When the narrator thinks the pomegranate is finally ripe, she persuades her mother to invite the MacGregors for the occasion. William arrives, looking a bit like the cracked pomegranate himself, his lips "full and thin-skinned" with their "blood, dull and dark around the pale groove" (581). Impervious to her romanticizing him or the fruit, he says the fruit is "bad" and she is "mad" for taking it so seriously, and he hits the tree with a stick so that the pomegranate "exploded in a scatter of crimson seeds, fermenting juice, and black ants" (582). Submissive to this gestured lesson in male sexuality, the narrator feigns unconcern, properly returning to the adults and their colonial teatime.

Like the god of the underworld, the boy separates Proserpine the pomegranate-eater from Ceres her mother, violently breaking the girl's identification with her mother as a sexual, maternal person by breaking her identification with her mother's exotic fruit. At the same time, as in the Proserpine myth, this rupture of the preoedipal mother-daughter bond places the daughter in an oedipal subordination to patriarchal culture and dominant values. Her Eden destroyed, its fruit uneaten, she joins the boy in humoring the adults; she too becomes a grownup, that is, socially-responsible person who hides her feelings and talks in proper clichés. She allows the dominant culture of home and family to define her and her experiences. Although the narrator adapts to her social situation, the story rebels against this conformity by stressing its falseness and the violence needed to bring it about. Morever, it idealizes the girl's frolicking with the boy on the veld; that innocent freedom intimates the possibilities for an authentic response to the nature of the colonized country in contrast to the mother's inauthenticity, her inability to perceive her actual surroundings because of her blinding nostalgia for the "home" country.

This story does not mention the fact that all its characters are whites who impose their culture not merely on a landscape new to them but more seriously on the black people displaced from that land, though Lessing's other African stories fill in this context. Her discontent and alienation, her sense of homelessness, pervade her canon, from the gentle critique of nostalgia in "Flavours of Exile" to the cosmic homelessness of her space fiction. As with Rhys and Stead, this discontent empowers her art. One of the simpler forms that the energies of exile takes is rage against the racist administration of southern Africa. This direct political attack, however, is complicated and deepened by nostalgia for "her" Africa, an Africa that never belonged to her yet whose loss she regrets. Even in "Flavours of Exile," in which the narrator lampoons her mother for enjoying "the language of nostalgia" (576), her own nostalgia exactly parallels her mother's, albeit with the poles of Africa and England reversed. The vegetables from the African vegetable garden, she says, tasted "as I have never found vegetables taste since" (575); thcy form a part of her own "inheritance of veld and sun" (577).

Lessing does not continue to feel her exile as estrangement, however. Despite her childhood rejection of England as part of her mother's stultifying and dead culture, she learns to feel England as home once she lives there. By coming home to England rather than "going home" to Africa, she succeeds where her mother failed; she both repeats her mother's desire and triumphs over her mother in so doing. In a recent essay entitled "Impertinent Daughters," Lessing complains about her mother: "had she, had my father, not escaped from England? Why, then, was she winding me back into that shroud?" (52–53). "I can't put myself in her place. It was the farm, the veld, that she hated, that trapped her. . . . But the farm, the veld, Africa is to me, quite simply, the luckiest thing that ever happened" (68). Thus Lessing uses her African "home" as leverage against the home her mother provided, not a happy home: "my memories of her are all of antagonism, and fighting, and feeling shut out" (61). By returning to England years ahead of her mother, she perhaps succeeds in shutting her mother out—at the same time that she writes celebrations of Africa that confute her mother's tastes. Yet her mother is also responsible for enabling her daughter to write, for endowing her with the dominant culture, especially the English literary canon, as her heritage: "it was my mother who introduced me to the world of literature into which I was about to escape from her" (68).

Writing itself becomes both home and exile for these three writers, marking their displacement from childhood homes but also replacing them with intimate invention, with places of their own. All three authors carried manuscripts around with them for years from country to country. Lessing and Stead brought manuscripts for their first works from the colonies to England; Rhys traveled with story-filled notebooks for decades. Ford Madox Ford's mistress Stella Bowen reminisced about Rhys, "when we met her she possessed nothing but a cardboard suit-case and the astonishing manuscript," which was "an unpublishably sordid novel of great sensitiveness and persuasiveness" (166). Like children's teddy bears, the women's manuscripts remained extensions of themselves that reassured them about home, that *were* their homes, at the same time that within the writing itself the experience of exile could be repeated, reunderstood, and mastered. For each writer, the psychological drama of breaking from an idealized imaginary mother-daughter union into heterosexual adulthood gets conflated with a story of exile, with longings for freedom and yearnings for a maternal home. The apparently universal story of growing up and leaving home reflects each writer's historical and psychological circumstances and acquires specific political reverberations.

History and female psychology, the psychology of empathy, each take a bow, endlessly upstaging each other as we shift the spotlight of our attention, each the explanation in terms of which the other can be constructed. I suggest that for these twentieth-century women writers, empathy is necessary to change history and so establish a meaningful female identity. This "identity" is not bourgeois male autonomy but a concept representing a process, part of which, one's sense of self, may involve a longing for coherence even as it represents itself as divided. Because female identity forms partly through relationships based originally on mother-daughter bonds, it is defined in terms of the world, not merely of the self. Fredric Jameson calls this pervasive but changing external "reality" by the term "history," that which is outside ourselves and resists our desires (102). This history has been a patriarchal one, inhibiting female growth. Therefore this world, this history of gender, class, and race oppressions in which every woman and man lives, must be changed in order that female authenticity—the sense of an identity that respects itself—be possible. Clearly this is a utopian ideal; however, the idea that self and authenticity are meaningless illusions or epiphenomena of discursive practices may itself be seen as a consequence of contemporary alienation. Despite their disclaimers of connection with organized feminism, these three writers are feminists in the specific sense that they perceive women living in a dystopian world, facing problems including that of forming an authentic self, problems not always shared with and sometimes caused by men. The three writers target the causes of oppression differently, and they do not agree on the direction or even the possibility of the changes that would be necessary to liberate women, in part because the history that oppresses women includes its patriarchal ideologies, like those of Freud and Marx, which promise human liberation and which these writers may themselves espouse. Because men and women internalize the values and beliefs that perpetuate sexist oppression, changing these internalized values is one prerequisite for change, although at times Stead and Lessing also believe in the necessity for direct political action. But to change people's minds, new information is not enough; they must be moved to feel the plight of others, especially of the oppressed, as their own. Perhaps more important, they must be moved to see that plight in a way that calls for change. This rhetorical effect implies psychological empathy. For these writers, then, women's fiction becomes a privileged arena for moral action and for creating the psychological prerequisites to historical change. Through their fiction, the authors establish those strategies of identification and distanciation that lead us to empathize with their characters and texts and so to imagine changing their and our social worlds.

II

HISTORICIZING EMPATHY
THE SHORT FICTION OF JEAN RHYS

Dense and allusive like James Joyce, unpretentious like Katherine Mansfield, and passionate like Tillie Olsen, Jean Rhys is a master of the twentieth-century short story, a form she wrote from the 1920s to the 1970s. Long neglected, she is still undervalued for her forty-six short stories and five novels, at least two of which stand with the top rank of modernist literature. Critics acknowledge that she is acute in the depiction of female consciousness; but this praise, often combined with a comment about the narrowness of her interests, has also been a cause of her neglect (see Mellown "Character and Themes"). Readers dislike her female heroes and, correctly thinking that they are autobiographical, tend to reject the author along with her characters. For Rosalind Miles, for example, these heroes are the "walking wounded" (55); for Peter Wolfe, they are "dull" characters, each a "dispossessed urban spinster" who lacks ideas, a job, or a man (9). Linda Bamber claims that "we" feel "irritation and disapproval" for Rhys's characters because "there is very little here to distance us from the bad mood of her work" (94, 100). That some readers reject Rhys is understandable, since her characters seem to ask for rejection, and this attitude brings us close to the central dynamic of Rhys's fiction. Her main theme is inclusion versus exclusion: it structures her work and provides the key to her rhetorical strategies; it also suggests the relationships her texts establish with their readers. In the course of her short fiction, the polarity between inclusion and exclusion breaks down; simple notions of exploiter and exploited become inadequate, and social distinctions develop more complex moral and political meanings. These developments occur both within the characters and in the relationship between narrator and reader: social inclusion develops into moral empathy.

Born as Ella Gwendolen Rees Williams in the West Indies in 1890 to a Welsh physician father and a Creole mother, Rhys went to a local convent for her education, then briefly to the Perse School and Academy of Dramatic Arts in England. In her autobiography *Smile Please*, she looks back to a privileged childhood filled with sensory bounty and dominated by black and white women, including her distant and disappointing mother. Her unpublished notebooks reveal one especially traumatic incident, her relationship at age fourteen with an elderly gentleman who carried on a prolonged sadomasochistic seduction through storytelling. He took the young girl for walks and told her about love: "a lover smiles at you. And beats you"; "cruelty submission that was the story." Rhys claimed she forgot this incident for years, but it made her sceptical of Freud. In Sylvia Beach's bookstore in Paris she read Freud's judgment that "women of this type will invariably say they were seduced when very young by an elderly man. In *every* case this story is fictitious." "No honey I thought, it is *not* fictitious in every case. Anyhow how do you know" (Tulsa black notebook). Rhys's adult experience of England and Europe was that of a colder, crueler society than the West Indies, a society dominated by men and their money. After her father died, leaving the family poor, she began a career in England as a chorus girl while still a teenager. Partially repeating her youthful experience with an older man, she had a first, devastating affair with a rich, middle-aged bachelor. She fell in love with him; he dropped her, paid for an abortion, and continued to subsidize her for several years. The years following World War I found her adrift on the Continent. She married the Dutch-French Jean Lenglet and had a son who died in infancy; a daughter Maryvonne, born in 1922, survived. Her husband went to jail for currency irregularities, the marriage dissolved, and Rhys started a series of liaisons and manuscripts under the name Jean Rhys that resulted in the publication of a volume of short stories in 1927, four novels from 1928 through 1939, and two subsequent marriages. She briefly revisited the Antilles in 1936 but lived primarily in England from the 1930s on, staying during World War II, at the end of which her second husband, Leslie Tilden-Smith, died. Her third husband, Max Hamer, was jailed for fraud; she herself spent a few days in jail on an assault charge in 1949. In her later years she was a sometimes charming, sometimes cantankerous drunk, isolated in a cabin in the English countryside and very poor. In obscurity and ill health, she received word in 1957 that an English actress wished to adapt *Good Morning, Midnight*, 1939, for the radio. Belated attention then encouraged her to complete *Wide Sargasso Sea*, 1966. Widowed again in 1966, she suffered ill health. Editors, mentors, and friends visited and encouraged her, though she retained a sense of herself as lonely and isolated. She continued to publish short stories almost until her death in 1979 (Angier, Athill, Wyndham).

For Rhys, the question of what her life means to the understanding of her fiction is especially acute, since the fiction is so heavily autobiographical. She both exacerbated and resisted the tendency to see her work and her life as coterminous, claiming everything she wrote began with a transcription of what really happened, sorting her fictions into autobiographical and not autobiographical categories, and writing an autobiography, *Smile*

Please, that repeats scenes and phrases from the fiction (*Smile* 7). Many negative responses to her work imply that living with her autobiographical characters is disconcerting, even embarrassing, for readers who blame their unease on her personality. Her editors and biographers often erase the boundaries between her life and fiction, until Carole Angier comfortably invents things that must have happened in Rhys's life to motivate fictional scenes.

A psychoanalytic approach may exaggerate this tendency to replace the work with analysis of the author. To an old-fashioned Freudian, Rhys might neatly illustrate the allegedly normal female attributes of passivity, narcissism, and masochism, perhaps connected to an "oral fixation" (see Spacks). Thus Staley invokes the term "negative narcissism" for Rhys's characters (53). They long for "warm, lovely food" even when they are anorectic (*Sleep* 138), and she herself was an alcoholic. To an Eriksonian, this oral imagery would relate to the characters' lack of trust in others and themselves. Other psychological labels fit Rhys and her characters. Beaten as a child, molested as an adolescent, Rhys repeatedly involved herself in painful situations, and her characters share some traits with incest victims (See Herman 96–108). She and her characters are also often depressed, even suicidal, and paranoid about their persecution by neighbors; they may appear as Laingian divided selves or as Horneyan neurotics whose insatiable demands for love drive people away (see Abel "Women and Schizophrenia," Herman, Plante 7–61).

From the perspective of self psychology, Rhys and many of her heroes manifest a "narcissistic personality disorder" with a weak sense of self and difficulties with self-esteem. Such people crave mirroring or idealizing relationships in which they feel merged with something more powerful than themselves. Rhys describes happiness this way, as that "fish in water feeling," a sense of effortless immersion which she associates with reading, with nature, and occasionally with sex (Rhys *Tigers Are Better Looking*, cited hereafter as *Tigers* 20, Plante 61). Inadequately mothered, the narcissistic woman can not be an empathic mother herself. Rhys thought of her mother as unresponsive to her need for love and of herself as a bad mother. Her first child died in infancy leaving her feeling guilty and inadequate, and she did not bring up her second child, her daughter Maryvonne, who lived with her father or at schools most of each year. Although Maryvonne speaks highly of vacations with her mother and although they corresponded tenderly, Rhys claimed she had been right to save her daughter from her; to Maryvonne she signed herself "your unworthy Mother" (*Letters* 156). As has often been noted, Rhys's heroes are either motherless or children of unresponsive mothers, like the comatose mother in *After Leaving Mr. Mackenzie*, 1930, and the mad mother in *Wide Sargasso Sea*, and the heroes fail to become mothers themselves. Alienation from mothering occurs early in their lives for Rhys's characters; the hero of "Goodby Marcus,

Goodbye Rose," 1976, decides after a frightening adolescent sexual experience that she is forever unfit for childrearing.

These "pathological" assessments of Rhys, however, minimize her accomplishments and stereotype her characters. She lived nearly ninety years, and her heroes, too, struggle on, assuring us that they are tougher than they look, admitting to being vain, weak cowards and liars, but also upholding their dignity as compassionate, truth-telling individuals. Moreover, these psychological labels have social as well as individual components, so that Rhys has seemed paradigmatic of the way that social prescriptions for women make women "mad." For example, Rhys spoke of her looks as her chief asset, but her narcissism in this regard was justified by her ability to attract male interest and support. She advised her daughter to "stay as pretty as you can and are. It works better than the staid people pretend" (*Letters* 117). As with the "narcissistic" evaluation of her appearance, the paranoid assessment that people were attacking her has social roots: she recounts instances of hostility directed toward her by blacks in the West Indies because her family had been slave owners and by whites in England who taunted her as though she were black (*Smile* 25, 39; Tulsa black notebook). Thus on both sides of the Atlantic she felt in the position of a member of a racial minority living among a resentful majority, a situation whose rage fuels much minority literature.

Rhys's use of her autobiography in fiction is not unreflective or mechanical. Autobiography provides her a way of testing others' generalizations about fiction and history against her own experience. She anchors her fiction in her own life not simply because she cannot see outside it, but because she must validate her rejection of prior literary views about women by comparing them with her memories. The most important context for her characters is that of the female life cycle. Her seven ages of woman are the innocent but violated child, the seductive working girl, the happy young mother, the abandoned mistress, the attempted suicide, the solitary old drunk, and the bewildered ghost. The persistent issue of rejection versus empathy assumes different shapes and means different things to the young girl violated by a dirty old man or to the solitary old woman rebuffed by a cruel younger woman. As Rhys ages, her fictional perspectives change, and the world she creates for her relatively similar characters grows more complex. Many critics entirely ignore this variety. A.C. Morrell claims that Rhys "told the same story 46 times" (243).

In addition to the context provided by the female life cycle, there is also the context of public history, to which Rhys is far more alert than has been recognized previously. Wolfe, for example, says Rhys's characters "live below history and below society" (24), and Angier calls Rhys herself "timeless" (16). In fact, however, her characters are embattled in World War I, adrift in the 1920s, depressed in the 1930s, resigned during World War II, and later alienated from postwar materialism and complacency. In her letters Rhys describes her efforts to get historical details accurate in her fiction, and she acknowledges that writers are always affected by their time and place (*Letters* 101, 169). A third set of contexts within which she writes is that of the literary tradition; she is a modernist whose work is dense with allusions to the literary canon, to her French and English predecessors and also to contemporaries. To understand her work in its full richness requires placing it within these contexts, which are themselves changing and intertwined—the women's age, the historical age, and the literary setting.

As Rhys ages, her female characters do not necessarily understand themselves any better, but the author grows in her ability to present them to us so that we can understand them. Her authorial self-concept changes, her identity as a woman writer matures, and the identifications she establishes between herself and her characters become more mediated. In her earlier work, the reader plays a role like an idealized mother who is sought to solace the authorially-identified hero's abandonment and loss. In the later work, though young women or "daughter" figures are often cruel and rejecting to the older women with whom we are asked to identify, Rhys shows a healing ability to let all her characters, young and old, make their independent way in the world. Like well-nurtured children, they can demonstrate their otherness without thereby being rejected. By her late fiction Rhys "mothers" her texts in this way, letting them leave her—often after long gestations—and even letting them contradict her or one another.

Rhys said that she lied but that her fiction told truth, especially the truths that life is unfair and social conventions mad. Fiction could redress this unfairness, not through the poetic justice of inventing a better world, but instead through the representation of an unfair world, which, unlike the social reality we normally perceive, obtrudes its unfairness upon us. She claimed she felt better about her losses, griefs, and humiliations as soon as she wrote them down (Athill 4, Tulsa black notebook). Such confessional release strives for knowledge and therefore for control. After the breakup of her first affair, she wrote the poem, "I didn't know/ I didn't know/ I didn't know" (*Smile* 92). Frequently she complained that no one had told her what life would be like. Her writing, then, acts to validate her perceptions by creating a world that operates according to the rules she perceives in society. This fiction aims at the moral result of distinguishing what is true, that is, what really happens, from what is "fair," that is, what people deserve, through empathy. In Rhys's later work, inclusion comes to comprehend exclusion rather than be opposed to it, and the spatial and social aspects of inclusion/exclusion deepen to a concern for the moral and esthetic meanings of including other's experiences in one's own. The issue of inclusion versus exclusion defines social insights about the treatment of poor women in a male-dominated society and it also becomes the crucial question of a distinctively female morality: whom does one accept, whom reject, and on what grounds?

The terms inclusion and exclusion make no sense without boundaries defining inside and outside. Rhys depicts several wholes, the boundaries of which are contested in her work. Three crucially guarded domains are the family, the social order, and the literary canon, and the hero defines her position by contesting these boundaries. Repeatedly she wants to be left alone but can't bear to be left out. She courts and fears rejection and abandonment, often precipitating both to forestall the cruelty of others. But prior to these social units is the boundary of the self. Rhys often registers questions about physical and psychological integrity through imagery of eating, sexuality, and pregnancy. However, division in the self is not represented solely by violation of body boundaries but also by splits in the narrative voice, which may internalize the dichotomy between a woman and her society. Rhys's narrators often claim to see themselves both from the inside and outside, split between being observers and participants. This duality, common in modern fiction, is perhaps especially acute in women's fiction because of what Rachel Blau DuPlessis calls women's "ambiguously (non)hegemonic" position within the dominant male culture, that is, because of women's subordination to the culture as a whole despite being partially integrated throughout its levels (DuPlessis "For the Etruscans" 275).

From her earliest to her latest works, Rhys's understanding of the conflicts between compassion and truth becomes more profound and therefore so do her representations of the artist: the artist must be an outsider, a truth-seeker and speaker, yet able to move her readers to a compassionate recognition of common bonds, especially among people who suffer.

Rhys's persistent theme of inclusion versus rejection varies the theme of conformity versus difference. Her heroes are rejected, exiled, excluded, expelled. They claim they want to be the "same" as everyone else, but they are treated as different. Furthermore, since they resent everyone else and feel themselves to be different, they reinforce their lack of sameness to others. A related progression in Rhys's work is the breakdown of polarities into multiplicities. From the beginning, Rhys is conscious of many hierarchies of powerful and powerless classes: white and black, male and female, young and old, rich and poor. As her work matures, she retains her "almost terrific sympathy with the underdog" but grows more subtle in her delineation of the powers of the weak (Ford 24). Rhys's heroes often debate whether women or men are crueller, but her ideas about men and women are not congruent. She expects more from women. She hopes for a bonding and sympathy which is considerably more disappointing when unfulfilled, more poignant and terrible, hence perceived as more cruel, because she expects women to be kinder than men are. Her early work focuses almost entirely on the difficult relations between men and the women they exploit, whereas the later work enmeshes its heroes in more complex and ambiguous relational webs. What makes her fiction, at its best, exciting despite the sad fate of most of her heroes, is its inclusionary relationship among author, narrator, and reader.

"Vienne"

The span between Rhys's earliest and her latest fictions is fifty years, with four of her five novels appearing in little more than a decade. To understand her full development, then, it is necessary to look at her short fiction, and her stories are accomplishments that reward close attention in themselves. By her first publication in 1924, Rhys was thirty-four years old, having lived in Europe for seventeen years, as long as her childhood in the West Indies. She had been carrying with her for a decade the notebook describing her first affair; this notebook established her claim to be a writer and inspired Ford Madox Ford's efforts to help her reach print. Her first published story, "Vienne," exists in three versions—a five-page sketch published in Ford Madox Ford's *Transatlantic Review* in 1924, a much longer version in Rhys's first volume of short stories, *The Left Bank*, in 1927, and a somewhat pruned reprint in *Tigers Are Better Looking*, 1966. The opening lines of the first version introduce Rhys's central preoccupations and constant themes, whereas the changes from version to version illustrate her moral and esthetic development.

The 1924 sketch has three sections—"the Dancer," "Fischel," and "The Spending Phase." Rhys's first printed words are already nostalgic, speaking of beauty and of loss.

> Funny how it's slipped away, Vienna. Nothing left but a few snapshots.
> Not a friend, not a pretty frock—nothing left of Vienna.
> Hot sun, my black frock, a hat with roses, music, lots of music—
> The little dancer at the "Parisien" with a Kirchner girl's legs and a little faun's face (*Transatlantic Review* 639).

Rhys frequently begins a piece in this quizzical tone, confusing place, time, and person speaking without breaking away from normal colloquial speech, so that we readers feel vaguely dislocated. Five sentence fragments in four paragraphs open the piece, imitating the staccato quality of "a few snapshots." The prose immerses us in a confusing wash of time and place where undeveloped, dreamlike characters float up to us and then disappear. Cities do not slip away, though people and their memories do. Vienna has lasted a long time, yet World War I did flatten cities, and many English-speaking readers may recall a European trip that recedes unevenly in the memory. The "few snapshots" that remain are not of enduring monuments or public sights. Instead, the narrator expands the phrase "nothing left" in an idiosyncratic way: "not a friend, not a pretty frock," and she undercuts the opposition between something and nothing by specifying the kind of somethings that seem almost nothing. Alliteratively, the phrase "not a friend, not a pretty frock" balances the personal and the apparently inanimate, though later we will discover that the "pretty frock" is essential to the narrator's sense of herself as pretty.

These musical opening lines, trochaic with an anapestic lilt, lead to "lots of music," which in turn leads to "the little dancer," a decorative part of the atmosphere who sounds more like "a pretty frock" than she does a "friend." Doubly "little," she has a mad German expressionist's legs and the face of a mythological creature on a Debussy afternoon. We appreciate her as a continental art object, then, and are not surprised that her snapshot bears a moralized caption: "She was so exquisite that girl that it clutched at one, gave one a pain, that anything so lovely could ever grow old, or die, or do ugly things—" (639). Rhys's first vision of another woman invokes an empathetic response, a painful one, which immediately shades into an esthetic appreciation of a lovely "thing" that presumably appeals to our *Transatlantic Review*-reading good taste. But the fates that await the little dancer are harsher than those facing an esthetic object; precisely her mortal personhood is painful. Aging is always a charged category in Rhys, and she sees historical epochs in terms of their specific impact on women's lives. For her, time treats men and women differently: women age faster and more perilously, going from innocence so valuable it constitutes an attractive nuisance to unvalued old age, whereas her young men are rarely innocent, and her old men remain both powerful and desirable. In this story, where we expect to hear that the pretty dancer may grow old and ugly, instead Rhys warns us that to age will be to do "ugly things." The sight of the pretty dancer makes the narrator think "ugly humanity" less ugly (640), but to appreciate women as esthetic objects may lead to acquisitive desire; objects can be bought. One man raves about the dancer; another "was afraid she would be too expensive" (640). Throughout Rhys's canon, morality has an esthetic dimension, and the rest of "Vienne" exposes its snapshot images of youth in dislocated Europe, of the temptations of despair, and of the ugliness of those who lack compassion. Memories fade, and the representation of change, too, changes, as the verbal "snapshots" condense to a few repeated views.

The other parts of "Vienne" explore the implications of a world where women are exchanged like cash and introduce the other stock characters of Rhys's early, somewhat melodramatic fictions. In "Fischel," the second section of the 1924 "Vienne," we meet the innocent ingenue's predator, the nasty older man who exploits women. Each night Fischel promenades through the city to choose a new woman. Fischel's villainy has political as well as sexual connotations: he flew German fighter planes in World War I. Rhys consistently connects wars between nations with the war between the sexes; all soldiers are brutes, and all men seem to be soldiers.

The third and final section of the 1924 "Vienne" brings in the most important Rhys character, a first-person autobiographical hero who is the victim of men, fate, circumstance, and her own good nature. Whereas the first two sections deal with men who exploit women as objects, this section explores value more directly, especially the value that money confers on those who have it to spend. Of course, spending and having work against one another, as the Rhys hero dramatizes. This section, "The Spending Phase," starts with an invocation to "the great god money," which makes "possible all that's nice in life—Youth and beauty, the envy of women, and the love of men—/ Even the luxury of a soul" (642). Thus this section revalues the beautiful young dancer in the first section: the narrator condemns those who treat her as an object, yet sees her, nonetheless, as having her values of youth and beauty established by the market in women. From the hubris of the rich this sketch foreshadows the humiliations of the poor who futilely beg for financial help. Rhys ends the story raging at all the haves in the name of all the have-nots: "And every second-rate fool can have their cheap little triumph over you—judge you with their little middle-class judgment" (645). Here the narrator is unencumbered by the ambiguities of judging others. The bourgeoisie despises the poor; the narrator despises the rich and respectable. Though it is "nice" to have money herself, those who can keep their money instead of spending it all are "cheap," "little," and "second-rate."

The version of "Vienne" published in *The Left Bank* in 1927 adds nine sections to the original three, three continuing the narrator's history after "The Spending Phase" and the other six introducing further vignettes of Vienna's colorful characters. Multiplying but not expanding their original cast are men who prey on women and women who do or don't succeed in turning the tables on men. A flashforward from the lavish spending phase adumbrates the narrator's coming poverty and produces an awkwardness in the narration, since the narrator tells about her humiliating experiences after she falls from respectability, then tacks on several scenes that take place before the fall. Thus she champions innocence, while not consistently speaking from either inside or outside it.

In this version of "Vienne," Rhys writes captions under her snapshots to direct our judgments and emphasize hers. Repeatedly male mistreatment of women is first described, then set in a larger political context. For example, after a giggling Japanese colonel calls European women "war material," Rhys proleptically connects male chauvinism and authoritarian nationalism: "the Japanese thought a lot of the German Army and the German way of keeping women in their place" (*Tigers* 220; checked against *Left Bank*. Quotations below will be cited from *Tigers* reprint if it is identical to the *Left Bank* text; otherwise, the earlier *Left Bank* text will be cited). In another snapshot, men who made money bring women "of the moment" to a fashionable hotel; men's money is an independent variable in her world while women are a dependent variable. Like the grace of God, cash blows where it lists, and Rhys invokes it as a god. Although seeing the cruelty of the system, the narrator ignores her perceptions when she herself is one of the favored ones. When she is temporarily rich and admired by men, the narrator says she was "cracky with joy of life that summer of 1921"

(*Tigers* 226). "Cracky" seems right; joys that will not last can drive one crazy, and a cracked ideal may shatter under reality's impact like Henry James's golden bowl.

The caption of another picture attacks the exploitation of women, not directly by men or by money, but by one of the ideas that upholds both patriarchy and capitalism: "if there's one hypocrisy I loathe more than another, it's the fiction of the 'good' woman and the 'bad' one" (*Tigers* 224). Rhys despises the "fiction" that divides women by pretending to be a natural morality rather than a social ideology maintaining gender and class distinctions, and she writes her own fictions in response. Although the narrator condemns one polarization that harms women, she upholds a polarized and self-righteous moral view herself, one that loathes hypocrisy.

The Rhys hero is liminal with respect to love and work, which intersect differently for men and for women: women get money from men, and men get women for money; sex and money are always interconnected. Since this is true for all women, there is no moral divide, only a difference in security and status, between the roles of wife/mother and of prostitute. In the stories as well as the novels, the Rhys hero paradoxically inhabits both and neither sides of female roles: as a wife, she is no wife—one whose husband is jailed or inaccessible; as a mother, she is no mother, because her child dies; as a worker, she is no worker—marginal, tenuous, about to be fired.

"Vienne" illustrates the ideas its captions summarize with anecdotes that flicker into brief movement like silent films. In one skirmish from the war between the sexes, Tillie the golddigger turns the tables on a man, making him pay her for a pearl necklace she pretends to have lost. The narrator gloats in vindictive female solidarity with Tillie "the avenger," "the Man Eater," in a passage that Rhys deleted from the 1966 version, perhaps because she found it too vengeful for her later sensibility (*Left Bank* 200). However, Tillie's story confuses the narrator, who first joins ranks with all women against all men, then with all victims against all oppressors: she greets Tillie's "fool," the victimized man, as a "brother Doormat in a world of Boots" in language that suggests male camaraderie (*Tigers* 230). Again the narrative voice switches from pathos to rage, as though the unclear moral stance creates confusions of narrative tone as well. The caption for this snapshot could serve for all of "Vienne," even for all of *The Left Bank*: " 'eat or be eaten' is the inexorable law of life" in this "detestable world" (*Tigers* 230).

The 1927 "Vienne" ends with a connected series of vignettes expanding the earlier "spending phase" into an autobiographical narrative that moves from prosperity to humiliation and flight. The narrator internalizes her earlier theme of women being exchanged like money by seeing herself as a function of money. In the fluid financial exchange market of 1921, the narrator and her husband are volatile currency whose value rises and then falls. She is euphoric when her exchange rate is high—"nice to have lots of money—nice, nice"—and she sees her own intimate relationships implicated in the universal mania for speculation: "I gambled when I married and I've won" (*Tigers* 231). She doesn't win for long, and the downswing of fortune's wheel leaves her lower than she was before because money has corrupted her. Combining critical self-analysis with self-justifying pity, she says that she "could never be poor again with courage or dignity" (232) and that she doesn't "want to work. Or wear ugly clothes" (236). Her revulsion from "ugly clothes" shows us how far she has moved from her original compassion for the innocent young dancer whom she feared might "do ugly things." The narrator's moral weakening leads her to contemplate suicide and the humiliation of begging, two motifs associated with recurrent painful scenes in her novels. When the narrator sinks to poverty, she immediately descends to moral irresponsibility, then to misogyny, and then to abject self-hatred:

> It's not my fault.
> Men have spoilt me—always disdaining my mind and concentrating on my body. Women have spoilt me with their senseless cruelties and stupidities. Can I help it if I've used my only weapon? . . .
> Lord, how I hate most women here. . . .
> They are animals, probably. Look at all the wise men who think so. . . .
> Even Jesus Christ was kind but cold and advised having as little as possible to do with them. . . .
> How lonely I am (236-37).

As a poor woman, she is lonely and miserable until she regains her value by identifying her body with an idealized female role, even though in so doing, she joins the men who disdain her mind in favor of her body. Pregnancy dispels her gloom; she enjoys a "placid dream of maternity" and "a calm sense of power" (239). But the power is illusory, enabling her merely to forget the depressing realities of her life: "one can become absorbed . . . exalted . . . lost" in pregnancy (239). By allowing herself to feel like a "Femme Sacrée" (239), a madonna, she reinforces the division between good and bad women that she previously designated a loathsome "fiction."

After her speculator husband loses his luck and his money, she accepts the sexist stereotypes that husband and wife should fill the roles of financial provider and little mother, and she taunts him for failing this notion of masculinity: "why can't you be a man and fight?" (242). Then, money gone, she drops her pretenses to bourgeois respectability and resumes the viewpoint of the down-and-outer, through which she feels her pregnancy as a sickness, not as a mystical exaltation. Her husband gives her a pearl necklace that was stolen or swindled; it recalls the pearls that Tillie pretended to lose, and accepting it makes the narrator one of Tillie's moral sisters.

Without money the narrator and her husband flee over a closed frontier and ricochet through Eastern Europe, breaking moral and geographic boundaries. She fears financial ruin because it will precipitate her fall from "good" woman to "bad woman," since a bad woman is a sexually available woman without money. She ends her story fantasizing about suicide and hysterically eager to "scream with laughter at the old hag Fate" (253), the female destiny that ages and judges women as hags.

In this tale, "snapshots" of others serve as a pretext for rambling reminiscences; the twenties' "joy of life" joylessly associates youth, flowers, and music with wine, pretty dresses, cars, and pearls. Rhys condemns the rich, but not the "nice" things their money can buy, and she is never so silly as to imply that the rich are more miserable than the poor. Men circulate women like cash; within this closed moral and financial circuit, a gold digger's pearl necklace reappears as the narrator's compensation for fleeing respectability.

In its earliest version, Rhys's fictional world is inconsistent regarding the meaning of action, the stance of the narrator, and the duplicity of the double standard. Equating acting with doing harm, the narrator describes herself as a passive observer immersed in social confusion. Although she sympathizes with others, neither she nor anyone else helps anyone else. She portrays her own potential goodness as negative and indirect, merely as her desire not to harm the vulnerable. To grow, to live in time, is to act, and she equates action with damage, with doing "ugly things." If all actions cause harm, then the most moral course is to be as inactive as possible, passively suffering from the actions of others. Many a Rhys hero represents herself as just such a passive victim, although the text may belie her self-image.

The narrator's passivity also leads to inconsistency in her fictional voice. Sometimes she speaks as innocent victim; sometimes a wiser, more experienced self contemplates her early innocence with affectionate patronage; sometimes she painfully criticises herself; and sometimes, in passages that Rhys later omitted, she lashes out at the reader as at another oppressing bourgeois. In the midst of all this, she describes the "calm power" of pregnancy as something between a hormonal high and a mystical state. These changes in voice do not smoothly indicate different states of the narrator's mind but seem superimposed between the viewpoints the narrator took "then" and those she takes "now."

Because her attitudes to sexual roles and the double standard are inconsistent, her moral pronouncements are contradictory. She sympathizes with women exploited by men, then with a man duped by a woman, but she insults her husband through sexual stereotypes: when he ceases to be rich and lucky, she calls him an unmanly coward. Although the division between good and bad women is fictitious, the division between eaters and eaten is not. The story divides people into only two categories: "nice" people who are fools to be "eaten"; and dangerous, contemptible respectable "good" eaters of others. The narrator establishes this simplified dichotomy even though she herself does not fit it: though a victim, she is not a fool, and she is not always nice. Thus Rhys reverses rather than dismantles the sexual and moral double standard, and she confusingly justifies women as both victims and predators. Rhys pities victims of gender and class oppression, but she does not always enlist our sympathies, alienating us from the narrator's judgments by her misogyny, self-pity, self-hatred, and sporadic vindictiveness. Arbitrarily, she shifts between empathetic inclusions and angry rejections of herself, us readers, and the people snapped in her fictional photographs, outbursts that she deleted in the later version. In 1966 she removes three character sketches, making the final story in *Tigers Are Better Looking* a much more concentrated narrative of the hero's flight from respectability than the 1927 version, but not changing its approach other than to delete some of the angrier phrases.

The Left Bank

Paradoxes of inclusion and rejection also structure the other, shorter stories of *The Left Bank*. At her simplest, Rhys urges us to accept those whom the world rejects, often members of the underclasses. They demand our compassion, though they are by nature incomprehensible, like the beautiful Arab in "Sidi" who can't communicate through the prison tapping code and so dies incommunicado. (This is originally Lenglet's story. *Letters* 283) "Trio" explicitly redefines inclusions: the lonely hero sees a loving black family from the West Indies, one of the few happy families in Rhys's fiction, and sentimentally announces, "these are my compatriots" (*Left Bank* 85); she tells us always to sympathize with such underdogs and to hate those at the top.

If we are to accept those society rejects, we are also to reject those it accepts. "The Spiritualist" satirically teaches this lesson. A sexist soldier neglects to buy a monument promised to his devoted mistress before her death. From the grave she hurls a marble block at him—but misses, as the revenge of women usually does. Rhys is particularly acerbic to rich people who patronize poor people. In "Villa D'Or," American millionaires say that "dollars aren't Art," while they believe that dollars can buy both art and the impoverished artists they keep as pets (*Left Bank* 162). In "Taking . . . a Friend to Dinner," Rhys records the voice of a lady bountiful but not that of the poor friend who hungrily eats through her monologue: "it is dreadful to try to help poor people. They will not help themselves." "One comfort. It is always people's own fault. . . . They lack. . . . Oh, Balance" (Rhys's ellipses, *Left Bank* 106, 108). Rhys makes this odious woman voice the criticisms often leveled at her passive heroes, but her satire is so one-sided that it fails to exorcise these complaints; we may condemn victim-blaming without being convinced that moral responsibility is irrelevant to our judg-

ments. Rhys blames those who blame her heroes in a reversal that excludes
them from our understanding. Later she rejected some of her angriest
stories, like this one and "The Spiritualist," when she reprinted others in
1966.

Many *Left Bank* sketches introduce us to the Rhys hero as a consistent
character who courts and expects our sympathy, even though she may
spurn it. Similarly, she courts and defies her own death: throughout Rhys's
work suicide defines one limit to her theme of inclusion. In "A Night,"
acceptance by a potential lover opposes her isolated despair, but only mo-
mentarily. She distracts herself from suicide by thinking of "the man I
could love. . . . What rot!" (111). As soon as she imagines herself loved,
loving, and accepted, she instantly censures her romantic sentiments,
though not her sentimental self-pity. Often, as here, her characters invite
rejection because they fear it so much they seek to control it by precipitating
it. Similarly, they seek and romanticize death because its loneliness terrifies
them; to counteract this loneliness, they fantasize death as enveloping
maternal darkness. In "The Blue Bird," a *liebestod* seems more attractive
than a lonely life; a woman laments missing her chance for a "sweet death"
(138) with her ruined lover. Isolation and rejection make the hero so miserable the narrator almost defies us to sympathize with her. In "In the Rue
de L'Arrivée" Rhys baldly defends a pure victim, a woman who "lacked
strength of character and was doomed to the fate of the feeble who have
not found a protector" (114). "A harmless creature pathetically incapable
of lies or intrigue or even of self-defense—till it was too late. She was also
sensual, curious, reckless" and aroused "curiosity in men" (115). The story
implies that "protectors" really help "harmless" women and puts us readers in the position of potential protectors. The story's conclusion states
Rhys's simplest view of feeling for others: "only the unhappy can either
give or take sympathy" (120–21). Rhys here limits empathy to the miserable, to fellow sufferers, those who can do no harm because they are too
weak; she seems to dare her readers to be unhappy enough to be understanding: if we reject her characters, presumably that is because we are not
sufficiently miserable.

"Mixing Cocktails" provides a childhood consciousness that explains the
etiology of these adult victims and shows how ambiguities about empathy
lead to ambiguities about action. A dreamy girl woolgathers until intrusive
"humanity" "must interfere" between the girl's thoughts and herself (*Tigers* 189). Clearly, a way of thinking that separates oneself from "humanity"
is an alienating one; when thoughts are separated from "self," the self is
mad or idiotic, like the Antoinettes of *Wide Sargasso Sea*. Rhys claims her
character in "Mixing Cocktails" is a "well-behaved little girl" who longs
"to be like Other People," the "ungetatable oddly cruel Other People"
(*Tigers* 189). But she does not seem to want to be "oddly cruel" herself.
Difference and exclusion define one another in an endless circle: the different are cruel; the cruel are different; one cannot like or be like them.

Then a voice interrupts the narrative flow as though we have been day-dreaming the story: "I am speaking to you" (*Tigers* 189), it says, identifying us readers with the little girl rather than with the conventional "other people." The story ends ironically as the hero concludes that action is better than dreaming. However, her one happy activity is mixing drinks, which make adults into dreamers, too.

Repeatedly the narrator excuses the sad women of *The Left Bank*, denying their moral responsibility while emphasizing their passive acceptance of their fates. This moral evasiveness complicates the reader's relation to the text. "It is always people's own fault," says the rich woman taking the down-and-outer to dinner, as though we well-fed readers will judge the rich woman defective in sympathy and deny our own suspicions that the hero's passivity contributed to her hungry fix (*Left Bank* 108). In "Vienne," the hero asserts, "it's not my fault" (*Tigers* 236). She's at the mercy of forces that her place and time set in play, forces larger than she is. She is also at the mercy of a human nature she defines as so predatory that her passivity is morally superior to action. If we question these characters' denial of responsibility, then, it is against the grain of the narrative. In these early stories Rhys condemns those who blame her victimized characters but offers no alternative moral or esthetic vision, and her stance appears contradictory. She blames the respectable middle-class and the authorities, even though it is "nicer" to be rich than not; her characters' animus thus seems to spring from exclusion, not from moral revulsion at corrupt wealth. In passages deleted in reprint, presumably because they seemed too crude, Rhys's hero repeats three things: that she is a defenseless victim; that women are cruel to her; and that she inspires passion in men, which she satisfies, although her own hunger for love remains unsated. These early sketches draw a competitive social arena where poor women vie for men with money while disowning responsibility for competing. Besides justifying herself, the Rhys narrator identifies with and attempts to enlist our sympathies for women, the poor, and members of other races, although in doing so she also supports racial stereotypes of otherness—the warm, sensual black people in "Trio," for example, and the mysterious Arab in "Sidi."

Of all the *Left Bank* stories, "Le Grosse Fifi" most successfully dramatizes Rhys's early notion that "bad" women are really better than good ones. The story lays out a clear and plausible, though unobtrusive, grid of inclusions and exclusions based on categories of age, class, sexual respectability, and national difference that enlist our sympathies in presumably unconventional directions. Roseau, a sad young woman named after a West Indian seaport, is convalescing on the Riviera after a disappointment in love. Placed like the middle heart on a five card, she forms triangles with two opposing couples. A coolly respectable English pair finds her interesting, while she grows curious about Fifi, a fat old French tart, and her young gigolo. Single and West Indian, she stands between English and

French cultures, the married couple and the mercenary one. The story evolves from this unstable formation, with Roseau moving away from respectability to side with Fifi. Roseau seems balanced between the two couples in historical style and in literary type as well. The proper English Olsens are young 1920s vacationers, the people of the future; middle-aged Fifi is still "Edwardian," an old courtesan living according to the pre-war code of her heyday. Roseau is neither of the past nor of the future, but adrift like most Rhys heroes, in a floating and disordered present. As a story, too, "Fifi" straddles older and newer literary traditions, clearly recalling de Maupassant's "Boule de Suif," in which respectable citizens use, then snub, a fat prostitute. (Rhys refers to this story in *Letters*, 99.) Fifi herself reads old-fashioned romantic poetry, which she finds consoling, while her passion unfolds like a turn-of-the-century melodrama—blood everywhere and her murdering lover sent to jail. After her death, her story enters the literature of the present, the sensational, debased style of the crime tabloid.

Roseau is both attracted and repelled by Fifi, who accepts the double standard and who incarnates so many stereotypes of the feminine role. Fifi does not question the code that judges her unlovable because she is old and ugly; she knows she must pay to keep her gigolo. When she reads Roseau a romantic poem of female dependency, Roseau recoils from hearing this "ruin of a woman voicing all her own moods" (*Tigers* 209): it is not the poetry itself that upsets her but its origin in a female voice similar to her own. She tries to reject Fifi as a vision of her own future, but instead finds herself defending the older woman against the priggish English couple. Fifi upsets Roseau by forecasting her bleak future as a woman who depends on men. However, Fifi also evokes in Roseau a psychologically more primitive dependency, one both more alluring and more threatening to her adult identity, and that is the dependency of a girl upon her mother. Like other *Left Bank* protagonists, Roseau lacks the "instinct of self-preservation" (*Left Bank* 186); she needs Fifi to comfort her. Unlike the woman in "On the Rue" who had "not found a protector," Roseau had a male "protector" whose withdrawal has increased her vulnerability. Hearing Roseau sobbing through a hotel room wall, Fifi enters, tucks Roseau into bed like a child, and gives her "the kindest, the most understanding kiss" (*Tigers* 205). From this infantile perspective Roseau sees Fifi as a "large, protecting person" as "kind as God" (206). Fifi, too, lacks "the instinct of self-preservation"; she jealously fights with her gigolo, who murders her. Thus Roseau projects on Fifi the stereotyped roles of both mother and whore. The conventional "bad woman" has a pure gold heart, yet society destroys this fat, nurturing mother figure. Because Fifi is as kind as God, a Magdalen turned Christ, she sacrifices herself for all our sins. Her death erases from view the damaging past baggage of prewar sexual values that still prevail, and it obliterates the reminder of the future that Roseau fears for herself, that of the unloved older woman.

Though sharing the limitation of other early stories that only the poor and unhappy can empathize with others, "Le Grosse Fifi" is more supple than most in having us alternately reject and identify with Roseau as she rejects and identifies with Fifi. These blurred identifications among women force us to reject the "fiction" of the "bad" woman, a fiction, Rhys implies, that other fictions in the literary canon too often support.

The Later Stories

Rhys's later short fictions show a substantial increase in range, in literary breadth, and in moral depth, and they develop our capacity to empathize with a whole situation, not just with an autobiographical hero. *Tigers Are Better Looking*, 1968, and *Sleep It Off, Lady*, 1976, collect stories written over decades. (Publication dates for individual stories are listed below unless other evidence dates them earlier.) Besides the general prejudice in favor of novels as more serious than short stories, the reputation of Rhys's short fictions has suffered from critics' desire to see a writer's *oeuvre* as a single work. Thus *The Left Bank* is perceived as prologue; the later stories, as epilogue to the novels. Because *Wide Sargasso Sea* is so good, so satisfying, and so clearly a culmination of themes and skills that Rhys develops in her first four novels, it is tempting to consider the late stories only as an appendix to that masterpiece, even though many of them were written earlier. However, this gives a misleading picture of Rhys's total accomplishment. Since *Wide Sargasso Sea* is an historical novel, it distracts attention from her mature interest in depicting the intersections between women's ages and the stages of contemporary history. Moreover, treating the later short stories as a piece collapses decades of Rhys's development.

Rhys inscribes history into her later fiction, carefully heeding the particular places and times in which her stories are set, especially to show changing conditions for women and the changing meanings of sexual codes from the 1890s to the 1970s. Rhys writes about much of history twice, while it is happening and then after a long retrospect. Though she does not paint clashing armies and revolting masses, she does represent what historical change means for women, and, contrastingly, for men, showing variations in sexual mores, sexual attitudes, and available work. Most of her heroes are of approximately her own generation—little girls in stories set in the 1890s, young women through the '20s, middle-aged women in the 30s, and isolated old women in the '60s and '70s.

Rhys's history starts, as she did, in the 1890s, in a stable, repressed colonial culture with a clear color bar and a similar bar separating public life from sexual secrets. Though most of her early stories describe the unanchored Europe of the 1920s, she set two sketches from *The Left Bank* in her West Indian childhood: as we have seen, "On Mixing Cocktails" evokes wistful nostalgia for an innocent childhood; "An Incident in the

Antilles" adopts a wry, distanced tone to satirize the pretensions of colonial and imperial cultures as exhibited in an island newspaper. In the novels between 1928 and 1939, Rhys uses the West Indian background as a recurrent symbol for childhood innocence, maternal warmth, and social cruelty.

The later fictions replace exoticism with reflection on the exotic, a topic fully developed in *Wide Sargasso Sea*. Similarly, in several late short stories, young girls learn about adult sexuality, violence, and racial and class antagonisms in a Victorian culture that strictly delimits proper behavior and suppresses expression of the improper: what is not supposed to occur is not supposed to be told. These late stories describe characters who cross the lines; old men make passes at little girls, white men marry black women, and these violations indicate mysterious cruelties in human, especially male, nature. The stories ask the reader to cross these lines, too, to admit the inadmissible and hear the inexpressible. For example, in "Goodby Marcus, Goodby Rose," 1976, a story closely related to an incident Rhys describes as autobiographical, handsome old Captain Cardew talks to twelve-year-old Phoebe like a grownup, a favor she appreciates. She is shocked, then, when suddenly "his hand . . . dived inside her blouse and clamped itself around one very small breast" (*Sleep* 25). She thinks, "he's making a great mistake" (25), but she feels blameworthy nonetheless. This is like the incident that, according to a notebook written in the 1930s, Rhys "forgot" for over thirty years (Tulsa black notebook). Her character Phoebe, however, expresses her violation rather than represses it. She even accepts it as part of her self-definition, deciding that her future as a "wicked" girl is "far more exciting" than as a married woman with children (29, 30). The perverse charm of the story springs from the violated girl's innocent speculations about her supposed wickedness and from the reader's less innocent, pleasurable pity for her moral confusion, a confusion we do not share, since we know that the old man, not the girl, is the "wicked" one.

Stories set and written in later decades capture the differing atmospheres of those periods, especially in terms of their varying sexual mores. For example, Rhys describes the cosmopolitan decadence of the 1920s in stories like "Night Out, 1925," in which a stingy man takes a respectable girl to a brothel to "stare and jeer" (*Sleep* 109). In contrast to early stories like "Vienne," the hero here can imagine and implement a relation to predatory men and exploited women other than watching the former and joining the latter. Instead, she gives the prostitutes a huge tip from her date's wallet, thus seizing his power to circulate money and women. The puzzled prostitutes react suspiciously, and the man abandons her. She has found feasible moral action, but not acceptance, though her own sense of identity is less compromised than in the earlier, more passive stories.

In "Tigers Are Better Looking," written by 1945, the 1930s depress a journalist for whom drink is more satisfying than "phoney talk about Communism" or the waxworks set up to celebrate George the Fifth's Jubilee in

1934 (*Tigers* 74, *Letters* 39). "Death" is "the only word that means anything," the journalist thinks (*Tigers* 84). He prides himself on seeing through the false ideologies of his time to the essentials of existence, but he doesn't realize his own advantage as a man in comparison to his friend Maudie, who is both more compassionate and more cynical than he. She knows that people are as cruel as beasts and less innocent: "tigers are better looking," as one of the journalist's friends tells him (74). Middle-age, depressing in itself, is far crueller when one is poor, female, and alone. As the century progresses, Rhys sees the social "Machine" inexorably classifying people, rejecting the misfits in behalf of "a stable, decent world. If you withhold information, or if you confuse me by jumping from one category to another, I can be extremely disagreeable" (*Tigers* 92–93). Chief of those who don't fit are old women detached from families or other ties. In "Rapunzel, Rapunzel," a solitary old woman in a convalescent home looks to her long hair "all intact, to comfort and reassure her that she was still herself" (*Sleep* 149). When a barber hacks off her hair in order to sell it, the old woman says "nobody will want me now" and promptly dies (153). Similarly, in "Sleep It Off, Lady," 1976, an "old, lonely and helpless" woman suffering from a heart condition faints while trying to move her heavy trash can. The neighbors have labeled her staggering gait as drunkenness, and a malign neighbor girl taunts the stricken old woman and lets her lie (*Sleep* 172).

In her early stories, Rhys's heroes courted death as an escape from human rejection and as an entrance into a dark, maternal power. In the stories written in her old age, death is a constant preoccupation, less attractively maternal than earlier and connected not merely with bodily breakdown but also with rejection and abandonment. In "The Attic," an old woman recovers her joy in life when a young man displays an interest in her. "We recognized each other, didn't we" (*Sleep* 162), he says, but he is not so much an admiring mirror as a needy sympathy-seeker like herself; he is not so young after all, and he is unhappily married. Although enjoying the renewed zest of a moment's flirtation, she realizes that her "one advantage" as an old woman is that "she could do exactly what she liked" (166), and this freedom requires being alone. In "The Sound of the River," an old couple is happy together, a rare situation in Rhys's fiction and a rare allusion to her own mostly-married condition. But this happiness is only an ironic prelude to loss: waking on a fine day in the country, the woman finds her husband dead. She thinks, "things are more powerful than people. I've always believed that. (You're not my daughter if you're afraid of a horse. You're not my daughter if you're afraid of being seasick. You're not my daughter if you're afraid of a shape of a hill, or the moon when it is growing old. In fact you're not my daughter)" (*Tigers* 151). Even in old age and in a story based on Rhys's second marriage, the Rhys hero internalizes the voice of a rejecting parent; like the Dickens and Bronte characters who punish children for not looking cheerful, this voice evokes the mysteries of adult authority in an alienating world. In another story an old woman achieves a victory over men, another rare occurrence in Rhys's fiction, but only by dying. Mother Mount Calvary in "The Bishop's Feast," written in 1960, defies the bishop's order to move away from the island where she had been Mother Superior of the narrator's convent school (*Letters* 186). Both a beloved mother and a woman who can stand up to male authority, even laugh at it, the nun must die to prevent the move, presumably with God as her ally. As in some of the earlier stories, death enables a last word against oppressors otherwise too powerful to deal with, and literature imitates heaven, recognizing and rewarding the just.

In Rhys's early stories, poor young women are used by older, richer men and women. In the late stories, vulnerable young girls are molested and vulnerable older women abandoned by a hypocritical and uncaring society. The Rhys life cycle has continuity but no renewal: the hero is always rejected by others, although sometimes she temporarily finds a comforting maternal presence, as Roseau does with "Le Grosse Fifi" and as Inez in "Outside the Machine," does with the vanilla-smelling old woman who secretly gives her money. However, Rhys's later fictions are less sentimental, less exclusively identified with their heroes' viewpoints than earlier, so that, for example, we understand why the neighbors dismiss the old lady as a drunk in "Sleep It Off Lady," even while we share her terror.

War Stories

Rhys's later short fictions play the continual sad narrative of a woman's lifetime against changing backdrops of public history. One way to appreciate her care in these discriminations is to compare "Till September, Petronella," a story written in the 1930s but set just before the "guns of August" at the outbreak of World War I, with a story set during World War II—"The Insect World," begun by 1959 but not finished until 1973 (*Letters* 39, 169–70).

In "Till September, Petronella," a story shortened from novel length, a man invites Petronella up from London to a country cottage (*Letters* 185). Hair recently bobbed, Petronella is a modern girl in 1914, and, although only an artist's model, a member of Bloomsbury's exciting bedsitter community of Bohemianism, modernism, and sexual ambiguity. Whereas visits to upper-class countryhouses are a staple of popular fiction that romanticizes the sexual encounters of upper-class men and working-class women, here we are closer to the clear shadows of a prolonged "dejeuner sur l'herbe," in which rich young men in full dress pose naked women in colorful rural settings. Petronella's hosts, well-off young men, an artist and a critic, discuss their jobs and blame themselves for prostituting their talents, though they do not object to prostituting the women. They have summoned Petronella and another woman as vacation playmates, but they are not really interested in them; instead, they revolve around one another in a sexual and professional competition that resembles a courtship, reading to one another about the "biological inferiority of women" and teasing and praising one another (*Tigers* 14).

Petronella resists being treated as a sexual and esthetic object. The men want the women to be "gay" and pretty for them and grow hostile when their plans are foiled. Petronella fights their objectification of her: "they're trying to make me like that but I'm not like that," she says (17). She also resists their assumption that she will fill the vacant sexual slot in the four-some by becoming mistress to the artist Marston, whom she finds physically repulsive because he is too soft. Instead, she is attracted to vicious, dominant Julian. Her own desires, then, internalize the sexist double standard that persecutes her. She refuses Marston, but this does not make Julian more available to her. Instead, Julian attacks her for refusing Marston, calling her a "ghastly cross between a barmaid and a chorus girl," a "female spider" (23). Instead of being as accommodating as the lower-class chorus girl and barmaid are supposed to be, she is an insect whose desires the men find dangerous. They despise her sexuality but turn nasty when they cannot direct it as they choose—not to give either man physical pleasure but to fulfill their need to dominate.

Petronella has worked as a model and an actress. Like Rhys, she failed as an actress because she couldn't perform on cue (*Smile* 90). Petronella quotes the lines she muffed, phony upper-class language about admission to the royal box at Ascot, from which she would be excluded in real life. The two upper-class young men are connoisseurs of art, and Petronella is one of their *objects d'art*. After she runs away from them, she meets a farmer who is also a ladies' man: a humbler, old-fashioned representative of the secret life, he knows that he must pay for women, but he also knows, as the younger men do not, that women like "a bit of loving" as well as "bracelets with blue stones" (*Tigers* 28). Back in London, still with "no money, no background, and no nous" (16), Petronella lets herself be picked up by another young man, for whom she acts the part of an acquisitive mistress, ending her story by condensing her roles of purchased object and of actress who can only repeat the same lines.

As a model, Petronella let herself be turned into art, and she fantasizes escaping her tawdry life by transforming it into a fairy tale: she will appear as a triumphant beauty in an opera box and so conquer a handsome prince. But when the two men at the country cottage sing "Tristan," she doesn't recognize that they romanticize their own death, not beauty or love for women. A despised Pygmalion's image, she resists the prospective horror of female aging by trying to freeze life into art, a process both alienating and narcissistic: she kisses her image in a mirror. Unlike deathly music or static art, books, she feels, are alive. Her recent French house-mate Estelle reminds her of long, fanciful Continental novels; Estelle's departure precipitates her depression at the opening of the story. Petronella says she likes to "gobble" up such novels, which surround her like a pleasant dream, even though they absorb her into their identity rather than helping her formulate her own (10). Her imagery of reading conflates gestation and happiness in a way that alludes to Minerva, goddess of wisdom, at the same time that it evokes a modern maternal theory of reader responses: "what is not there you put in afterwards, for it is alive, this book, and it grows in your head" (10).

Petronella fears time is passing too quickly; it will soon be too late to escape her confined world through youthful beauty. The thought of becoming an ugly old woman so depresses her that she cheerfully contemplates suicide as though she can imagine controlling her life only by ending it. When she leaves the summer cottage, its calendar reads July, 1914. Personal time, the time of the female life cycle, and public, historical time intersect ominously. Petronella thinks old women hate her for being young, yet they are less dangerous to her than the rich young men who are "spoiling for a fight" to end the tedium of their empty lives (20). The church clock seems to chime, "there's a good time coming for the ladies" (33), although Petronella feels only despair. Will the coming World War be good for the ladies? Will what's "good . . . for the ladies" be good for poor girls who are not ladies? Warm, French Estelle has left London, and perhaps with her the easy cosmopolitan camaraderie that characterized prewar society. Petronelia ends sadly waiting for the clock to strike. The young men claim they will see her in the city after their summer vacation, "till September, Petronella." But the guns of August will intervene, the men will go off, and the young woman will face the autumnal possibilities of aging alone. "Petronella" connects the war of 1914 with the battle between the sexes and with men's desire to blow everything up out of sheer self-loathing (see Staley 123). The first World War, destroyer of a generation of men and deflater of male grand illusions, will have different repercussions for women, although as male self-confidence collapses, men will increasingly project their competition with each other onto women.

In contrast to her anticipatory and allusive treatment of World War I, Rhys's picture of World War II is much more graphic and direct, showing women on the homefront under bombardment, suffering the effects of foreign aggression, class antagonism, and pervasive sexism. "The Insect World" focuses on the tense emotional dynamics between two women housemates during the blitz. One is solid; the other paranoid, weak, and confused. Like "Till September, Petronella," the story connects world war with the battle between the sexes, but in World War II men have vanished from the home front, though misogyny has not. The only man's words that the neurotic working girl Audrey hears are the marginal notations of her second-hand paperback's prior possessor. Apparently reading soft porn provokes his hatred of women: "women are unspeakable abominations," he writes in 1942 with a fury that tears the page, like that of Woolf's furious professor in A Room of One's Own (Sleep 132; Woolf 31). Audrey and Monica connect this virulent misogyny with the psychology of war: some people's hatred for others is "the horror everybody pretended did not exist, the horror that was responsible for all the other horrors" (132). Monica links misogyny and fascism, opining that the Germans want to make their women feel ugly in order to make them more submissive; Audrey claims England treats its women no better. Everywhere people manipulate and diminish women's self-esteem, like the salesgirl who persuaded Audrey to buy an ugly, ill-fitting dress on the grounds that it was "unpatriotic to make so much fuss about what she wore" (134).

While the men are invisibly abroad killing one another, the women work as typists in government offices at home. The overworked Audrey has a backache from sitting at her desk all day, and she envies a pregnant friend who doesn't have to work because her husband in the armed forces supports her. Audrey welcomes the war, at least as a leveler of class pretensions, but fears it will keep her from finding a husband. Her "real and especial reason for loathing the war" is that it "had already gobbled up several years" and, at twenty-nine, she "dreaded growing old" (130). Unlike most Rhys heroes, therefore, she is considerably younger than her author was at the same historical period. Audrey's roommate is an "optimist five years younger" than she, as though, in Audrey's resentful mind, youth and optimism are interchangeable (130). Fear and self-hatred shape Audrey's attitudes toward women. She has internalized the misogyny she reads and sees around her: "it was funny how she hated most women" (139). When a young woman jostles an old one in the tube, Audrey responds in a panic, even though the plucky old woman catches herself; "her face, though, was very white. So was Audrey's. Perhaps her heart kept turning over. So did Audrey's" (140). Audrey's hatred obviously springs from her identification with the old woman, and Rhys's empathy includes both women, even in their desire to exclude each other and reject their common identity.

Audrey both craves and rejects nurturance from other women. The hungrier she feels, the harder she finds it is to say, she's "ravenous" (136). She thinks all day about "warm lovely food" but fidgets rather than eats when cheerful Monica cooks dinner for her (138). She's thin as a girl, and her anorexia apparently springs from an alienation from her body, a fear of growing up and of growing old that we more frequently associate with adolescents. Like food, sleep is a troubled maternal presence to her. She drowses musing, "She (who?) sent the gentle sleep from Heaven" (143).

Audrey's ambivalence about food carries over to her ambivalence about reading. Both incorporate something into the self, and Audrey fears growth. On the other hand, she experiences happiness only as fusion with a whole larger than herself, though she expresses this desire for narcissistic fusion in esthetic rather than infantile terms: "she could give herself up to the written word as naturally as a good dancer to music or a fine swimmer to water" (129). She thinks almost any book is "better than life," offering hope and providing pleasure, even though most books lie and the recognition of the lies undercuts her pleasure in the imaginary hope. Therefore, finishing a book makes her feel full, then hollow: reading gives her "indigestion" rather than continuing to live in her mind as a muse or fetus, as it did for Petronella (129).

Audrey's current indigestible book is *Nothing So Blue*. The title connotes a story both risque and sad; the blue unknown can be natural as sea and sky; the "blue" woman may be one who thinks too much. With tongue-in-cheek self-reflexivity, Rhys makes Audrey's disturbing book parody her own *Wide Sargasso Sea*. "Whitely horrible" insects, nasty "jiggers" swarm in an uncomfortable tropics where the natives are cruel and vindictive (133). "Though he didn't really want to" the "hero simply had to make love to" "this horrible girl" (132). Audrey connects sexuality, compulsion, and swarming insects. In a hysterical frenzy, she tells Monica about the novel's insect cities. Monica tries to calm her, calling her roommate an "old girl," and Audrey attacks her (145). Rhys said it took her years to find "the final, well meant remark that drove the poor girl frantic in the end" (*Letters* 170). For Audrey, being an "old girl" is equivalent to being damned to "everlasting hell" and both equal being women during wartime, shaped by the food and "segregation" into sexless worker drones like the terrifying "jiggers" (144–45).

Like other Rhys heroes, Audrey has a divided, painful consciousness. She thinks of herself as "twins" (see Abel "Women and Schizophrenia"). One of the twins is a conformist; the other rejects things as they are. Audrey's twin selves appear in the story as the two roommates—pleasant, accepting Monica, who is easier on the nerves, and grim Audrey. They are antithetical; they don't bond. We can identify with both. We can understand the pain in Audrey's persecuted mind and also stand outside her, sharing her "twin" viewpoint. Audrey's non-conforming side feels lost, betrayed, forsaken, "a wanderer in a very dark wood. The other told her that all she accepted so meekly was quite mad, potty" (131, see Nebeker 156, 196). This passage connects the psychology typical of Rhys's women—paranoid, masochistic, anxious for a lost mother—with a sweeping indictment of "normal" social arrangements. To accept a world that makes people feel so lost is mad. Conservative pessimists may believe we need a strict social order to suppress our mortal sin and guide us through the dark wood. But Rhys is a radical pessimist, disillusioned since her youthful phase of "G.K. Chesterton" socialism (Plante 14). Although she offers no vision for a better society, she indicts the "potty" misogyny, nationalism, and class divisions that brought war and "all the other horrors" of this century.

Rhys carefully differentiates the social milieux and characters' psychology of "The Insect World" from those in "Till September, Petronella." Petronella's storybook name contrasts with Audrey's crass working-class one, that of a foolish bumpkin in *As You Like It*. Petronella the poor model sees prostitution as the only other job available to her in 1914. Audrey, the 1940's government typist, imagines her alternative as marriage and motherhood. Petronella loses herself in long French novels; Audrey in cheap Penguins and second-hand pornography. Men treat Petronella solely as a sexual object; the coming war, World War I, will explode from repression, from male self-loathing, and from the battle beween the sexes. In contrast, Audrey is sexually frustrated and bitter, with no men in her life. Hypocritical Edwardian England has changed to a culture that mass produces porn while segregating men who kill from women who work. The misogyny remains: Petronella's tormentors read to her about the "natural inferiority of women"; Audrey's marginal predecessor thinks women are an "abomination." Because men treat her only as a sexual object, Petronella punishes herself by acting like one. In contrast, Audrey lashes out at her twin self, the other woman. In "Petronella," men itch to fight in their tedious world. "The Insect World" develops a nightmarish analogy between insects and worker drones riding the tube, and the jiggers which lay eggs in people's skin inspire Audrey with a paranoid fear of invasion that recalls the anticommunism, racism, and anti-Semitism of the 1940s. Audrey's private paranoia seems entirely sensible as the psychology of the air raid victim. She wanders through bombed streets, superstitiously thinking "if the siren goes when I'm in this street it'll mean that it's all U.P. with me" (140). Random death menaces the Londoners like the "man with a strange blank face and no eyebrows" (140) who got into a cinema ladies' room, familiar, domesticated, indecorous, perhaps even comic, but nonetheless terrifying. Hardly the soothing maternal presence to which earlier Rhys heroes looked as a last refuge from exploitation and misery in a sexist society, here death in war is a part of that sexist society.

The early Rhys stories introduce us to a disheartened young woman who, like many an adolescent, perceives herself as lonely, misunderstood, uniquely sensitive and uniquely miserable. She experiences life as exile and sex as war. Feeling misunderstood herself, she is compassionate toward underdogs but not toward respectable citizens. Thus her limited empathy extends only to those already like herself. In contrast to those who judge that Rhys does not develop as a short story writer (Wolfe 32), I claim that her later works retain the ability to immerse us in characters' humiliation and rejection, but they are also able to show us a moral world more complex than its characters can see for themselves and so extend empathy to people who are not simply victims.

The Late Stories: Truth, Texts, and Empathy

In her late work Rhys uses her personal experience not as a closed box out of which she cannot venture, but as a clarifying lens which tests the reports of others. She respects the text's power over our minds but distrusts textual distortion. We may never know the truth; but we know there are lies, just as, in her world, we can identify wickedness more easily than know the good. Thus for Rhys style becomes a moral issue, a question of saying hard truths rather than pretty lies. The insight that style is moral can help us understand the deepening of her later work when compared to her earlier fiction. In "Vienne," the worst "fiction" was the division between "good" women and "bad" ones (*Tigers* 224), a fiction that conventional literary fictions often uphold. "Le Grosse Fifi" develops a somewhat more subtle criticism of texts' power over people and of the inauthenticity of these texts. Fifi escapes confronting her disloyal gigolo by reading sentimental poetry: "I have laid my life in the hands of my lover" (*Tigers* 209). The language sounds false, overblown. But Fifi does lay her life in the hands of her lover: the gigolo murders her, and the newspaper's sensational account, "yet another drama of jealousy," is more false to Fifi's character than the romantic verse (*Tigers* 215). The story's central character Roseau is not involved in this battle of texts, however, and her need for consolation is not clearly connected to the narrator's desire for truth, as it is in the later stories.

In the later fiction, the disparity between texts and truth, language and experience becomes a dominant theme that the narrative voice dramatizes as well as reports. In "Heat," a newspaper story about a volcanic eruption bears no resemblance to the narrator's experience: "it wasn't like that at all" (*Sleep* 41). "Again the Antilles" describes a newspaper feud between a white landowner and a black firebrand who attributes a Chaucer quotation to Shakespeare. The Englishman gets his Chaucer right, but he calls his opponents "damn niggers" (*Tigers* 194). Although those who own the press assure themselves of the last word, the owners of the literary tradition do not own the truth. The black nationalist understands his situation as well as the patronizing Englishman does his, even though the canon with which he is imperfectly familiar provides the imperialist justification for continuing to regard him as a cultural inferior. In other cases, Rhys describes black art as more personally immediate than white art, just as she describes women's texts as more personal and probing than men's public documents. As Sasha thinks in *Good Morning, Midnight*, her story "would have to be written by a man" "to be accepted as authentic" (161).

"Let Them Call It Jazz," 1960, highlights the contradiction between an art of direct personal relationship and art as a cultural commodity (*Letters* 184). In that story, a poor black West Indian woman in England says "I don't belong nowhere really, and I haven't money to buy my way to belonging" (*Tigers* 70). Incarcerated in Holloway women's prison for making too much noise in a white neighborhood, she hears a voice singing from a cell above her. "But when that girl sing, she sing to me, and she sing for me. I was there because I was *meant* to be there" (*Tigers* 70–71), she claims, and she keeps the imprisoned woman's song alive by continuing to sing it. A commercial musician hears her and finds the tune catchy: he gives the black woman five pounds for it. He does not want to sing it himself, but to make more money by selling it for popular consumption. In contrast to commercial music, the women's song crosses the distance between the two women with its immediate voiced presence, giving hope to women imprisoned in a white, middle class, male-dominated society.

Even when fragmented down to single words or names, texts hold magical power in Rhys's world. Her heroes change their names to change their luck, and Rochester maddens Antoinette in *Wide Sargasso Sea* by calling her by the wrong name. In Rhys's fiction, words may be stronger than death. Inspired by the black people's belief that the dead receive letters, a white girl writes a letter to "My Dear Darling Mr. Ramage," an Englishman who committed suicide and on whom she had a crush, in "Pioneers, Oh, Pioneers," 1966 (*Letters* 298). When the girl's mother, trying to thwart such nonsense, throws the letter out the window, the narrative voice, though ambiguous, seems to endorse the self-determination of the text over the common sense view: the letter goes "bouncing purposefully down the street. As if it knew exactly where it was going" (*Sleep* 22).

One sustained treatment of the complex power of texts is the story, "The Day They Burned the Books," 1953 (*Letters* 101). Although the title implies a scene of vigilante repression, the story concerns a domestic vendetta by a black widow against her racist white husband and is told by a young white girl, a friend of the couple's son, Eddie. Mr. Sawyer abused his pretty wife, the mother whom Eddie loves dearly. He also loves his father's books, but guiltily feels that this affection for his white English heritage implies hatred for his mother, who is black like himself. The cultural war between the parents continues within Eddie after his father's death. His mother "can't make up a story to save her life," but she makes up lies about people she knows, her own domestic fictions (*Tigers* 47). She despises all books, but especially books by women, whom she regards as traitors who have gone over to the white male cause: the narrator sees in Mrs. Sawyer's eyes that men who wrote books "could be mercifully shot; women must be tortured" (46); in fact, Mrs. Sawyer burns all her husband's books that are not fancy enough to sell. The narrator admires Eddie for questioning the idea of "home," meaning England, and its supposed perfections, an idea derived from books like those in Mr. Sawyer's library. Mrs. Sawyer allows each of the children to keep one book from the literary pyre. Eddie saves *Kim* from his mother's book burning, as though to seal himself an agent for Kipling's apology for British imperialism. The narrator, a frightened and alienated child, thinks of books as comforting, "warm and alive" and preferable to most people (47). Her book from Mr. Sawyer's library is *Fort comme la Mort*. What is strong as death? The father's hoard of great European literature or the black mother's hatred for her oppressors? Or, perhaps, as in the de Maupassant novel, love? Between the white and black traditions, the two children cry and share their books and therefore feel that they are married to one another. In her letters, Rhys referred to herself in 1964 as "fort comme la mort," but wasn't sure she "got over" what she meant by the reference in the story (*Letters* 258, 105).

In "The Day they Burned the Books," European literature has an oppressive imperial role, with its victims turning against one another and the black widow burning books by women writers like witches at the stake. In "The Lotus," written before 1945, Rhys writes about a woman author who is treated as a sort of witch (*Letters* 39). The story is bitter self-parody, reusing the Rhys figures of the lonely old woman and the cruel, rejecting young one in one of her powerful but uncomfortable efforts to expand our empathetic elasticity without sentimentality. Lotus, a drunk old woman, is writing a novel about a "girl who gets seduced" (*Tigers* 115)—a summary that might serve for Rhys's own *Voyage in the Dark* as well as many other works. The subject evokes the knowing laughter of a respectable young couple who apprehensively befriend the old writer, a neighbor in their building. She recites to them a campily sentimental poem she has written, to which the younger woman responds that she hates "slop" and that people get what they deserve in life, a belief that throughout Rhys's work characterizes those whose pleasant circumstances never cause them to question their deserts (120). Lotus shows her young friends twenty-year-old photos of herself to prove that once she "had everything" (123); pathetically, "everything" means only good looks, which vanished long ago, taking her self-esteem with them. Drunk and sick, the old lady runs out into the street with "nothing on" (125), not so much a demonstration of the poor forked animal of naked humanity as of the pitiful reduction of woman to sexual object. The end of the story involves exposure, but the more naked it is, the more ambiguous it is. Lotus describes her novel about a betrayed woman, but the text she exposes is her old, betrayed, naked female body. It seems to be the core of her story and of her devalued identity as a woman, an identity that is both narcissistic and representative. Although she is clearly a self-pitying and difficult woman, the story encourages us toward empathy with her, not for her histrionic victimization by wicked seducers, but for our common aging and mortal condition. The narrative voice treats Lotus, who cadges drinks through transparent lies, as though she were a difficult elderly relative, and the story thus imitates a family that includes and forgives an impossible old mother.

"Fishy Waters," 1976, one of Rhys's late stories with a West Indian setting, combines wonder at the mysteries of human cruelty with empathy for both victims and perpetrators and with a sophisticated attention to the mysteries of unknowable textuality. It is a story of many lies and one truth—a black girl about the age of puberty has been beaten, perhaps sexually molested. Though it seems to conclude with wonder when facing the dark heart of humanity, it does not leave its readers at the edge of a fashionable abyss. Instead, it takes its compassionate stand for all those who are lonely and needy, but especially for those who are poor or black or female or old or young. Ultimately it insists that empathy cannot wait for factual truth and that the empathy at the heart of women's fiction *is* its basic truth. The beating she suffered is so traumatic that the child victim can't speak of it. There is no evidence and no apparent motive, and, in fact, the crime is one for which the concept of motive seems meaningless. The only suspects are two adult white men. The central incident is an example of wickedness that magnifies the sense of incestuous violation felt by a young girl harassed by an older man. In "Goodbye Marcus, Goodbye Rose," a frightened girl, like many actual victims of child abuse, feels too ashamed and blameworthy to speak of such an incident, though, of course, the story's narrator spills the secret, and the story is told entirely from the girl's point of view. In "Fishy Waters" we never hear from the violated girl, and so our curiosity, anger, and compassion are more diffusely directed.

Set in the 1890s, the story consists of several letters. The first four are public expressions of indignation sent to a newspaper about the trial of a poor, drunk, and unpopular English socialist carpenter for child molesting. In earlier versions, the story began more directly with the central incident; Rhys added this framing perspective later (Tulsa red notebook). These letters submerge the individual facts of the case under a welter of references to the island's slave past and to political positions based on race, class, and national origin. The editor comments that these are "fishy waters," which means that something is rotten but perhaps also that something submerged will be valuable when brought up into the air. Then the story shifts to a different kind of correspondence and to differing literary conventions. Maggie Penrice, a colonial wife new to the island, writes her English friend Caroline that "your letter rescued me from a mood of great depression" (*Sleep* 46). This is private, female correspondence about emotions, not about West Indian history: "it will be such a relief to tell you about something that I don't care to discuss with people here" (46). We normally think of writing as a more public, less intimate form than conversation between friends, but here the letter seems an extension of the diary, more private and potentially more revealing than direct talk because the writer need never see the face of the reader. In her letters Maggie describes her version of the events in the trial. Her husband Matthew Penrice, a leading citizen of the colony, and another leading citizen, a doctor, are the two key witnesses. Then the story returns to public texts with a newspaper account of the trial. A letter from the carpenter to the court, read by his lawyer, constitutes his defense. The judge seems fair. The decent white doctor tries to treat his black patients, including the beaten girl, humanely, and he denies that the "result of illiteracy is an uncomplicated mind" (57); however, he does not want to consider the possibility that the victimized girl has been intimidated into silence. Because the evidence is inadequate, the judge sends the carpenter back to England, and the case closes.

After the public trial is a private trial, as after the public letters there was Maggie's private letter. Local rumors claim that Maggie's respectable husband beat the girl and then hustled her off in the care of an old black woman, a former servant indebted to him, to prevent her talking; the same rumors charge that he deliberately framed the unpopular carpenter. The beaten girl's adoptive mother reports that "she is getting quite fat and pretty and hardly ever wakes up screaming" (63). These second-hand screams are all we ever hear from the girl herself, the one undeniable and innocent victim. But as Maggie watches her husband pretend to read, she is "trying to fight the overwhelming certainty that the man she was looking at was a complete stranger" (66). In "Pioneers, Oh, Pioneers," malicious gossip alleged that white Mr. Ramage murdered his black wife. He was so distraught at this charge that he committed suicide, only to be posthumously exonerated when his runaway wife reappeared. Blacks are not necessarily less malicious, callous, or treacherous than whites in Rhys's fiction, nor more so. Her fiction is antiracist when pointing out the racism of others; in the later fiction, it is less sentimental about black people than earlier, though it still falls into stereotypes, and some of Rhys's unpublished later views regressed to conventional racism ("Imperial Road" typescript 1973, Tulsa green notebook). In "Fishy Waters," the gossips' informal system of information, based on black female domestic servants' knowledge of their employers' habits, may turn out to be correct in its suspicions of evil and its disdain for hypocritical respectability. On the day of the crime Penrice inexplicably left his house two hours early. The gossips blame him for the attack, and the gossips may know more about Penrice than his wife does.

In this story Rhys does not give us access to the minds of victim or criminal but instead to the mind of Maggie Penrice, an indirect victim of male aggression. Matthew Penrice acts the role of a benevolent husband who indulges his frail wife's fancies. His own secret fancies may be less benign if they have indeed resulted in the violation of the black girl and the deportation of the English carpenter. In *Wide Sargasso Sea*, English Rochester fears female sexuality and needs to repress his desire for his wife by oppressing her. In "Fishy Waters," the desire that results in the assault is monstrous, evil and perverse, but we do not know in whom it arises or why, and we can only surmise that the elegant Penrice committed this crime in the colonies in the same way that respectable Victorian husbands in England sought to amuse themselves with working girl prostitutes or flagellant boys.

The girl's adoptive mother delivers the one clear moral judgment in the story: "a very wicked person did that," and the narrative invites us to share this maternal concern (54). The public case cries out for justice; the private approach, for empathy—for the girl, the persecuted carpenter, the struggling judge, the woman who adopts the haunted child, even for the repressed criminal who cannot admit what he has done, and finally for the colonial wife plunged into a social world constructed along rules she doesn't understand, so that her relationship to her husband is mediated by strange customs and unreliable texts as well as by the unreliable human heart.

Like many of Rhys's late fictions, "Fishy Waters" presents us with pastiches of style and a potpourri of public and private literary conventions. Whereas most of the earlier stories were straightforward anecdotes, the later ones indulge in more sophisticated framing and distancing devices. This development is not merely technical, since such devices make us repeatedly redefine ourselves and our empathic positions as eavesdroppers on some one else's mental letters. "Fishy Waters" faces us with both collusion and confrontation in public and private styles. Politically, the upper class white Englishman appears to have private power over his white wife, whom he humors; public power over the working-class socialist English carpenter; and an undefined authoritative yet personal power over the black girl. A white man's attack on a poor black girl represents the depth of wickedness, but evil is not necessarily male or white. The nurturing black woman may also help the cover-up. The judge and police seem honorable. Rhys draws a social and moral world far more complex than that in *The Left Bank*, in which she simply championed underdogs and vilified "little middle-class judgment." In "Fishy Waters," the victim screams but doesn't speak. The perpetrator, whoever he is, speaks but lies: although we will never be able to decide who is right or where truth resides, in her later work Rhys shows us that we must empathize with others nonetheless.

III

EMPATHIZING POLITICS
CHRISTINA STEAD'S FICTION

In an interview published in 1973, Stead said that she is a "bad mother" to her writings. "Once the baby's born, I don't even think about it. It must fight for itself" (Whitehead 232). She thus describes herself as a literary mother as abandoning her texts but also as forcing them to sturdy independence, perhaps as her own mother had both fostered and abandoned her by dying when Christina was an infant. She did not consider herself a motherless child, however, but rather one "mothered" by her father, the Australian naturalist David Stead, the most important influence on her life and the model for her most famous character, "the man who loved children." Stead repeatedly connects her early childhood experiences, her attitudes to writing, and her progressive politics. Her political ideals responded to her psychological needs, particularly her utopian, sometimes contradictory, longings for egalitarian community and for individual autonomy. However she also founded her writing on the insight that individual psychological needs arise from the political pressures of capitalist patriarchy and fuel aspirations for freedom. Unlike Rhys's, her work does not trace a coherent line of development but tries out a number of strategies in the attempt to record society and human experience as she sees them. These strategies include oedipal struggle and fraternal bonding as well as maternal empathy, always in a self-conscious political and historical context.

Stead was born in a suburb of Sydney, Australia, in 1902, where her family cherished a private patrilineal literary myth about its establishment in Australia: inspired by *Great Expectations*, her jolly carpenter grandfather left England to make his fortune in Australia (Lidoff 3, Beston "Brief Biography"). She expressed her own origins, too, in somewhat mythic terms, claiming that her father "married, a child was born, and Ellen died. For two years or so, we had a very merry household" which her aunt and young cousin joined (*Ocean of Story*, cited hereafter as *Ocean*, 487). Her father was a self-made naturalist who worked for the fisheries department; in her reminiscences, her golden time of special closeness with her father is also a time of immersion in language, in the "ocean of story" he told her at bedtime, "magical" stories that created the "hope of recognizing and having explained our own experience" (*Ocean* 3, 6–7):

> you see my mother died when I was a baby and he sort of mothered me, and I was the first child. He was a very young man, and he used to come in every night when I went to bed and tell me these amazing stories—about nature mostly, and the backblocks, aborigines, geography, geology, fish, anything that he was thinking about; so that when he went away and I wasn't asleep yet, the room would begin to talk to me. . . . (Whitehead 242)

David Stead's stories animated the universe for baby Christina, so that when her father left her room, "I at once heard other voices. . . . The chest of drawers usually began, 'I am so heavy. . . . ' They were a morose, selfish, grumpy lot. I must have been their own natures" (*Ocean* 6). Stead's world from the beginning is one in which identity is achieved through language and through struggle; the individual voice can speak only by contesting the power over it, even as it denies and projects this perception. "Oddly enough," Stead said in an interview, the "conversations" of her childhood furniture were all about "oppression" (Wetherell 20).

Her father's remarriage and the rapid birth of six younger half-siblings put an end to this period in Stead's childhood. She became the "cradle rocker and message runner and the one who sang the sleep and told tales" for the younger children, but thought of herself as the family's "eldest son" rather than as a surrogate mother, and she later associates herself with both maternal power and with fraternal bonding (*Ocean* 6, Lidoff 209). Her early loss of her mother relates to an adult psychology in which issues of autonomy and empathy remain important and conflictual. On the other hand, her favorite legends are fraternal, telling of Oliver's love for Roland, True Heinrich's loyal heart, and Clovis's bonded sons (*Ocean* 9, Lidoff 202). She told stories at home and was effortlessly good at school, which she calls the child's "first valuable break from the family" (Lidoff 185). As a young teen she had a crush on a woman teacher for whom she wrote a cycle of poems. She went to teacher's college and taught a class of mentally-handicapped children, then went to night secretarial college and later worked as a secretary while saving the money for a "traveling scholarship" to Europe where she hoped to find a university life "howling with philosophical arguments" (Lidoff 190).

On her arrival in London, she found a job with the firm of her husband-to-be William James Blake, born Blech, a married American Marxist businessman, who hired her, in her various accounts, because she was carrying a volume of Bertrand Russell, because she was shy and serious, or because he felt pity for her thinness (Lidoff 193, Baer). Eight years her senior, a prolific writer of historical novels and Marxist exposition, and an eager conversationalist, Blake admired Stead, encouraged her to publish her work, and served as her political teacher, brother-in-arms, and lifelong companion, her "great friend, devoted and true" (*Ocean* 502). She described him as "a most eloquent man with an organized, well-stocked memory, remarkable," "much more gifted than myself" (Stead, letter to Patterson 19 June 1975). "Meeting a man who was my equal and like me, admired me and taught me so much, kind of introduced me to life, was the great freedom for me. You can't live alone. Freedom is association with other people, and especially with a sexual partner, a companion, a mate" (Whitehead 247).

Stead wrote *Seven Poor Men of Sydney*, published 1935, in her first, sick year in England. A publisher accepted it on the stipulation that she write something else first, so she dashed off *Salzburg Tales*, 1934, followed by *The Beauties and Furies*, 1936. Stead and Blake lived in France from 1929 to 1935 and worked in a bank that provided the setting for *House of All Nations*, 1938, then went to the United States, living mostly in New York, from 1937 to 1947, with a short stay screenwriting in Hollywood in 1943. During this time she wrote the autobiographical novels, *The Man Who Loved Children*, 1940, and *For Love Alone*, 1944, and she gave her next three novels American settings: *Letty Fox: Her Luck*, 1946; *A Little Tea, a Little Chat*, 1948; and *The People with the Dogs*, 1952. During the McCarthy years, Stead and Blake lived in hotels and rented rooms throughout Europe; much of the time they were extremely poor, getting by on translations and reviews, their two typewriters clacking together: "we never thought of having a home," she wrote; "home was where the other was" (*Ocean* 512).

In 1952, at age fifty, she married Blake and they settled in England. The reissue of *The Man Who Loved Children* with a laudatory afterword by Randall Jarrell in 1965 revived her reputation. *Cotter's England*, known in the United States as *Dark Places of the Heart*, appeared in 1966. When Blake died in 1968, his death was a terrible blow; five years later she said, "our writing didn't affect each other but of course our interrelationship did. It's taken me all this time . . . to get over his death. . . . I had to begin like an imbecile (Lidoff 219). *The Little Hotel: A Novel*, and *Miss Herbert (The Suburban Wife)*, begun decades earlier, appeared in 1975 and 1976. In 1974 she returned to Australia to live with her brother Gilbert, publishing stories and memoirs until her death in 1983. *Ocean of Story*, an anthology of fiction and essays, and the novel *I'm Dying Laughing: The Humourist* appeared posthumously in 1985 and 1987.

In her later years Stead claimed that she was "not a political person," meaning that she was not herself an organizational leader or joiner, and most critics have taken her at her word (Lidoff 182). R. G. Geering, her literary executor, defensively comments that "despite her political radicalism, she never became an apologist for any political group, never compromised her art by writing propaganda. She began and ended her writing life as an individual artist—an amateur in the best sense of the word" (*Ocean* 637). This defense diminishes Stead; many of her best works are deeply concerned with political issues without being "propaganda." Moreover, her journalistic writings in the 1930s and 1940s closely follow the Communist Party's official line. Although her faith in the U.S.S.R. later diminished, she remained attracted to the "marvellous people," the great "patriots" on the left (Lidoff 182), and she retained a Marxist perspective on world politics and economics throughout her life. In 1935, she suggested that the solution to "the problems of most serious liberal-minded writers outside the U.S.S.R." was to take "lessons from workmen"; since World War I had "smashed the bourgeois machine," progressive writers had only to dissect "the morbid tissues of the [capitalist] social anatomy" to be assured they were "cohabiting with the future" ("Writers Take Sides" 454–56). After Blake's death, she tended to attribute her association with left circles to his influence. Nonetheless, in 1971, she vigorously attacked the United States war against Viet Nam and praised that small nation for "constructing its future": "in socialist nations, it is a principle that if the people are called upon, they will respond and work out their own solutions" ("What Goal in Mind" 128, 119, 120). Shortly before her death, she eulogized leftist writer Stanley Burnshaw as a Communist idealist, a category that still earned her respect: Burnshaw, she felt, suffered from "this stepmother reality" but believed he should "face it and become one with it" ("Some Deep Spell" 136).

If Stead saw reality as a harsh stepmother, she categorized desire as a longing for the maternal, and she subsumed women's attachments to other women under Marxist interpretations of women's lot. Like Rhys and Lessing, she rebuffed attempts to celebrate her as a precursor of second-wave feminism and rejected what she understood to be its aims: "it's not a genuine movement. It's totally, purely middle class. . . . And of course they all have chars!" (Lidoff 207). Nevertheless, she upheld socialist feminist demands like equal pay for women and rights for housewives. Recognizing that women were less well represented in literature than men because "the long literary tradition, thousands of years old, had enabled men completely to express themselves, while women feared to do so," she claimed that her "object was by no means to write for women, or to discuss feminine problems, but to depict society as it was" (*Ocean* 547). Understanding the women's liberation movement as equivalent to female separatism, she traced its origins to infantile yearnings:

> I think that with many women the Women's Movement has something to do with a hang-over of their longing to be in the shelter of their mother's care and love, you see. This didn't happen with me, it was my father who took on this job, and that probably explains something (Whitehead 248).

Infantile fear of maternal power, not longing for the maternal, explains cultural attitudes toward women in a society that divides people into powerful and powerless classes and that arrogates childrearing to women:

> . . . the woman in the home, so weak and ailing, often moneyless, power-
> less . . . yet has the awful power of hunger and suck, gives life and holds
> off death, sets out her law, defies *their* law for our sake, . . . a magic woman
> sheltering this small creature, ourselves, obliged to live in the country of the
> giants. Mothers and fathers can and do maim and kill; and children have
> their moments of fear with even the kindest of parents. But the man's power
> is evident: the woman's is stranger. . . . Behind the concept of woman's
> strangeness is the idea that a woman may do anything: she is below society,
> not bound by its law, unpredictable; an attribute given to every member of
> the league of the unfortunate (*Ocean* 529–30).

All "slaves" have a similar perspective, yet each social group has its own
experience and hence its own views: "who denies that . . . a cosmonaut,
an Arab, a Jew, a coal miner, a housewife, will each see the same event
differently? So it is likely that a woman, most women, will see things
differently from a man, most men" (*Ocean* 534).

Thus Stead opposed what she defined as separatist and regressive feminism to progressive Marxism, just as she opposed the engulfing power of
the infantile care-giver to male-defined political power. "The awful power
of hunger and suck," a phrase blending child and mother in one frightening
unit, indicates that fear of engulfment against which Stead's daughterly
characters fight. In these battles for freedom and selfhood, the child needs
its own healthy narcissism in order not to be overwhelmed by the dominating self-interests of adults: for Stead, the opposite of empathy is narcissism; the female self fears being sucked in or dominated by a selfish
parent, not being excluded or rejected as in Rhys, and its struggle for
identity is so furious that it can only rarely attain the generosity of empathy.

Stead said she believed the only important thing about writing was character, that she was interested in character rather than plot (Wetherell 26).
This is true of her work and yet misleading, since characterization, the
representation of individual identity in fiction, remains a recurrent problem
in her work. Her characters face decomposition from two opposing directions, directions we might see as marshalled under the banners of Freud
and Marx. The characters may lose their external identity and appear as
random intersections of libidinous drives, or they may lose inner coherence
and appear merely as social surfaces, the sum of their economic and historical determinants. Thus with Stead, though she resists such labels, the
problem of defining a relationship between the individual and history becomes the problem of defining female identity under capitalist patriarchy.

Stead's characters manifest their identity in speech more than in action;
they are walking mouths. Fragments of psychological drive often appear
in Stead's imagery rather than through character, whereas the "objective"
forces of history push her plots and receive exposition as chunks of authorial wisdom or as the wise words of a character modeled on her husband.
Her best realized characters, on the other hand, cohere through their in-

dividual linguistic styles, like Henny and Sam in *The Man Who Loved Children* and Emily in *I'm Dying Laughing*. Although much of Stead's fiction seems "objective," focusing on public issues and on characters observed from the outside, recurrent psychological issues related to preoedipal parent-child dynamics, especially the dangers of narcissism and the necessity for autonomy, shape her work from the inside.

Female identity in Stead's work is constantly struggling for definition against overwhelming forces—in her earliest and some of her latest work, the disruptions of female sexuality and the engulfing power of parents. One of her best works, *House of All Nations*, escapes the problems of female identity through male identification, and it has therefore received little attention from feminist critics. The subsequent autobiographical novels *The Man Who Loved Children* and *For Love Alone* directly portray female identity in formation. Several of her late novels with female protagonists, especially *The Little Hotel*, *Dark Places of the Heart* and *I'm Dying Laughing*, dramatize the dangers to female autonomy from engulfment by the other and the destruction of both self and other through women's manipulative empathy.

Unlike Rhys and Lessing, Stead does not write her best in short fiction, and this chapter does not restrict itself to her short stories. She published stories ranging from a few pages to long novellas, but she rarely organized a story as a complete action, a moment of understanding, or even as a slice of life. Rhys's stories seem perfect for their length; Lessing's stories, various in both subject matter and accomplishment, vividly create characters, ideas, and situations. With Stead, however, raggedy anecdotes search for meanings; characters search for actions; jokes lack punchlines; or punchlines need stories to rest on. Many of the stories published in the posthumous volume *Ocean of Story* are sketches toward the longer pieces. However, like Rhys and Lessing, her earliest writings were short stories and therefore shed light on the first stage of her career.

Women's Tales, Men's Ends

In *For Love Alone*, the autobiographical Teresa writes about the "sorrows of women." Although Stead's first novel, *Seven Poor Men of Sydney*, bewails the sorrows of poor men, her earliest writings, three stories composed in Australia and included in *The Salzburg Tales*, do indeed chronicle women's woes: "The Morpeth Tower," "On the Road," and "The Triskelion" (*Ocean* 498). The *Salzburg Tales* assign a wide variety of short fiction to fictional speakers in the tradition of *The Canterbury Tales*. Although most of the storytellers in the book are men, women narrate these three stories—a schoolgirl, an Australian schoolteacher, and a "doctoress." All three stories focus on female sexuality as a frightening and destructive force.

"The Morpeth Tower" is a two-page series of poetic images, like those

Louisa tells her younger siblings in *The Man Who Loved Children*, about a woman in a tower:

> The music rises high . . . the tower becomes clumsily human in form, seizes the lady's hair and begins to draw a bow across it: the lady cries in pain, and her cries are the cries of a violin.(*Salzburg Tales* 298)

As in a dream, the tower, "like a demon rider" (298), leaps on a black horse, one of Stead's frequent symbols for rampant sexuality; Louisa Pollitt mistakes her heartbeats for galloping horse hooves and tells her siblings about a vanishing horse. In a girl's nightmare of sexual and pregnancy imagery, the Morpeth tower opens and closes, reveals and hides a woman inside it, rides a wild horse at night, and returns to its normal appearance as calmly as parents overheard in the night appear at breakfast in the morning.

In contrast to these childish images, Stead gives the Australian school-teacher a parable about the difficulties of female desire that turns the same imagery of mountain, horse, and path into an allegory about women's choices. Two single women in their thirties ride together up the "rough and bestial" Mount Solitary, while speaking of the miseries and boredoms of their lives (349). Passionate Rachel attempts a suicide jump, but sensible Lilias pulls her back. Referring to a Goya etching which shows a ringless woman struggling between a "sloth and a black horse, each waiting to make her his prey" (348), Lilias claims she wishes to avoid passion and "get old as quickly as possible to take my ease. . . . With good luck I shall be in a year or two perfectly resigned, and I will be able to enter the warm and indolent country of my heart" (351). Though she is a strong woman with loyal women friends, her fate seems quite as sad as tempestuous Rachel's. But neither Lilias's "sloth" nor Rachel's "black horse" of unfulfilled passion can alleviate the "horrors" in these women's lives (351). Although Stead said she wrote her first schoolgirl poetry to praise a woman teacher, she represses the idea of female attractiveness to other women throughout her adult writing, and her women together remain women alone.

Stead assigns the wild story of the Triskellion to the "doctoress," another professional woman, who claims it is only a simple "case history," because she has "no time for romance" (172). Thus, like the women in the school-teacher's tale, she repudiates desire, though her story seethes with sexual imagery. This odd "case history" probes the origins of blind, retarded Arnold and his symbolic talisman, a gold "triskellion" or wheel with three spokes shaped like men's legs. Arnold turns out to be the afflicted byblow of his depraved, teenaged mother and her yet more depraved incestuous father, simultaneously his father and grandfather, who molested and murdered another young girl before his jealous daughter murdered him. Arnold marries, but his working-class wife throws him out because he is "sick" (176); all night he pesters her with his hands "running, like a pyannist doing his scales" (177). Stead codes these fantasies in a different language from that which she uses for social description, one dense with images, loose in syntax, and unconnected to individual character; the several characters and the narrator of this story speak in the same style so that they blur into one another. A woman in the story says, "I hate nature: it is full of cries and tears like a female madhouse" (185). Like sexuality, nature in these three stories is malign and perverse, excessive, frightening, and anthropomorphic. In these early stories, Stead attributes terrible fates to women who succumb to desire and wretched ones to women who don't, and female identity is subsumed under instinctual forces.

The later stories of the *Salzburg Tales*, too, link sex with death and mutilation and marriage with boredom and violence. In "The Volcano" an adulterous sculptor carries the heart of his dead mistress in a knapsack before flinging it and himself into a volcano. In "The Prodigy," a young female musician is robbed, "ravished and killed, and the body flung into a thicket" (275). The male musician who tells this tale moralizes, "what is wilder, more reckless and weaker than a rebellious woman? History, reason, and intuition all tell her she must fail in this world of men" (276). Men in similar stories seduce women or drop them with narrative impunity. Thus Stead's fiction begins by assuming that female heterosexuality is inevitable but dangerous and that heterosexual institutions, especially marriage and the family, are intolerable. Women's lot makes women rebel, but this rebellion is doomed by "history, reason, and intuition . . . in this world of men." Since Stead sees women as so torn by sexuality and so alienated in a patriarchal society, she seeks the control offered by reason, the assurance offered by history, by turning to "this world of men."

At the same time that she presents women's desires as anarchic and destructive, she expands another analysis of women's condition, a simple Marxist analysis, presumably what she thinks "reason, history, and intuition" tell a woman. The schoolboy in *The Salzburg Tales* says, "men, women . . . they are the same animal: do we have to use these old gaslight distinctions. . . . There are only two kinds in our society, rich, poor, master, servant, proprietor and pensioner; and all the foibles of women that we laugh at in secret, are the foibles of a dependent class. Women are open-hearted, good, ambitious, capable as we are, given the same economic opportunity" (259). Moreover, "all oppressed are oppressors, like the servant who passes on his master's discontent to his inferior" (168). On the one hand, then, women as a category do not exist: they are merely a species of exploited men. On the other, Stead's imagery treats women very differently from men, subject to and punished by their bodies and their sexuality, and some of her characters announce a basic polarity between the sexes that results in inevitable antagonism. A widow in *The Salzburg Tales* exclaims, "what is sadder than the eternal difference, the eternal misunderstanding between the sexes?" (246–47). Catherine Bagenault of *Seven*

Poor Men of Sydney futilely tries to find a way out of this double bind; "I've fought all my life for male objectives in men's terms. I am neither man nor woman, rich nor poor, elegant nor worker, philistine nor artist. That's why I fight so hard and suffer so much and get nowhere" (247–48).

Difference and misunderstanding characterize relations between generations as well as those between the sexes, and Stead repeatedly chronicles marital abuse and parental neglect, the exploitative power relationships within the family. In *The Salzburg Tales*, the Marionettist abandons his famiy for fifteen years but is surprised when his wife, running the business without him, does not welcome him back. The public stenographer, another independent woman, tells a tale about her horrible father, an eccentric schoolmaster who humiliated his first wife by his open affair with a local teenager. He bullies his adult sons, keeps them ignorant, taunts their stupidity, plays practical jokes, and alternately wheedles and abuses them. The stenographer explains that one of her laborer brothers tried to learn Egyptian hieroglyphics from pictures in an encyclopedia. When she asked him to decipher his scrawlings, he danced her round the room: "it says We ALL hate the Old Man. We ALL hate the Old Man!" "We are a devoted family," the stenographer concludes peacefully (404). A manipulative, overbearing father recurs throughout Stead's work, and the manic glee of *The Salzburg Tales* as a whole, like that of the laboring son in this story, comes from the writer's sense of liberation in decoding the dangerous truth: "We ALL hate the Old Man"—whether the "Old Man" is one's boss, pious conceptions of God, or each family's father, and the "devoted family" is a sibling band united by common hatred of the father. Stead's deep anti-authoritarianism makes her distrustful of power but susceptible to the attractions of comrades-in-arms who can unite to overthrow the *status quo*.

Stead came to literary maturity during the great depression, and class is always a major determinant of her character's thoughts and actions: poverty warps most of the characters of *Seven Poor Men of Sydney* and later of *For Love Alone* and *Dark Places of the Heart*, but it also leads a few to stoic independence. Wealth confines the rich even more tightly than poverty does the poor, although even the egotistical monomaniacs of *House of All Nations*, *A Little Tea, a Little Chat*, and *The Little Hotel* occasionally lapse into generosity. In this respect, Stead's fictional economics are far more flexible than her '30s polemical line. In 1936 she criticized William Saroyan for his soft love of "our lady poverty" and his ahistorical humanism, calling him "the Pied Piper of the common denominator" ("The Impartial Young Man" 25). Her 1935 report on the first international Congress of Writers for the defense of culture stands for a polarized position, calling on all writers to fight "the armies of reaction": "in all countries but one," [the Soviet Union], "the pauperization of the middle-class, militarization and barbarism of the upper class and rationalization, enfeebling and unemployment of the lower classes have withdrawn from the writer his ready public" ("The Writers Take Sides" 453). In such a time "the frightful insistence of economic questions" leaves writers "quite at sea," unless they follow the party compass and "give up their poetic solitudes and soft self-probings" in order to "enter the political arena" and "take lessons from workmen" (453–54). Throughout the dour analysis of the contemporary situation rings exhilaration: capitalism, reflected in soft bourgeois modernist art, lies in its death throes. Unlike Rhys, she is not mentored in introspection or the technical devices that convey interiority in great modernist fiction, but joins the leftist antimodernist reaction that returns to older traditions of realism and of individual character in the name of progressive human values.

Banking and Brotherhood: *House of All Nations*

With her leftist exhilaration, Stead turns with insight and enthusiasm to the magic of men and money in her wonderful book of 1938, *House of All Nations*. It is a confident book, confident of the economic and historical forces killing capitalism and confident that "artists are sensitized plates," "indicators and interpreters" of their times ("The Writers Take Sides" 454). Because "every man's economic interest primes his intelligence," working writers of the '30s can believe they are "cohabiting with the future," looking proudly down on the older writers who suffer the "desperate pessimism" of "the generation of defeat" and assured of their own ability to understand all people as simple representatives of economic forces: "the French liberal says of the East, 'What passes in their mysterious heads?' The answer is, the same as passes in men of the same class in your own land" (454,456,461,462). Although economic interest presumably supersedes individual identity, Stead in *House of All Nations* observes and reports a dazzling array of men who overflow the ideology that purports to understand them.

Thickly surrounded by leftist politics while working at a Parisian bank in the 1930s, Stead conquers the usually all-male preserve of high finance in *House of All Nations*, her first entirely successful novel. Tightly structured, coherent, and a good seller, it announces its seriousness in ways traditional to the male canon by treating a public subject of recognized importance, the European economic crisis, on a scale that recalls a Hollywood epic; one hundred and twenty-five characters jostle in one hundred and four chapters. This enormous novel records a few years between the heydey and bankruptcy of a private, speculative Parisian bank catering to a rich, reckless international money crowd. Jules Bertillion, whose motto is "no one ever had enough money," owns and manages the bank. He claims "it's easy to make money. You put up the sign BANK and someone walks in and hands you his money. The facade is everything" *House of All Nations* (11). The action opens in 1931, when Jules is rich from betting on disaster. However, craving excitement, he agrees to a huge bet on the exchange rate of the pound, a sort of contemporary upper-class financial duel. When

England goes off the gold standard in 1936, he loses most of the bank's funds but survives by speculative juggling until a greedy employee steals his books, which show the bank's illegal but profitable dealings. Rather than face the law, Jules steals what's left in the vault and escapes to Estonia. Although the novel is comic and satiric, the forces dooming Jules combine a tragic external fate, England's currency policies, with Jules' personal hybris, the character flaw that causes him to bet and so defy the prudent advice of Michel Alphendéry, his brilliant and loyal Marxist employee and one of the Stead characters modeled on Blake.

Despite its vast cast and subsidiary plots, the novel has only a few main characters and actions. Stead labels her many short chapters "scenes" and sets most of them within the claustrophobic inner offices of the bank. Dialogue carries the action as men pit themselves against one another, the stock markets, and the exchange rates. The effect is that people are seen from the outside and in their own terms, as though underscoring the novel's historicity and objectivity. The hustlers love explaining their deals, but they also enjoy lying and mystification; occasionally, Stead stops the plot to explain the characters' financial schemes to us and to unveil their deceits.

The narrative point of view is that of an omniscient insider. It discriminates between Argentine and Chilean playboys, for example, but rarely follows the bank's customers out its doors into the rest of their lives. Compared to the hodgepodge structures of *The Salzburg Tales* and *Seven Poor Men of Sydney* and the mannered intensity of her other early novel, *The Furies and the Beauties*, *House of All Nations* is an astonishing performance. Stead banishes her earlier obsessions with incest and mutilation and focuses this novel's loyalties, betrayals, and power plays exclusively on Lady Fortune, who is presumably free of the anarchic fragmentations of female psychology and sexuality. Jules' character creates his situation, which sweeps us along in suspense, at the same time that the author fulfills her self-proclaimed social duty to explicate historical forces in society. Stead always claimed maximum verisimilitude and minimal invention for *House of All Nations*; she said she wrote up what clients and employers told her when she was a confidential secretary. Because they didn't take writers seriously, she said, they revealed themselves to her fully (Whitehead 238); probably they did not take women seriously either. From the belly of capitalism's lying whale, Stead reports the beast's failing digestion.

At its simplest and sometimes most powerful, *House of All Nations* exposes capitalist exploitation. The bank's wealthy patrons make their money wickedly. Pedro Pedrillo flies to Paris from the Argentine where he spends weeks in the saddle "whipping the peons when they were troublesome" (529). The merchant Daniel Cambo sells cut-rate goods he acquires cheaply from disaster-struck people. Such marketing is far more profitable than manufacturing, he explains: "buy everything below cost from people whose capital has been lost. . . . See: deal in human dreck, not dreck goods!" (258). The wheat dealer Henri Leon loves others' misfortunes, chortling, "you can only make a fortune in a war!" (402). Stead lets the allegorically-named Adam Constant, a Marxist bank teller, denounce the bank most clearly. He plans to write a grand exposé based on his experiences in the bank, to write, that is, a novel like *House of All Nations*:

> My dream is, that one day I will get them all down. . . . I want to show the waste, the insane freaks of these money men, the cynicism and egotism of their life, the way they gambol amidst plates of gold. . . . I'll show that they are not brilliant, not romantic, not delightful, not intelligent; that they have no other object but their personal success and safety. Although, of course, there are plenty of living intelligences among them, sidetracked talents . . . but all, all compliant and prostituted. . . . (87)

These rich men believe the truths of the revolutionaries, but hide them: " 'knowledge, money, real love, power', they say, 'are too good for the people. These things are divine, we must keep them all to ourselves.' And they debase learning, coinage, sex, democratic control to fool the people . . . " (88).

Clearly intended as a satire on banking and capitalism, *House of All Nations* is also a deft crime novel in which our sympathies extend to Jules, "the charmer who deceived," as he finagles his heist (768). The narrator tells us Jules was a "robber by instinct, sharpshooter of commerce by career, nourished by corruption . . . child of his age . . . born to profit greatly by it, without understanding it in the least. He had only one interpretation of history and politics, an economic one" (93). Stead, too, has only one interpretation of history, an economic one, although hers is a different economics from Jules'. For him, the one law is that everyone is greedy: "if all the rich men in the world divided up their money amongst themselves, there wouldn't be enough to go round" (11). He doesn't fear Stalin, Mussolini, or Hitler because he assumes the people at the top always play the same game, but he is baffled, even repulsed, by Alphendéry's disinterested honesty.

Although capitalism is dying, economic institutions crumbling, fascism winning, and war hovering on the horizon, the Marxist characters enjoy the bank. "It is fascinating living among the Cro-Magnons" (84), Constant says. Blake claimed the 1929 crash confirmed Marxist theory, though he also admitted he had not foreseen the crucial event of *House of All Nations*, England's going off gold (Blake 382,298). This long-range Marxism gives the book a more cheerful tone than one might expect. Although published in 1938 and including events through Hitler's rise to power, it both foresees and downplays disaster, interpreting fascism as merely an upper-class expedient to shore up markets. Alphendéry explains the coming war as a phase in the decline of capitalism, one of "three quick sweeps between the last war and the next"—the Russian revolution of 1917, the "expropriation of the American bourgeoisie" via the stock market crash of 1929, and the "smashing of the German bourgeoisie" by Hitler (111). However, Hitler's success does at last shake the novel's leftists and even its capitalists.

> At this moment the wing of terror spread its shadow over Europe, and the governing classes, in despair since 1929, began to see that Fascism was not simply an expedient to be used on a lackadaisical southern people, but a real salvation for their property. At this time the socialist friends of Alphendéry began to tremble; the wisest predicted ten years of black reaction; the conservatives predicted a hundred years of domination (620–21) .

The end of *House of All Nations* foreshadows World War II: "all the clients banded themselves together in national protective associations, and thus the next European war began in little" (748–49).

Thus the book foresees but underestimates "the next European war," just as it underestimates anti-Semitism and national prejudices. The Jewish-born Marxist Alphendéry does not recognize any categories other than economic ones. To him, "the Jew" is "just a bourgeois" with "a head for finance, money monopolies, learning, family organization, love of law and medicine, rationalism, democracy, a complete organization of property round the family," and "Bolshevism" is "Izzy, Jake, and Manny forming a labor union in the sweatshop. So the boss runs back to Judaism"; because Alphendéry sees religion purely as a mystifying device by the upper classes, he advises, "let us forget the Jew . . . let's remember humanity" (171–72).

One of Alphendéry's few truly depressed moments occurs when he thinks his dire predictions for capitalism may be based on wish fulfillment, not historical fact: "I belong to those who want to see the great change in their lifetimes and so I overlook the truth that our overlords will not give up the ghost without trying to strangle us to death first. . . . They have a hundred tricks up their sleeves before they'll lose and then, the last trick, machine guns" (460). By taking a Marxist view of history seriously, Stead can shape her tale of a bank's collapse so that it represents the end of capitalism. This assurance gives the novel much of its strength, its conviction that the case history we read has wider reverberations. As one socialist sympathizer in the novel taunts her capitalist father, "we have neither art, learning, science, nor refinement yet on our side. You have them all. We have nothing but history" (45).

Much of the novel's good cheer springs from its focus on the comic squabbling among the greedy capitalists, not on the poor oppressed masses. When the bank finally goes under, very few decent people get hurt. The bank's customers are all the upper ten thousand, the "idle rich and speculators" of the globe (28). As Blake writes, "Capitalism develops large parasitic groups of investors—'the idle rich'—and yet shakes them off like snow from a bough" (Blake 391). No poor widows or orphans are ruined by the bank's fall. In contrast, socialism in the novel is represented as communal, egalitarian, and idealistic. Alphendéry says he has "mankind to live for" (*House of All Nations* 200), and Adam Constant rhapsodizes about "fellow feeling": the clay of all living men is on fire . . . with the same life" (82, 83). Yet the brotherhood of men excludes and marginalizes women, who do not appear as full persons in the novel. Stead seems so ambivalent or indifferent about them that she loses track of them, for example, by referring to Alphendéry as though he is single, then speaking of his long unhappy marriage, as though the success of her identification with a male-oriented historical view implies the misogyny of that view as well.

The novel solves the problem of female identity in a way traditional to the male canon and to orthodox Marxist theory, by abolishing women as persons, letting them serve instead as occasional metaphorical vortices. Perhaps the most fully drawn women in the book, Marianne Raccamond, is a relentlessly ambitious harpy. Stead repeatedly draws female desire and self assertion as monstrous and disgusting, and also as disruptive to the naturally harmonious—if competitive—relationships among men. Fidelity and fertility are important values in the novel, but most of the women are unfaithful and childless. The title metaphor of the book rests on an equation between capitalism and prostitution, since the "House of All Nations" is a Parisian brothel, a metaphor that blames the prostitutes, not the johns. (Stead referred to the book as "Harlot's House," *Ocean* 523; Blake calls the stock exchange an "old wanton," 384). Jules believes "every woman is a whore, but the whores are the ones who never learned the game," just as "every banker is a poker shark" (*House of All Nations* 309). Everyone, including Jules, considers his marital virtue trivial in comparison to his financial promiscuity: "I sleep with my own wife, true; but I sleep with other people's money" (350).

Stead decenters issues of female identity in *House of All Nations* and appropriates a male-identified narrative voice, for example, in apostrophizing "sweet gold" as having "everything that man desires in a wife" (140). Alphendéry's secret is that he "loves men" (236), and it is the secret of the novel as well, a novel about male bonding not only among political comrades but even more strongly between Alphendéry and his class enemies, the banking Bertillon brothers. As we have seen, the novel marginalizes women as people and admits them chiefly as metaphoric counters for male economic power. On the other hand, it invests male comradeship with erotic force. Alphendéry is "a man who loved men's company and knew how to bring out the best in them . . . he got a lot of affection and a lot of business" (247). He and Jules' brother William Bertillon do the day-to-day work of the bank, working together so closely that they understand one another completely: they "knew each other as well as a husband and wife, long, but not too long, married. They talked much of the day in glances" (532). Jules' reckless inventiveness earns him Alphendéry's total admiration and devotion. "Money has flowed to you, but your joy has been in inventing schemes"; "the beauty of this place is you, Jules. Its soul is you" (201, 202). Alphendéry speaks of Jules in idealized and erotic terms, like a faithful wife: "I suppose I'm old-fashioned or timid, but I love you, Jules" (203); "I stay here like a fool because I'm loyal to Jules, whom I love dearly" (452).

Although they are eventually left jobless, the bank's workers enjoy a pleasant life under the genial Jules, who contributes generously to employee wedding presents, keeps impoverished incompetents on the payroll, and treats many employees as valuable co-conspirators. Unlike the overpaid Raccamond, faithful Alphendéry draws a modest salary and is touched when Jules buys him a gold pencil for his birthday. Though he made Jules twenty million francs, he is pleased with an occasional bonus and willingly donates his money to bolster Jules when the bank is failing. Thus, although the bank represents late capitalism, it perversely and charmingly mimics an ideal utopian community. When the police and bankruptcy courts try to figure out the bank's situation, no one can tell them who the bank's general manager was or how its chain of command operated. Rather, this brothers' business works at best like a convivial men's club, like a genuine fraternity.

House of All Nations is a homosocial novel. Alphendéry supports his old mother and unfaithful wife, but he loves men—poor oppressed humanity and his charming, amoral employer Jules. His ideal relationship is a brotherhood that he shares even more with the capitalists at the bank than with his communist comrades. Privately Stead shared a "brother" fantasy with Blake, her model for Alphendéry. She said she had a puppet alter ego named Nello, after the younger brother in Edmond Goncourt's *The Brothers Zemganno*, a tribute to his love for his brother (Lidoff 217).

Alphendéry loves Jules, and though this love is misguided, the narrative voice often shares the infatuation, describing Jules as potent, fertile, and beautiful. This creates an interesting situation for the reader. Reading a satire, we don't identify with Jules, the shallow schemer. Despite our criticism, however, we do become loyal to the bank, hoping for its escape from bankruptcy; as in a heist film, we hope the charming thieves get away with the swag, because we identify with Alphendéry's loyalty to Jules. Embodying an idealized masculine, rather than a feminine psychology, the novel puts loyalty at issue here, even love, but not empathy: Alphendéry can't understand Jules' narcissism, nor Jules, Alphendéry's love. Yet Michel's loyalty seems noble, and we reprehend Jules far more for betraying Alphendéry than for absconding with the bank's gold deposits. This narrative identification makes the novel a richer experience for the reader than the self-assured satire on capitalist greed that Adam Constant says he wishes to write and that the novel sometimes pretends to be.

Alphendéry loves men, but his form of both courtship and consummation is speech. For example, he enjoys matchmaking two moneymakers, "his eyes glossy with his personal passion, exposition" (30). He speaks on behalf of socialist causes, too, winning "a following of young disputatious

student-workers and old socialist wisebeards" (599). His comrades praise
him as "a changed man," "a socialist orator of the grand school" (600). All
of Stead's work shows her fascination with language but also her profound
distrust of a medium that is used chiefly to deceive and dominate. The
money-seekers at the bank are also yarn spinners. Leon the wheat merchant
speaks in a private telegraphic code, which only Alphendéry can understand. Jules lies from the love of lying. The outlandish Theodor Bomba
adapts his style to match that of the person he is trying to manipulate, and
the novel endorses this virtuosity, even in a hypocritical fraud, as equivalent to a knowledge of human nature: "he knew men very well" (437).

Stead describes her childhood as formed through listening to her father's
bedtime tales, the "ocean of story" that combines facts, myths, and fictions
(*Ocean* 3–5). The reader of a Stead novel is often in the position of the
tucked-in child, flooded by speech. Often Stead's talkers embarrass, be-
leaguer, and humiliate their listeners, a fact which may account for the
difficulty many readers have in finishing her books. In *House of All Nations*,
however, we identify with the willing listener. Alphendéry talks as an act
of love to instruct his friends, and his therapeutic and comradely speech
sometimes fuses with the novel's narrative voice. In this way the novel
seems sympathetic rather than merely didactic as Stead identifies with her
life companion's Marxist discourse.

Female Quests

In *House of All Nations* Stead merges her voice in the voice of another,
neither a woman's voice nor that of the dominating father, but instead the
voice of a brother comrade, a male rebel, a man who loves men. This
creative immersion perhaps helped to consolidate her own powers for her
next and finest fiction, *The Man Who Loved Children*, discussed in chapter
five. After that book she writes her next, most explicitly autobiographical
novel, *For Love Alone*, when she is old enough to be her hero's mother.
The narrator's identification with her character is very close, even though
she adjusts her characters to fit the historical period. Stead herself reached
England in 1928 at the age of twenty-six, but she makes her hero Teresa
twenty-three when she arrives in London in 1936, a date when her personal
poverty fits the depressed state of London and her sexual awakening can
accompany the daring bravado of a lover who fights for the Republic in
the Spanish Civil War. At the opening of the novel Teresa, named like the
author-saint who inspired George Eliot, is only nineteen.

Structured as a conventional novel of development, a triumph of character over circumstances, *For Love Alone* records its hero's progress from
impoverished adolescence in Australia to happy marriage in England. The
novel's opening sections juxtapose the motifs of cultural exile and the patriarchal oppressions of home with unusual clarity, setting them out in

prologue and text, respectively. The prologue, "Sea People," portrays Australia as a topsy-turvy world, still defined by the English norm: "in the part of the world Teresa came from, winter is in July" and Christmas dinners are set "near the tall pine tree loaded with gifts and tinsel as in the old country" (*For Love Alone* xi). Australia is "a great Ithaca" (xii), and the colonial woman will have to leave home on her own epic quest, as the novel's first scene makes clear. The chapter begins with the imposing figure of Teresa's father "naked . . . in the doorway" (3). His first words admonish his daughters to emulate an aboriginal woman he saw "sitting on the ground nursing her black baby, . . . herself . . . black as a hat, with a strong, supple oily skin, finer than white women's skins" (3). He claims that the black woman admires him, and he makes her an object lesson for his daughters. "What do we look for in women—understanding!" he pontificates. "In the rough and tumble of man's world, the law of the jungle is often the only law observed, but in the peace and sanctity of the man's home, he feels the love that is close to angels!" His home should be his castle, his refuge; he shouts at his daughters to clean his boots to insure his comfort (8). He insults Teresa by calling her "a little tramp" (6) because she does not cater to him. Simply, somewhat crudely, Stead underscores the domineering banality of the father's use of cultural myths—myths that assert white cultural superiority and that treat black people and white women as like the land, nature to be exploited so that it serves, nurtures, and enhances white men. When her father teases that she has "ants in her pants and bats in her belfry," Teresa responds fiercely, "you offend my honour! I would kill anyone who offends my honour" (11); one of her brothers sneers that female honor is something other than she thinks. "I'll go away," she announces; "I have suffered too much" (13).

Teresa escapes from her father's domination through paid work, then through voluntary subservience to her perverse Latin tutor, Jonathan Crow. He inspires her with a taste for intellectual ferment, and she decides to follow him to England. Absent, he becomes the sage of her penny-pinching deprivation as a teacher and secretary, inspiring a heroic journey to follow him. Having become a secretary, she saves wages by denying herself food, clothing, and all pleasures, including tramfare to work. She thus "walks" the distance to London in three years. After she gets to London, the process reverses, with deprivation, work, family, and love played out in relation to her choice of men. Having enticed Teresa to follow him to England, Crow enjoys rejecting her, and she experiences her chastity as humiliation, not self-sufficiency. Jonathan says free love is impossible because "women are not free. . . . Does property want to be property?" (217). Teresa's goals and actions are often male-defined, and she guides her decisions by asking herself what a man would do in a similar situation. In her quest for Jonathan's love, she feels like "a gallant and a brave man" longing "to win a wife" (246). Humiliated by Crow, she believes she is to blame for not taking a more active role in the courtship, and she quotes to herself "none but the brave deserve the fair" as though she is a gentleman (212). The sexual double standard is a social reality for her and also a moral enigma. Stead described Teresa as "self-integrated" (Wetherell 22), and the "honor" she would kill to defend is something like integrity, not sexual chastity.

Teresa gets a secretarial job from an American businessman in London, Jim Quick, who promptly falls in love with her. She cannot fully reciprocate his love, however, until she rejects the constraints of fidelity, becoming free and ennobled through sexual choice. When in love, she changes dramatically. "She began to think she could master men," and she surmises that if women loved freely "an abyss would open in the principal shopping street of every town" (454). Her affair with a Spanish freedom fighter defines her own, equally revolutionary rebellion. By the end of the novel, she has acquired a family of leftist comrades in addition to the still-devoted Quick; she is writing fiction; and she plans to return to paid employment, unlike the women of her Australian childhood who could work or marry but not both. Teresa thinks of literature by men as telling the truth about passion, but not literature by women: "her world existed and was recognized by men. But why not by women? She found nothing in the few works of women she could find that was what they must have felt" (74). Clearly this novel intends to tell us what women "must have felt" and so increase our identification with the writer hero.

Having gone from an encyclopedic masculine and Marxist analysis of society to an empathetic reimmersion in her personal history, Stead turned outward again to chronicle the effects of world war on a variety of Americans—a sexually adventurous New York secretary in *Letty Fox, Her Luck*; the horrible capitalist womanizer Robbie Grant in *A Little Tea, a Little Chat*; and the bemused, benign Edward Massine in *The People with the Dogs*. The postwar period was a disappointment for Stead: the working classes joined in suspicion of the Reds; left movements were disbanding and demoralized; popular Freudian psychologizing was on the rise. Individual and national self-interest seemed to propel history rather than socialist community or Marxist determinism, and sexual polarization further eroded the possibilities of equality.

Stead's intensity faltered without the firm ideology of *House of All Nations* or the clear autobiographical impulses of *The Man Who Loved Children* and *For Love Alone*, though she continued to explore the social implications of individual egotism. Moreover, her later books failed to sell. During the fourteen-year gap between *The People with the Dogs* and *Dark Places of the Heart*, she wrote pieces toward *The Little Hotel*, *Miss Herbert (Suburban Wife)*, and *I'm Dying Laughing*. *House of All Nations* and the autobiographical novels solved the problem of female identity in history: the former by abolishing it and the latter by identifying the daughter's needs for autonomy with a rebellious political tradition. The maternal protagonists of the later novels are estranged from themselves and from the progressive forces of history.

Mrs. Trollope in *The Little Hotel* achieves autonomy for herself through empathy with other women, and she at least removes herself from the predatory sterility of postwar capitalist speculation; however, the heroes of both *Dark Places of the Heart* and *I'm Dying Laughing* pervert both socialist and maternal responsibility for others and so become responsible for some of history's failures.

Because of the delayed publication of Stead's later works, it is difficult to trace her responses to history. However, we can discern a shift from women's issues in her earliest stories to male politics in the 1930s, and another shift after World War II as she tries to connect the historical era with women's new experiences. Rhys was set up and knocked down by the romantic anarchy of Europe between the wars, when men enjoyed free love and women suffered the double standard. Doubting the fashionable ideologies of political liberalism and literary modernism, she contented herself with describing her feelings and the social insults that provoked them. For Lessing, antagonism to the racist society of her youth and bewilderment at the violence of World War II decisively shaped her evolving political views. For Stead, class rather than gender or race remained the most important category for understanding society. In her and the century's twenties, she was poor and hungry, translating her hunger for freedom and knowledge into physical deprivation by starving herself. The great depression with its egotistical scrabble and its boom and bust psychology marked her outlook thereafter. Briefly in the 1930s, a Marxist enthusiasm buoys her narrative, persuading her that the imminent demise of capitalism will herald a new era. After World War II, renewed prosperity depressed her more than prewar depression; capitalism kept breathing on the heart-lung machines of McCarthyism and consumerism. She and Blake were not so prosperous. They stayed poor and peripatetic, living in European hotel rooms, eating out of cans, and typing away at translations and odd literary jobs.

The Little Hotel

Stead claimed she wrote *The Little Hotel* in the late 1940s, publishing two stories later incorporated into it, "The Hotel Keeper's Story" in 1952, and "The Woman in the Bed" in 1968. By the time she issued the whole book in 1974, it was her shortest, tightest, and most structurally sophisticated novel and the only one with a sympathetic maternal heroine. Her episode as a scriptwriter in Hollywood perhaps influenced its structure, which resembles that of the "Grand Hotel" movies of the 1930s. Mme. Bonnard the hotelkeeper frames the stories about her guests, beginning with the mad "Mayor of B" and ending with another mad guest. In between, two relationships dissolve, one tragically, the other comically. Mme. Blaise loses her war against her husband, who murders her, and Mrs. Trollope wins her money and freedom from her lover of twenty years, Mr. Wilkins. Friendship and treachery link the two women, and female identity consolidates for good and for ill in the disrupted atmosphere of postwar Europe.

Stead's revisions of this novel indicate successive stages of her narrative decisions and construct different author-reader relationships at each stage. In 1952, Mme. Bonnard identifies herself as a woman who bonds with other women and who cares chiefly about events in the female life cycle. She wonders about one guest "whether she was divorced and remarried, or otherwise" (*Ocean* 293) and longs for a female friend like her girlhood confidante who married a German. Her husband is a Nazi sympathizer who defends Germans as "modern, orderly people whose only object was to bring backward countries up-to-date and to prevent the disorder malignantly stirred up by the communists" (297). A Swiss neutral, Mme. Bonnard replies sarcastically, "well, then, we must invade all other countries and teach them hotel-keeping, banking and how to make watches" (300). Mrs. Trollope, one of the hotel's guests, thinks the odd "Mayor of B" suffers from collaborator's guilt: "I suppose he drank and made merry with the Germans and now he has gone mad" (305). The story thus sketches war-torn Europe settling down to live with grief and guilt, like that which drove the "Mayor of B" mad, while many of the attitudes that led to the war remain. In contrast, the 1968 version, "The Woman in the Bed," is written in the third person and focuses on Mrs. Trollope and the emotional dynamics of female dependency. In the 1974 novel, the story of the "Mayor of B" weaves in and out of other tales and ends with his spectacular appearance outdoors "entirely naked, except for his hat and muffler" (*The Little Hotel* 58), but the novel omits the political punchline that is the reason for his madness. Instead, the 1974 novel shows female identity constrained by the diminished options available to postwar women, combining the personal and the political aspects of the novel to emphasize the former. *The Little Hotel* also develops Stead's first female character who can be empathetic to others while at the same time attracting our empathy.

As we have seen, Stead sometimes resisted the idea that she wrote for women or in a specifically female literary tradition. She and Blake edited an anthology in 1945, *Modern Women in Love*, in which they disapproved of Katherine Mansfield and Virginia Woolf while praising Joyce, Lawrence, and Forster. Yet *The Little Hotel* begins the sustained attention to women that runs through the end of Stead's career. The women guests at the hotel are mostly unpleasant characters cut loose from their families. The guests seek, reject, and manipulate each other's company. Mme. Bonnard's woman friend insults her child and flirts with her husband; the servant Clara, a "restless intriguer" (42), sends poison pen letters to foment trouble; and the sick spinster Miss Chillard domineers over her poor old mother as though she were a paid companion. Other family relations in the novel are equally perverse. Mme. Blaise hates her daughter and neurotically loves her son: "I prefer him to love men . . . and once he is corrupted he will never turn back; he may marry but he will hate and torture the bitch. My daughter's a clown. . . . I never wanted a daughter; they are all frumps" (92).

Lilia Trollope is the only character who tries to help other women, and in response they often snub and humiliate her, calling her racist names because her mother was part-Javanese. Living permanently in a hotel, motherly Mrs. Trollope chafes for something to do. Her lover Mr. Wilkins does not permit her to work; he himself enjoys moneyed idleness, napping, reading the financial papers, charting currency fluctuations, and dawdling near road repairs where he gets "real amusement out of watching the men at work" (28). Boredom and loneliness afflict Mrs. Trollope: "I must love people," she tells the hotelkeeper (50), recalling Alphendéry's love of men, though she can love women as well. She pities the meddling servant Clara because "jealousy and loneliness are cruel diseases" (54). "People suffer and we call them names; but all the time they are suffering" (141). "I want to be free," she cries. "Life seems very small to me this way. . . . I can't go on all my life trying to love people at the *table d'hote.*" (73).

Mrs. Trollope even befriends the terrible Mme. Blaise, a rich woman who never takes off her clothes, washes, or sleeps with her husband, a physician who supplies her with narcotics. She steals money from Mrs. Trollope's purse and alternately abuses her friend and commandeers her attention. She tells her husband to "leech all we can out of the damned ruined robber Empire" represented by Mr. Wilkins and Mrs. Trollope, those "little salesmen and their half-caste mistresses running here to be safe from doomsday and thinking themselves our equals" (102). Mme. Blaise is also a treacherous war profiteer, stealing the American holdings of German friends who entrusted her with their savings. She justifies herself: "I got it from Nazis. . . . It's mine. Everyone's against Nazis now" (102). The Blaises are a wonderfully vicious comic creation, a married couple interdependent in sadistic cynicism. The husband admits he hates his wife, whom he married for her money, and she insults him in return. "All marriage is hell," he says (92), and eventually murders her.

"But all love affairs hold surprises," the narrator tells us, "including those of such long standing that they resemble marriages. Mr. Wilkins remained [Mrs. Trollope's] lover, lived beside her, but made her engage their lodging wherever they lived and pay their rent" (89). "The odd thing about this was that Mrs. Trollope was an heiress, richer than" Mr. Wilkins, but "you are always astonished at how people can muddle their lives" (16). This non-marriage is a fine study of a plausible, moderate decaying relationship; we watch this old romance fade into banality. Mr. Wilkins is a pleasant, ordinary man, no longer a gallant lover but a self-centered old fellow who reads the newspaper at the table, ignores his mistress's desperate pleas that he pay attention to her, and refuses to marry her. Like many other Stead women, Mrs. Trollope is passive, compliant, and frightened of scenes, hence easily exploited. Mr. Wilkins insists they live abroad to save her capital: she wishes to live with her children in England, expostulating, "I cannot live for the exchanges" (94). "Oh, what is the use of money when it is no use?" she asks. "Our money is shut up and we are in jail because we must stay with it. . . . The money has us" (73).

Of mixed blood and tarnished reputation, Mrs. Trollope cannot be a snob like many wealthy women around her. Her lover treats her like a child, and she has developed typically feminine habits of pleasing, clinging, and sympathizing with others. "We are one flesh," Mrs. Trollope tells Mr. Wilkins "with deep emotion," while he callously replies, "and one fortune" (119). However, she does not succumb to feeling like a victim. She has had a grand passion, which she never minimizes, but "she was ashamed when she compared her dreamed life of true love, happiness, hope and trust with the insignificance of her present life" (108). She fears her lover's growing indifference but also the horror of a dependent old age: "supposing she ended up like that, with her little aches and pains, in a narrow poor hotel room, despised and harassed? . . . She had a terrible choice to make, to choose between Robert and some sort of freedom" (119). Ultimately her sense of "honor" (115) and her future determine her to action. Her money provides her one opportunity to freedom, yet she does not act like a man with money, despite Stead's earlier subordination of gender to class issues; she does not conform her life to the exchange rates. Among Stead's many depressed, dependent, and unhappy women, Mrs. Trollope is unique in seizing control of her situation without attempting to control anyone else, and so in achieving an autonomous female identity in middle age. "I would rather trust myself than anyone" (96), she decides. "I cannot believe that life is meant to be ugly. . . . I am going to strike out for myself now" (141–42). She is a rare success story in the Stead canon—a decent person who does not impose on others.

The 1952 story that was the first published version of material for *The Little Hotel* shows World War II's effects on European minds. The 1968 version highlights Mrs. Trollope's emancipation, contrasting it with Mme. Blaise's married misery and with the lonely helplessness of the spinster invalid. In the 1974 novel, Stead successfully combines the political and domestic interests of the earlier two stories. While focusing on Mrs. Trollope and Mme. Blaise, the novel casts the hotel's characters as representatives of the displaced ruling classes of postwar Europe. The inhabitants of *The Little Hotel* are landlocked on their ship of fools, far from the battlefield. Stead does not show the war's devastation directly, but, like Rhys, concentrates on the dangerous attitudes that led to world war and continue to divide and confuse people. Servants and guests are torn by racism and national prejudice. The hellish Blaises echo Nazi arrogance and brutality although they betray their old Nazi friends in order to keep their wealth. The rich guests rail against Britain's labor government and fear the communists who might take away their money. Madame Blaise asks, "Why don't the Americans use the atom bomb on the Russians now? A surprise attack" (14). They are comfortable with modest wars and capitalist dictatorships. Mr. Wilkins wishes he "could get some dictator or president to declare that Switzerland is going to be first victim in the next war—so that the Swiss franc would drop and we could get it cheap—then we would be rich, transfer back into dollars, go abroad" (86); and silly Princess Bili plans to go to "South America where they have dictators and an organized society and excellent servants and I am going to get married. . . . Your money is safe with a dictator. He keeps the greedy people down, those who want to nationalize everything" (96–97). Mr. Wilkins left Malaya because he thought colonialism was doomed, yet he is last heard from starting a new business in South Africa.

The Little Hotel depicts a postwar Europe where shabbily genteel exiles decline into uselessness. Like many of the hotel's guests, capitalism seems to be an unhealthy but malingering invalid, bossing its servants and refusing to give up the ghost. However, human change is more likely here than earlier in *House of All Nations*, in which the gods of fortune revealed each character's static essence. *The Little Hotel* follows the more optimistic model of the novel of development, like *For Love Alone*, in which the individual can change, overcome social obstacles, and exert personal choice.

Lost Women

In contrast to *The Little Hotel*, the characters of Stead's later fiction are locked into lonely individualism, exerting their wills but unable to grow or to empathize with others. Women in *Miss Herbert, The Puzzleheaded Girl, Dark Places of the Heart*, and *I'm Dying Laughing* have lost their balance, achieving independence only through alienation, and intimacy only through symbiosis. This fiction focuses on emotional anarchy and isolation, and it returns to Stead's early concern with irrational desire.

For Stead, like Lessing, the fifties and sixties were a perplexing period of lost values, in which young people seemed to be fugitives from engagement and hence enemies to the committed older generation. When a man in *The Puzzleheaded Girl* tells a listless woman that "a little drama might wake you up," "she looked at him, bored, horrified. 'What? I was here just after the war, working with people from concentration camps' " (79). History has made individual stories meaningless, and no "little drama" of private life can compete with the holocaust. The entire culture seems simultaneously bored and horrified in its aftermath. Yet its sexual roles seem to have regressed; the "feminine mystique" affects Europe as well as the United States, and the young woman is a compulsive sexual tease.

Like Rhys and Lessing, Stead blames bland, pitiless postwar youth as shallow, greedy people without ideals and thinks the postwar family is something new and noxious, fostered by popular Freudianism, "mommism," and consumer ideals, and split along generational and gender lines. Rhys and Lessing dramatize a mother's horror at the possibility her own children might reject her, whereas the childless Stead draws spoiled children and monstrous, conflicted mothers. "I don't go about thinking about the fate of women," Stead said of one late story; "it just came out that way" (Lidoff 215).

Stead's *Cotter's England* or *Dark Places of the Heart* is a dark countertext to her earlier work. It is a novel of malignant female bonding that reverses the male camaraderie of *House of All Nations*. It is also a novel of malformed female development that reverses the optimistic outcome of *For Love Alone*. In *For Love Alone*, the woman hero was right to conquer her society by will; by *Dark Places of the Heart*, female ego is a terrible, destructive force, and people officially on the left no longer represent its values. Unlike some other writers who held communist sympathies in the 1930s, Stead does not blame Marxist ideology for the failure of western socialism; instead she blames left opportunists who put personal satisfaction above class advancement.

The novel follows the breakdown of Nellie Cook's family, marriage, friends, and work. The twin and related climaxes are the suicide to which she drives her young friend Caroline Wooler, the sacrificial lamb of Lamb Street, and the lesbian bachannal that precedes it, a vision of the ultimate collapse of marriage, family, and women's self-esteem and female identity as well. Nellie undermines Caroline's trust in herself, seducing her into a symbiotic union in which Caroline loses her individuality. Nellie confuses Caroline's gender identity and redefines her sexual choices. She demeans Caroline's job in housing as pathetically reformist, until Caroline quits the job, and Nellie also isolates Caroline from her family and other friends. Her destruction of Caroline's identity becomes murder. In a hideous parody of maternal love, Nellie croons about the beauty of self-sacrifice and incites Caroline to suicide: "her face shining with the light of a planet" Nellie asks Caroline, "Will you die for me. . . . It would be a great triumph. . . . What I need is the confidence your beautiful sacrifice would give me. Then I would be the thing I am meant to be, the great leader" (*Cotter's England* 266).

Nellie succeeds as the wicked stepmother is never supposed to, by killing her Cinderella. In contrast to *The Man Who Loved Children*, which murders the bad mother to let the daughter live, here the bad mother kills her daughter, not by rejection but by smothering overpossession, as a vampire sucks another's will into her own. Nellie claims she's "trying to free" her women friends "from themselves; that's the only freedom" (175); her brother replies that she is really seeking her own power: "you dabble in their lives as if their lives were puddles. . . . You're just trying to get a lot of personal influence" (176). Nellie claims her feeling for Caroline is pure love and friendship and that she understands her completely: "you'll never know what she knows and I see it through her eyes, through love. . . . And she clings to me. . . . She's such a credulous loving child" (179). Caroline succumbs to Nellie "who had taken her up, haunted her, and ruined her. She was walking away from her, but Nellie was someone she carried with her, as you carry a bad parent always with you" (294).

Nellie proves the importance of empathy by her obscene perversions of manipulative understanding, augmenting other women's weaknesses in order to break them to her will. She is an artist of bad empathy, projecting her own desires and understanding on the other only to destroy her: "she can make you see things her way, though you know it wasn't so," another woman says (145). The innocent androgynous quality of Teresa's identification with men in *For Love Alone* becomes evil and perverse in Nellie, who puts on an airman's suit to take advantage of her protégé Caroline in a weird lesbian orgy. Nellie claims she lightens the burden of women abandoned by men, but instead she exacerbates their woes, telling them how unreliable men are and making the women feel unattractive, old, and undesirable. She says "men cannot see women. They see them with a purpose, an aim, not with pitiful love" (182), although she, too, has her hidden purposes. Pretending to help poor women, she preys on them, gathering women into a sort of half-way house where they must depend on her, and she tries to disrupt everyone else's heterosexual bonds.

Wicked witch and devouring mother of the Left, Nellie seems headed for dissolution in lung disease, sleeplessness, and divorce. Ironically her estranged husband George, a labor organizer, sends for her while he is traveling in Europe and then dies, so that Nellie ends triumphant with all the credit of being a devoted widow. "Nellie had invited [her brother] Tom to that foreign funeral and they had brought back a photograph: Nellie gay with success as a hero's widow and Tom smiling, hand in hand" (352).

Built on contradictions, the novel provides no solutions. Nellie's social criticism is only a means for personal advancement, but social constraint, especially grinding poverty, has diminished the characters and should be fought. More explicitly than *For Love Alone*, the novel questions the purposes of literature. Teresa writes about the "sorrows of women" as an act of compassion and solidarity with other women after she has seen and escaped the fate of most women who are dependent on men for money and love. Nellie talks about the sorrows of women, too, but rejects women writers, including her friend Caroline. Nellie's writing trashes the working class as well. Although she is working-class herself and allegedly their champion, she doesn't believe in the the workers, whom she calls "walk-ons in all this glorious history" (38). She claims she writes "stark staring reality, straight in the face," but she means just the opposite, given her advice for the labor writer: "no destruction, nothing depressing. The lives of the workers are depressing enough. You want to cover it with a rosy veil, a mystery" (38). Nellie "was always talking about introspection by which she meant drool; and confession, by which she meant spinning interesting lies, or sifting out people's secrets. To her that was truth. . . . She had a horror and suspicion of naked fact" (270).

Dark Places of the Heart draws a grimmer world than Stead's earlier fictions. No decency prevails in it, and people's virtuous emotions merely make them prey for others. The novel does not see the 1960s as a time of renewed political activity and youthful exuberance but rather springs from the despair of the 1950s radical for whom the Left has lost leadership and credibility with the workers. One Labour Party organizer comments dispiritedly in the novel: "for fear of the landlord, they think it's bad manners to talk about the bomb; and when I say your children will be destroyed, burnt up, they shut the door in my face, because I must be a bad woman" (72).

Although Stead's work is not strikingly experimental or avant-garde, *Dark Places of the Heart* does seem bizarre and dreamlike and raises the more general question of whether female realism is quite the same as male realism. Women writers primarily committed to showing a social milieu in its full range may also be committed to writing a language true to women's feelings, a language for which the words of the social surface are inadequate.

In contrast to Stead's earlier novels of female development, here female will and self-assertion do not assure freedom and meaningful intimacy. Instead, the breakdown of marriage and heterosexuality indicates a breakdown in the social order. The notion of individual progress or growth dissipates as the novels' heroes become less realistic and less autobiographical. Teresa Hawkins' quest in *For Love Alone* could take the shape of a novel of development, its hero marrying but retaining her identity and her freedom. However Stead's later, older female heroes face uncharted middle age with neither social goals like marriage nor individual illusions, like happiness, to drive them forward. Mrs. Trollope achieves a belated independence by holding on to her ideals and by empathizing with other women, whereas Nellie Cook perverts political ideals and manipulates other women through a dangerous empathy that seeks to understand others for her ends, not theirs.

I'm Dying Laughing is Stead's only book to consider seriously and at length her most important esthetic preoccupation, the connection between writing and politics. This issue defines her identity as a female writer on the left, even though, in her interviews after Blake's death, she claimed to be only a transcriber of real people, neither a creative novelist nor a politically motivated writer (Wetherell 24–25). The chapter "U.N.O.—1945," published as a story in 1962 and revised in the posthumous book, discusses the relationships of writing to ideology, of writing to money, of money to ideology, and of writing, money, and ideas to public historical changes and to the private changes within a long-term relationship. "U.N.O." details the squabbling marriage of Emily and Stephen Howard, rich left-wing writers living in Hollywood. Although based on common goals and mutual interdependencies, their union is breaking up over the multiple contradictions between their situation and their ideals. The story opens with the couple quarreling about their reports on the founding conference of the United Nations. Like the organization they write about, the Howards have ideals for a peaceful, harmonious, and just world that cannot be realized because self-interest divides people into hostile camps. Like the world, the Howards are settling into a difficult "cold war."

Stephen Howard comes from a rich family, and he wants them to consider him a success, that is, a money-maker. He writes dry, analytic, political articles but urges his wife to make money with her movie scripts and popular fiction. If she won't, he fears poverty, though his ideas about poverty are comically upper class—replacing the Portuguese butler with "a char smelling of boiled rag" and getting an apartment "with no towelrails" (*I'm Dying* 52). Stephen became a radical at Princeton in order to feel superior to his classmates, and he still does not believe in the working class: "what are we fighting for? Not to make people like the workers are now. Good grief! I had 'a love the worker' phase; but I wasn't sincere. I walked along working-class streets and saw their stores and their baby-carriages and hated 'em. I wouldn't raise anyone to be like them" (67).

Stephen's political contradictions are closely related to his ambivalence toward his plebian wife, who dominates the novel. He idealizes her as "potent," "genuine," "strong and meaningful" because when he met her she was wearing an "awful dress" (69). She is his "revenge" against the genteel despondency of his set, his connection to humanity, and his romantic mission: "and I live for you. . . . My life drives me into sterility; I can't give and nothing bears for me. But you did" (70). He expects his wife, like his politics, to justify him, but he doesn't want to examine these things too closely. He follows the party line and believes "ideas are civil war" (66), caricaturing himself as "a radical dandy . . . with laughable ineffectiveness exhorting a stone-deaf working class out of the blind alley of pork-chop opportunism to lead them down the blind alley of rigid righteousness" (72).

Emily Wilkes is her husband's complement, equally self-contradictory though she looks "goddam earthy" "like a Polish peasant" and comes from a "little Arkansas sharecropper's shanty" (63, 64, 52). Even when she can make it easily, she treats money with contempt as that "filthy reeking stuff" (71). Without respecting the mass market, Hollywood, or American popular taste, she writes "Hh-umour and Pp-athos for the commuters and hayseeds" (52). Instead, she believes in the family and in revolutionary Marxism, though her actions belie her words. She worries about her children's dental appointments even when planning to leave her husband, and she sentimentally wishes to be Jewish to enjoy their "beautiful family life" (65). "Family love is the only true selfless love," she says; "it's natural communism . . . and everything is arranged naturally, without codes and without policing" (66). She cites Debs, the Haymarket martyrs, and Sacco and Vanzetti to back up her belief in "the whole of revolutionary history" while she calls the butler to carry her bags (64).

Stephen wants her to be a "shining—red—light" (68), and the ambiguity fits: she is both prostituting her talents and championing progressive "Red" ideals. She rejects her husband's dependence on her, saying "you mustn't found your life on one person" (70), yet she depends on him: "I'm secretly afraid you'll leave me and get some decent woman who never sold out. . . . You're my whole life, my rayzon d'ayter. If we haven't got each other, we've got nothing" (68). She's cheerful when churning out another story about a "freckle face in the big city" (74) or a script idea "so cheap I blushed for shame" (52), yet she also revolts at her own hypocrisy. For her, money and truth run in opposite directions. She knows the Truth, but she sells out. Only poverty guarantees purity: "in Europe contributors to radical sheets go without soles to their shoes and gnaw a dry crust in freezing attic rooms; and we live on the plunder of the land" (50). Along with the rest of the United States, American radicalism has grown too rich, and the Howards fear letting their chldren "grow up like Clem Blake's, eating out of cans with many a fly twixt the can and the lip," presumably Stead's tribute to the impoverished integrity she shared with Blake (67).

Emily's great ambition is to expose the failing left. She still believes in Russia as strong, perhaps invincible, and the American working class as a socialist's dream turning into a nightmare of cooptation: "Oh, God! And we have to be on the *wrong* side in the bad time coming! To be in America, to like America, to want to be an American and to be wrong, to be martyred by Americans" (73). She wants to write an "epitaph of American socialism" (72): "look at the size of the labour union movement! . . . Organised millions of conscious workers. . . . Or is it already too late? Are there too many labour opportunists, too many finks and goons?" (71); "or are we what's wrong with it, the goddamn middle-class opportunists" (*Ocean* 249). While Stephen looks for "theoretical errors," she blames "essential human weaknesses," "ignorance and self-indulgence." Her bitterness battles her revolutionary optimism, her hope that the book could help revive socialism: "it would be for the real rebels, the real labour movement, against all vampires . . . Socialism can't die! . . . But it can die—suffocated, here! By us!" (*I'm Dying* 72).

Like Emily, though more honorably, Stead despairs in the postwar decades as the Left, knowing the truth about capitalism and history, fails to keep its moral advantage and so fails to win the working classes. In her late interviews, Stead denies being a "polemic writer," though her work always assumes a materialist, basically Marxist view of history (Wetherell 24, Stead "What Goal"). *I'm Dying Laughing* is presumably the novel Emily wants to write and never will, just as *House of All Nations* is the satire about capitalism that Adam Constant wants to write. Emily knows that the failure to live one's beliefs means living a lie, even though she continues her

profitable lying fictions. For an adult education class, she summarizes her
ideas about truth and literature: an ambulance chaser introduced her to
the poetry of William Blake, and she knew a landlord who rented out
condemned houses; the fact that he recited John Donne's poetry was no
excuse when his buildings fell down on the occupants. "The choice will
come, the choice has come" she tells the workers; "one day it will be as
obvious as the cop's club and you will weep by teargas, because it is then
too late to choose" (74). The rich landlord and ambulance chaser uphold
an elite English literature that does not affect their lives, that allows them,
in fact, to feel superior to their victims. But this misappropriation does not
condemn the poets, and Emily ends her speech to the workers by quoting
Blake the Romantic poet, after whom Stead's husband renamed himself:

> But Palambron called down a Great Solemn Assembly . . .
> That he who will not defend Truth, may be compelled to
> Defend a Lie, that he may be snared and caught and taken (72) .

Clearly Emily believes, with Stead, that the truth can be known, that it
must be defended, and that the American postwar Left had failed in that
task, even though Emily will also fail in living up to her convictions.

The marriage of the Howards symbolizes the confused, corrupt American
left, and it is also one of Stead's mutually self-destructive dependencies.
Emily worries about the nation but is ambivalent about nurturance and
autonomy. She is a good cook for her family, but she scorns feeding "corn-
meal mush to full-bellied Bible belters" (52). Disgusted with the American
public as "stupid, cruel, and food crazy" (51), she nonetheless puts recipes
in her fiction. Stead's young women often starve themselves, while her
good characters bring food to others. Emily associates food with the love
she craves: "do you think you can buy me back with a stick of
candy? . . . The only thing you could buy me with then was affection. I
loved people. They didn't love back" (64). Alphendéry, Letty Fox, and
Mrs. Trollope, too, say they love people. Rarely are they loved in return,
except by us readers.

In persistent preoedipal imagery, Stead's characters hunger for truth,
freedom, justice, and love—and are not fed. The epigraph for the first
portion of the book is Rabelais's "I'm thirsty" (1). Stephen says he can
understand the anticommunist Russian renegades who "write lies for
bread. . . . It's the infant screaming for its mother" (71). Capitalism is
doomed; we are at the end of something. "Let's face it," says Emily, "that
time, the day before yesterday, was IT, *die Ende, Schluss, Fini* " (71). The
end is still coming; catastrophes like the Great Depression validate the sense
of Marxist apocalypse, but late in Stead's life, she has little confidence that
something wonderful will grow from the ashes. Her good characters, male
and female, are "maternally" nurturant. They love and feed others without

reward. They love humanity, but humanity, a selfish, power-mad lot, do not love back.

According to Stead's literary executor, R. G. Geering, who edited *I'm Dying Laughing* from several manuscripts, Stead began the novel in the 1940s and finished a draft by 1966, but was then persuaded to continue revising it in order to clarify its political background (vi-vii). She therefore added the first chapters of the current book, which introduce Stephen to Emily on a boat to Europe in 1935. These opening chapters confuse some details—Emily has several birthplaces and social origins and an adopted child who abruptly disappears—but they also extend the story back to the Depression, with its galvanizing impetus to the left. In Paris Stephen woos Emily, a lively young journalist, with the heady enthusiasm generated by hearing writers like Aragon, Forster, and Thomas Mann at the International Writers Conference that had impressed Stead, too. Then the novel jumps ahead to Hollywood in 1945 where Party members invite the Howards to a dinner party, only to denounce their deviationist politics and bad parenting. They resettle in New York with a fashionable radical set as the McCarthyist "witch-hunters" move closer, then emigrate to Paris, where they live extravagantly while trying to ingratiate themselves with local Communist leaders and heroes of the Resistance.

Like others of Stead's best fictions, *I'm Dying Laughing* fills in a broad, bustling panorama despite its tight focus on a few main characters, and it moves quickly despite its bulk, like a rambunctious rhinocerous. The novel builds to a dramatic climax as Emily, a top beginning to topple, loses her shaky equilibrium and careens wildly from mood to mood, from role to role, as wife, mother, popular writer, political purist, and opportunist. The one role in which she does not lose faith is her ability to write. She airily dismisses the postwar misogyny that argues women can't be artists because "if women don't have children, their art's cramped, and if they do, they don't have art. So men have the art" (81); she replies that being a woman artist is no more difficult than being a "wage earner in a factory with kids at home, or a working mother or an unmarried mother" (81). Her insecurity, though, is that her husband will leave her for a prettier, more conventional woman. Early in her career she wishes to "get inside someone else and be someone else" for even half an hour in order to understand "the baffling, puzzling, beloved others" (33), but when she is in Europe faced with the tortured and heroic survivors of World War II, she gives up on empathy and decides it is better not to try to understand other people. As she becomes more isolated from her family and colleagues, she nonetheless succeeds in writing a serious political novel set in the French Revolution, with Marie Antoinette as its tragic hero. While delirious from fights with her husband, silly flirtations, incestuous infatuation, drugs, and financial pressures, her real problem remains moral: without the courage to uphold her beliefs against public opinion and financial advantage, she is left a self-hating renegade who names names of former comrades. Mad with despair, she destroys her book and drifts crazily after Stephen's suicide.

Emily and Stephen's tragedy is that of a generation but not of an ideology; this novel condemns corrupt Marxists, not Marxism. As a serious, satiric political novel, *I'm Dying Laughing* is an anomaly, and one can understand why Stead delayed its publication: it might offend both the right and the left. Moreover, it is a *roman à clef*. Ruth McKinney, author of *My Sister Eileen*, the model for Emily, did not die until 1972, and friends of Stead can identify other characters in the book as well (Lidoff 182 and two anonymous sources). Whereas much literature by people once on the left divides into biting anticommunist diatribe or tight-lipped loyalism, Stead simply assumes that socialists should be moral people and then grieves over the unworthy. This also distinguishes her work from leftist novels about poor folks ground down by capitalist oppression like Tillie Olsen's *Yonnondio* (1974; written in the thirties) or Harriet Arnow's *Dollmaker*, 1954, and also from the self-righteous denunciations of what Lillian Hellman calls *Scoundrel Time*, 1976. Despite its completion years after Stalin's atrocities became public knowledge, *I'm Dying Laughing* does not attack the Soviet Union, and it portrays the follies of American communism as indigenous contradictions rather than as the result of Russian influence. The "American dilemma," according to Emily, is that "you believe sincerely in Washington, Jefferson, Lincoln; and also know you'll get your nose bloodied if not worse, if you don't believe in Rockefeller, Mellon, General Motors and Sears Roebuck" (16). "Other countries have a history; we have nothing but contradictions" (13), Emily says, seeing America as a reflection of her contradictory self.

According to Stead, the book portrayed the almost religious "passion" of two Americans who "wanted to be on the side of the angels, good Communists, good people, and also to be very rich. Well, of course . . . they came to a bad end" (vi–vii original elision; Lidoff 181). Stead draws Emily as a complex and tragic character, precisely because her accomplishments and contradictions as a woman writer exceed those of an allegorically greedy or corrupt political hypocrite. As a popular writer, Emily helps create the meretricious consumer culture that will distract the workers and women like herself, who like recipes and happy endings, from the injustices of capitalism.

Emily grows neither into empathetic maturity, like Lilia Trollope, nor into manipulative monstrousity, like Nellie Cook, but self-destructs into her own contradictions. Stead said the woman on whom she based Emily was a "Danton in skirts," a corrupt but persuasive revolutionist, and Emily alludes to herself as Lady Macbeth, Madame du Farge, and as the hero and author of a new *American Tragedy* of the left (Whitehead 246). Stead called Emily "a great character who goes astray" and the novel a "tragedy. It's about Miss America too, about the American girl" (Raskin 77).

Because her characters are so intense, verbose, and unrelenting, many readers feel overwhelmed by Stead's fiction. Several friends have told me they dropped *The Man Who Loved Children* after a few chapters. On the other hand, those who read the novel all through are always enthusiastic: once one has entered the Pollit family, one comes to know it in a special way, vividly but not sentimentally. *I'm Dying Laughing*, too, places the reader embarassingly close to its characters, especially Emily. She is an astonishing and unusual female hero, a vigorous original who is both manipulative and dependent, a woman writer *not* modeled on her author, and a credible genius who is not idealized. Ultimately, reading through Stead's novels is like attending a marathon encounter weekend—one feels fatigued and triumphant at the end and a comrade of all one's fellow travelers in the experience.

Last Stories

Stead's last stories return to her childhood experiences, although a few celebrate later events. For example, after Blake's death she wrote "A Street Idyll," 1972, in honor of her marriage, in which a couple together for forty years greet each other on the street with "rapturous intimate smiles"; "they were not alike, they looked like strangers to each other; and they had never lost this look; reared in different countries, different traditions" (*Ocean* 400, 401). The sketch is tender, a memorial to the web of intimacy they shared, "a quick-weaving, thick-netting web. . . . It tugged like the moon at waters, sucked like a drain, had already grown part of them like barnacles on rocks . . . nothing fatal in it" (401), which Stead said shattered when Blake died. The disclaimer seems necessary to separate this beneficent fusion from manipulative regressive mergers like those in *Dark Places of the Heart*. This blissful marriage, unlike those in the rest of her fiction, is not a hierarchical economic institution but its own utopian counter-culture: "they had nothing but good to say of marriage. It was the best state for men and women; there was calm and thrilling joy, there was forgiveness, solace, peace, certain home and country, without passport, rent book, marching, petitions" (398).

Other late Stead stories reinvoke, often in very naked fashion, psychological issues that more covertly underlie her earlier novels. For example, "Uncle Morgan at the Nats," 1976, shows an "expatiating" naturalist father, like Sam in *The Man Who Loved Children* without Sam's mitigating charm (*Ocean* 111). Morgan's energetic talk about stomach rumbling and flatulence is more vulgar, his decayed narcissism more apparent, as he fusses about his false teeth and muses about girls who used to stroke his hair. The main feature of this late story, however, is its obvious patriarchal sadism. Angry at being displaced as chairman of the Naturalists' Society, Morgan demands that his three-year-old niece put her "hand in the fire for your Uncle Morgan" (103). When his furious wife rushes to protect her niece, he complains of "whim-men" and their "whimsies" (102). His children recognize Morgan's linguistic gifts as tools of domination. One son calls his father both "Morgan the Gorgan" and "Morgan the Organ"—a monster of mellifluous and dogmatic sound (102, 106). As in her earliest tales, the exuberance here derives from vengeance against a tyrannical father: "we ALL hate the Old Man."

In "The Milk Run," 1972, nostalgia flows like a muddy clay road, and psychological issues recede from oedipal antagonisms to preoedipal longings. A seven-year-old boy ventures past a bully to grandmother's house for milk; on his way back he spills the milk, and looking for it, finds a gold coin, as though in a parable of Freudian oral and anal stages. His parents don't believe his account, and he even doubts himself. The story ends with a displaced yearning for maternal nurture: "he would rush out when the milkman came, glorying in the spurting, foaming quarts that they took in, in two big jugs. . . . 'Two quarts, please,' his mother always said, standing in her long pink dressing-gown, her black hair fluffed out. Oh, the milk! The flowing milk" (*Ocean* 39). Whether milk is worth trading for gold, whether telling the truth is worth being abandoned by those you love—"The Milk Run" places these questions in a nostalgic, filtered context of childhood memory that reveals a hidden subtext, a persistent, romanticized longing for the preoedipal mother. Thus even for this predominantly father-raised and sometimes male-identified woman writer, crucial issues of female identity based on the earliest mother-daughter bonds resurface at nodal points in her work.

Missing her mother, mothered by her father and husband, surrounded, manipulated, and empowered by language, Stead found political views congruent with her psychological perspective. Committed to individual choice on the side of the exploited, she condemned wily weaklings and could brilliantly mimic the exploiters. Despite late denials that she was a political person, she understood history through Marxist economics, and economics and politics as moral forces. Her empathy is rare but sunny in a grim social world, and concerns about female identity recur in her work from its beginning to its end without resolution, held to a subordinate place by firm moral and political convictions: "the choice is coming; the choice has come." Perhaps her conviction that individual choice can triumph over debilitating circumstances of gender, culture, and generation, that is, over "stepmother reality," is her strongest legacy. She puts her beliefs into her literary practice, choosing not to empathize with but rather to observe her most threatening characters and choosing male-identified forms when the conventional choices available to women seem too limited. At the end of her career, like Rhys and Lessing, she contemplates her fiction self-reflexively, convinced that lies about society need exposing, whatever the slippery opacities of truth.

IV

GENDERED CHOICES
HISTORY AND EMPATHY IN THE
SHORT FICTION OF DORIS LESSING

For the twentieth-century writer, the short story may serve some of the same functions that the verse pastoral served for classical and Renaissance authors. The pastoral was traditionally a small form, distanced from the writer's self, and simplified in point of view. It grounded the author both with respect to nature and to the literary heritage and also celebrated a place, idealizing its landscapes as it idealized other origins—the past and the lower classes. It dealt with the claims of country versus city, ambition, the role of the poet, love, and death. Yet it was also a duplicitous form, a sophisticated simulation of the simple from the viewpoint of the worldly, often used to satirize the worldly in contrast to the simple or to allegorize urban social conflicts as harmless country matters. After composing pastorals, classical writers could expand into more comprehensive forms—ultimately, the epic. Without taking Virgil as a model, the modern writer's career may have a comparable shape. James Joyce's canon is paradigmatic: first, a set of short stories that taken together define a specific place, while each separately is a well-crafted vignette; then an autobiographical *bildungsroman* , suggestive, tense, and anguished; then, the culminating epics, written in exile, comprehensive of a nation, the human condition, and the literary past.

The short story has been an especially congenial form for twentieth-century women writers, whether or not they cherish epic ambitions. One thinks, for example, of Katherine Mansfield, Katherine Ann Porter, and Isak Dinesen. Small, unthreatening, often centered on a single character and leading up to a single revelation, the short story may seem an ideal form for the woman whose time and attention are distracted or whose ambition falters. Rhys follows the Joycean pattern with her early, wandering stories, then the four autobiographical novels, and late in her career, the comprehensive masterwork, though she also continued to write stories. Stead, who wrote tales both early and late, evades pattern with her quirky, long-nurtured, and sporadic productivity. Lessing, despite her mid-century debut and anti-modernist ideologies, also follows Joyce's model, and in this respect one may see English colonialism as fostering a modern pastoral, as Alexandrian and Roman imperialism fostered the classical genre.

A cunning exile devoted to art, Lessing began writing short stories about her childhood Africa. She consolidated her career with a series of autobiographical novels, the *Children of Violence* quintet, and *The Golden Notebook*, a comprehensive novel of female subjectivity. Now she is compiling a many-volumed cosmological epic space fiction. However, this schema omits several novels and the stories set in Europe, and it underestimates the continuing importance of her short fiction, which many critics consider her finest writing (Sprague and Tiger 5). Whereas her novels sometimes appear didactic, disproportioned, or flat, her short stories are often more finely crafted and broader ranging, achieving a forceful emotional impact or evoking a character, situation, or idea with a grace and concision achieved only rarely in her novels. These are the qualities she praises in her most overt tribute to another author, the short story entitled "Homage to Isaac Babel." Joyce Carol Oates pays tribute to "how beautifully the craftsmanship of her many short stories illuminated lives, the most secret and guarded of private lives, in a style that was never self-conscious or contrived" (883).

Lessing was born in 1919 in Persia, now Iran, of English parents who were profoundly affected by World War I. Her father Alfred Taylor had been injured, and her mother Emily Maud McVeagh was his nurse. "Home" for Lessing was neither Persia nor the England her mother nostalgically longed for, but the land-locked veldt of Southern Rhodesia, now Zimbabwe, to which her parents moved when she was five and where they remained throughout her youth despite their marginal success as farmers. She left school early, worked at various women's jobs, married and divorced twice, and bore three children, two of whom she left with their father, her first husband. During World War II she became politically active with an idealistic pro-communist group. In 1949, she emigrated to England with her son by her second marriage and established herself as a fiction writer, theater critic, journalist, and left activist. She joined the English Communist Party in 1952 and left it about five years later. Her thought from the 1960s on has been influenced by Jungian and Laingian psychoanalysis and by Sufi mysticism (Bertelson 3–12). In 1966 Lessing said that she was "too prolific" a writer (*Small Personal Voice*, cited hereafter as *SPV*, 78); by 1988 she had published seventeen novels, some poems and plays, seven volumes of non-fiction, and over seventy short stories.

In the preface to her *African Stories*, 1965, she described herself as an "addict" to the short story form who would write them "even if there really wasn't any home for them," even if they found "no market" (x). She thus signalled her short stories as privileged forms of self-expression, freer, perhaps, than the novels and reflecting her identity as an exile, homeless and ambivalent about seeking commercial approval. On the other hand, one of the advantages of "home" is that one can behave there in ways not permitted outside. "Home" is the privileged site of the private emotions, like the adult sexual passions bemusedly observed by young characters in "Old John's Place," 1951, or "Getting Off the Altitude," 1957. But "home" is also the place where one can get away with flying into a temper. Lessing sometimes encourages us to empathize with her characters, sometimes incites our antagonism against them. She commends as her favorite stories several that provoke especially nasty emotions—the "cold and detached . . . toughy" "One Off the Short List," 1963 (*SPV* 53) or "Black Madonna," 1964, which is full of "bile" against Southern Rhodesia as she "knew and hated it" (*African Stories* x)—stories whose protagonists include a racist white African and a self-satisfied rapist. Although many of her stories appear autobiographical, she often insists on her stories' separation from herself, saying, for example, that "Each Other," 1963, dealing with incest, is "not autobiographical at all" and "To Room Nineteen," 1963, is "all too typical of so many Europeans and Americans" (*SPV* 54). The stories provide an arena in which Lessing can enact the interplay between self and other, the individual and her or his circumstances, that can be more detached, playful, and experimental than the more committed long fiction. Lessing recently spoke of her stories as "something small crystallized out" of the long transformative writing process (Bertelson 103).

Like Rhys and Stead, Lessing alternates in her fiction between self-expression and attempting to capture the other, most simply at first by writing vignettes shaded with local color. These early works assume that a vivid mimesis will insure the reader's duplication of the author's attitudes—often attitudes of rejection toward her subjects. Domination and empathy, the values of "market" and of "home" or of empire and colony, of sophisticated city and of pastoral retreat—and often of men and women—struggle with each other throughout Lessing's work. Domination and empathy may work to cross purposes when the narrative dominates its subject matter in such a way as to break the empathic identification between reader and characters, often by turning the tables on a dominating person and so exposing the social order that person represents. Lessing's narratives, in turn, struggle against both domination and empathy, seeking the autonomy of an individual identity, which is also the desire for a story of one's own, a story within a meaningful history.

First Forks—Through the Fifties

In the 1964 introduction to her *African Stories*, Lessing saw her first literary choices as gender-coded:.

> *The Pig* and *The Trinket Box* are two of my earliest. I see them as two forks of a road. The second—intense, careful, self-conscious, mannered—could

have led to the kind of writing usually described as "feminine." The style of *The Pig* is straight, broad, direct; is much less beguiling, but is the highway to the kind of writing that has the freedom to develop as it likes. (x)

Indeed, most of her early work takes the implicitly "masculine" road of "The Pig" toward social realism, a road along which masses could march to a better future, in contrast to the "beguiling," seductive, and apparently backward-looking "feminine" modernist path with its "self-conscious" insistence on female difference (see Hanson).

Her overt rejection of the "feminine" path in writing accords with her persistent denial that she is a feminist and with her tendency to describe "larger" issues than gender in her work. Unlike Rhys, race, not sex, is the primary category through which she begins to organize her experiences of otherness and of injustice, even of the inequities of class, which is the primary category for Stead. Yet, as we shall see in analyzing the "feminine" line in her short stories in relation to the "masculine" line over the four decades of her career to date, Lessing's two paths repeatedly intersect; both address interactions among empathy and domination, female identity and male authority, and both struggle to resolve the contradictions between opposed sets of psychological needs and the historical outlooks that they imply.

Lessing's earliest story in the rejected "feminine" category, "The Trinket Box," written in Africa in the 1940s, was not printed in the earliest collections of her African stories and admitted later only with a disclaimer, not destroyed but defensively denied. Although Lessing chastises the story for its style, it may be its woman-centered content that is truly disturbing, the gender-specific existential dilemma: what does a woman's life mean? This early, rejected story confronts questions about female identity squarely and centrally. Does a woman who devotes herself to others have a self? How can a woman with no sexual life claim happiness? What or who does her autonomy threaten? Lessing carries the unease of these questions into the story's interrogative style, which asks ten questions on its first page, one of which echoes the child's question to her parents, "where did it all begin?" (*African* 26). Perhaps Lessing, who was developing her reputation as a writer in the early 1950s, rejected identification with these questions; Aunt Maud is her first portrait of a "free woman," that is, of a woman unattached to a man, but she is a doomed and diminished creature, and after writing about her, Lessing drops the subject for over a decade.

Little happens in the story. Aunt Maud, an unassuming old spinster who served her relatives as an unpaid companion and domestic help, dies leaving only a box of valueless trinkets, carefully labeled for their many recipients. Although Maud's name recalls those of Lessing's own mother and grandmother, it is Maud's apparent rejection of such familial roles that defines her. The story begins with a bland narrative tone, discussing the possibilities of other stories embedded within this one: "Yes, but it was only recently, when it became clear that Aunt Maud really could not last much longer, that people began to ask all those questions which should have been asked, it seems now, so long ago" (26). The narrator's defensive "yes, but" turns its guilt about unasked questions onto us readers, and the time shifts from "only recently" to "now" to "long ago" implicate us in puzzling out a coherent story from Maud's life, the task the narrator sets herself as well. Maud has lived so long that she is a part of history, but not a history the narrator can understand. Perhaps women's history deliberately avoids public events: when asked about Oscar Wilde, Maud refers vaguely to an "interesting book" in the library, not to a scandal she lived through (26). The narrator imagines that Maud sees herself, too, as a fiction rather than as a person, as a "character in a historical play" rather than as a participant in change (26).

Although a "character" both literary and historical, Maud won't take center stage; she declines attention, even in death. The narrator approves Maud's self-effacing autonomy, yet she surprisingly deduces from it that the old lady's stoic generosity incited others to sadism: "we are forced to know that the thought of her aches and pains put warmth" into those who hired her as a companion (27). This narrative "we" seems to be the collective of Maud's surviving, mostly female relatives, though it also ambiguously includes the author and us readers, and the "mannered" quality that Lessing disavows in the story comes largely from this plural narrative voice. The old relatives Maud serves feel their mortality less when they have her, frail and uncomplaining, at their sides, a permanent scapegoat for the indignities of living. After each extended visit in which she has acted as the unpaid servant, Maud sends her relatives presents which they resent: giving and taking are always difficult in Lessing's world, even though they are among the main ways people relate to one another. Typically, women give, and, although they resent men and other women who take from them, they prefer the covert dominance of giving to being takers themselves. In addition, Maud's gifts arouse antagonism because of their aptness, which seems sinister to the narrator: "how did she come to know our most secret wants?" (28).

The narrator dislikes being understood by this peripheral woman as though understanding is a kind of domination. The old lady's ability to empathize without asking for a return threatens the narrator, who judges that "it is all intolerable" and harangues Maud: "how could you stand, year in and year out, pouring out your treasures of affection to people who hardly noticed you?" (28). The narrator seems to regard it as "intolerable" for *her*, not for Maud, that Maud's generous understanding was not reciprocated. Throughout Lessing's work, people's needs for love battle with their longings for autonomy, and she describes herself as a girl as independent and critical but longing for love ("Impertinent Daughters" 61, 68). In this story a woman who seems not to need love shames others by giving rather than needing. But Maud's threat may also be that she usurps the power of the author by understanding others without being available to be understood herself; she presents her heirs with posthumous evidence of her understanding and concern which they cannot reciprocate. Though refusing marriage and motherhood, she has acquired the frightening maternal power of understanding others who do not wish to be understood, and hence, implicitly, exposed. It is a relief to the narrator when Maud dies "as a leaf shrivels" (29).

After Maud's death, her survivors describe her as a "casket of memories" who hoarded the reminiscenses they wanted, and they are affronted when the casket snaps shut on them: "it is monstrous that a human being who has survived miraculously and precariously so many decades of wars, illnesses, and accidents should die at last, leaving behind nothing" (30). This is one of Lessing's first statements about the intractability of history, which goes on and on without our understanding it and without it adding up to anything. The fury here, directed against the woman, not the wars, illnesses, and accidents, might seem to be that evoked by a woman who has refused to mother. The narrator futilely awaits "that one thing, the perfect word of forgiveness that will leave us healed and whole" (30–31) and interprets the old woman's death as an aggressive act, a deliberate withdrawal of parental support. But perhaps more fundamentally the fury attacks the obliquity of the relation between history and women's lives. A staunch believer in the Victorian heresies that became Lessing's causes and then, according to her, the dominant ideas of the twentieth century, socialism and feminism, Maud did not preach her beliefs. Despite all she has lived through, despite being cast as a historical character, she refuses to tell stories, to answer questions, to frame herself within a public and historical narrative. A woman who has no story has no history. Endlessly and quietly involved in female services, Aunt Maud refuses to make anecdotes of herself or to place herself in terms of the public stage. Lessing's professed beliefs throughout her career all oppose the threatening idea that each life sums zero and that each generation can do no more than repeat the last. This desire for a progressive history is also, of course, a desire for narrative, for shapely and intelligible stories. By refusing either to tell or to make herself into a story, the old lady resists narrative, defining a female anti-story and anti-history in opposition to the stories the narrator wants, conventional stories about adventure or romance.

Perhaps Maud *does* reveal her truth though she does so covertly in "the order of the words" of her last sentence: "I put everything right when people became so kind and I knew I was ill" (31). Her "terrible knowledge" (31) is people's—and fate's—indifference to others, especially to unattached women: "protest, is that what we are feeling," "a dull and sorrowful rage" because "we all feel . . . ' No, no! It can't all be for nothing!' " (32). The narrator shies away from this "feminine" "protest," sublimating her rage into heroic posturing, a sort of female mimicking of Churchillian patriotism in adversity.

> So it comes to this: we are grown proud and honest out of the knowledge
> of her honesty and pride and, measuring ourselves against her, we allow
> ourselves to feel only the small, persistent, but gently humorous anger she
> must have felt. Only anger, that is permissible. . . . But against what?
> Against what? (32).

Even the obscure can serve us as exemplary objects, and Aunt Maud proves
to be a treasure-trove, a trinket box, of exemplary attitudes and permissible
emotions.

If Maud will not tell her own story, she will have stories told about her.
If we cannot empathize with her, at least we can resist her understanding
of us by making her an object lesson about women's lives. The narrator
expects us to share, first, her bafflement at Maud's life, then her confidence
that she has unlocked the box of Maud's secrets. This knowledge reverses
Maud's maternal power over us; we become little Maud's big parents: "now
it seems that we hold Aunt Maud in the hollow of our palms. That was
what she was; now we know her" (32), and now, presumably, we can
write her, replacing her muted voice and story with our own. Understanding Maud at last means that we will feel as she felt, her "persistent but
gently humorous anger." But the story in fact creates and incites this anger,
directing it back at the female collective represented by the narrative "we,"
including the reader, and at Maud herself for colluding with society's marginalization of women.

If Maud's death expresses women's fears of becoming our mothers, the
end of the story insists that we must become her. A retroactive moral
missionary, Maud saves us through selfless martyrdom: "we are grown
proud and honest out of the knowledge of her honesty and pride" (32).
But is the "anger" we feel "measuring ourselves against her" an anger
against her for making us feel "small"? Both angry at Maud and angry in
her behalf, the collective narrative voice enacts ambivalences redolent of
mother-daughter psychological dynamics.

Lessing deprecates the style of "The Trinket Box," though it is not a
more artificial style than that she employs in "The Pig," 1948, which she
favors over it. She may have been uncomfortable with Maud's "box" as
too obvious a Freudian symbol, or with the story's exclusive concentration
on female identity, untempered by the explicit racial context that distances
and justifies other early African stories. However, it is more likely that the
collective female narrator troubled her, encapsulating as it does the central
difficulty of the female child's development as described by object relations
theorists and of Lessing's development by her own account, that is, the
daughter's differentiation of an individual identity from the symbiotic "we"
of herself and her dominating mother: "I can't remember a time when I
wasn't fighting with my poor mother" (Bertelson 100, Lessing "My Mother's Life" 236–38). Her late work repeatedly returns to this problem of
individuality in collectivity, ultimately finding virtue and bliss in a cosmic

"substance of we feeling" (see Spafford). In literary terms, too, this feminine "we" may have seemed dangerous to Lessing in linking her with Virginia Woolf's fluid and apparently plotless female modernism, a style that postwar leftist writers considered elitist and reactionary.

Responding to '50s misogyny, Lessing rejects her earliest "feminine" writing without explicitly gender-coding its opposite, so that she accepts the implicitly "masculine" style of postwar realism as simply generic. She associates the apparently guileless masculine style of "The Pig," the "road" she was glad to take when starting her career, with open adventure, quest, and freedom. Like a male infant, the young "masculine" story must separate from its mother to develop independently, and Lessing as a young artist first feels comfortable with neat stories that conform to a "masculine" esthetic of realism, action, and male-defined serious issues.

Unlike "The Trinket Box," "The Pig" begins in a flat third person voice with no hint of interchange between author and reader: "the farmer paid his laborers on a Saturday evening when the sun went down" (*African* 33). The story places an ordered social world before us, ranked by class and race; the farmer is white and arrogant; his laborers, black, retiring, and apparently subservient. Together they stand silhouetted against the night sky, as though in a timeless tableau, "for all this had happened before, every year for years past" (33). The nameless farmer genuinely loves the fertile land: "how good those fields of strong young plants looked" (33). The landscape of the story evokes comfortably familiar colonial and mythological associations: the white, light world of the "civilized" farmer against the dark land and its mysterious people, and all this made eternal, rather than being seen as a fairly recent historical development of European colonialism in Africa. The farmer associates the natives with the land, and with sexuality, youth, virility, darkness, and the "theft" of taking the fruit of their labors, corn grown on land stolen from them. The story's moral landscape seems as simply contrasted as the silhouetted scene, though in reverse: the farmer is an exploiter; the Africans, his victims. After setting this scene, the story drops the white farmer and moves to its black protagonist, a "tall elderly man with a mild face" (34). Despite his dignity, Jonas cannot redress the power imbalance between the farmer and himself; he is coerced into following the white man's orders to guard the corn "against theft by his own people" (35) and to shoot anything that moves through the field at night, "and if it turns out to be a human pig, then so much the worse" (34).

As the narrative moves into the old black man's mind, its style simplifies to a Hemingway-like swagger. The old man has an unfaithful young wife: "once he had snatched up a stick, in despair, to beat her with; then he had thrown it down. He was old, and the other man was young, and beating her could not cure his heartache" (35). This style is as intense, self-conscious, and mannered as that of "The Trinket Box," but mannered according to the conventions of the masculine plain style: short phrases, paratactic syntax, monosyllabic diction, rhetorical repetitions. The old man remembers with pleasure a waterbuck he shot, and as he imagines the "blood, and the limp dead body of the buck," he thinks of "the young man laughing with his wife" (37). We are hardly surprised, then, when after nights of jealous vigil, Jonas follows his wife's lover after a tryst and shoots him in the cornfields: " 'a pig,' said Jonas aloud to the listening moon. . . . / He wanted to hear how it would sound when he said it again, telling how he had shot blind into the grunting, invisible herd" (39). Like a joke, the story ends on a pun, here a moral one. The white man commissions murder to retain control over his property, the food his blacks grow that they wish to eat though he will not. Instead of protecting his people, black Jonas follows the immoral white command in order to retain control over what he considers his property, the wife that the lover can enjoy as he no longer can. The dying lover grunts and thrashes, reduced to the physical level of a pig while the old man sinks to second-hand white swinishness.

Like Lessing's first novel, *The Grass Is Singing*, "The Pig" places a woman in a situation that would produce anger but expresses that anger through a murderous black man whose aggression is justified by racist oppression: the reader should blame black brutality on white colonial brutalization. However, despite the story's assertively masculine stance, it encodes a covert feminist protest at the cross-racial male solidarity and violence used to keep women in place. Critic Michael Thorpe inadvertently acknowledges this male solidarity when he praises "The Pig" for its "universally intelligible" treatment of jealousy (27). No women murder men in Lessing's works, but men of both races kill women, as in "The Nuisance," 1951; "Hunger," 1953; and "Plants and Girls," 1957. However, to read these stories as attacks on sexism avoids recognizing that they participate in tacit sexist literary conventions that invite the reader to collude in the imaginary destruction of women.

Racial injustice provides Lessing with her first model for understanding oppression in general. Her earliest published works display a steady knowledge about what happens when some people treat other people as objects, projecting their own desires upon them and encouraging them to act out their own worst impulses. She also understands the degrading consequences for women of accommodating to a patriarchal society, but she treats this issue as secondary.

By taking the "masculine" road in writing short stories, Lessing joined the unmarked, paradigmatically male dominant tradition of the postwar decade. She also found a way to shape her short fiction, setting up stories in terms of conflicts between men, sometimes white and black men, about women who could be, and often were, destroyed. These simple plots seem controlled and well-crafted in comparison to the more amorphous and dangerous "feminine" stories. Lessing's early African stories in her "masculine" mode display explicit insights about racial injustice, but present sexual roles more covertly. A maternal metaphor about authorship implies a special affinity between a woman writer and her female characters, which Lessing flirts with and rejects in the narrative "we" of "The Trinket Box." In the "masculine" stories she develops a related, though opposite technique, which might be called projective disidentification, the device of getting "inside" another person whose consciousness seems alien, then exposing that character while apparently sympathizing with it. This is a device that works toward domination rather than toward empathy with its object, and Lessing seems to find it a useful way to distance herself from her characters. She uses this technique first and least successfully to create black men; later, for white men and antipathetic white women.

As she saw it in the 1960s, Lessing charted two possibilities for herself as a beginning writer in the 1940s: one was female modernism with its sensitivity, fluid characters and narrators, and an interior focus; the other, male-dominant realism, a fiction of neat plot, clear beginnings and endings, and of discrete characters who deftly represent political positions. Death in the "feminine" stories raises questions about individual identity and the meaning of life, about the connections between maternity and mortality; in contrast, death in the "masculine" stories is a result of human will. Through most of the 1950s she stayed close to the second track, sustained by a Marxist ideology that upheld the social usefulness of a realist esthetic. However, despite her either/or rhetoric, her actual practice tends toward both/and; her fiction oscillates between positions that it declares "correct" and others that it disavows, and her oppositions covertly admit their excluded categories. The binary division between "masculine" and "feminine" oversimplifies the categories; the "masculine" stories might more accurately be called oedipal in their triangular rivalries, whereas her "feminine" line often explores preoedipal anxieties about identity and the dominating powers of empathy. The story "Traitors," 1951, for example, graphically portrays children's conflicted familial loyalties as sisters move from a position behind their mother's chair to one behind their father's. Throughout Lessing's fiction, this oscillation continues, though the values of the male and female poles change in the course of her and the century's history, and the stories thus dramatize a daughter's development through a looping process that incorporates and rejects variously reimagined paternal and maternal models. In her afterward to Olive Schreiner's *The Story of an African Farm*, 1968, Lessing claimed that the creation of a woman novelist often arose from "a balance between father and mother where the practicality, the ordinary sense, cleverness, and worldly ambition is on the side of the mother; and the father's life is . . . weighted with dreams and ideas and imaginings" (*SPV* 108).

While the daughter stands behind her father's chair, Lessing writes realistic, oedipal stories that treat chronological narrative unproblematically. The illusion of verisimilitude arises from using conventions that signal the complexity of people's inner lives. Typically, Lessing paints with a primary palette of a few intense emotions—anger and resentment predominate, but she also attributes to her characters fear, hunger, sexual jealousy, longing for affection, and ecstatic joy in communion with nature. We are to believe that people are complex but that she and we can understand this complexity better than her characters can understand themselves. For example, in "Hunger," 1953, she describes strong, contradictory and rapidly shifting emotions:

> He waits for her to turn—if she does and thanks him, then he will shout at her; already he feels the anger crowding his throat. And when she does not turn he feels even more anger, and a hot blackness rocks across his eyes. He cannot endure that anyone, not even his mother, should understand why he creeps like a thief to do a kind thing. (*African* 432)

That is, being understood, Lessing thinks, feels like being dominated, because being understood is like being a mother's child. By representing themselves as understanding the characters, Lessing's narrators assume an ambivalent maternal position toward them, even in apparently "masculine" stories like "Hunger."

Lessing characterized this novella as a failure because in it she tried too hard to follow the dictates of one of her cultural fathers, the Communist Party, and so produced a stillborn child, an almost deliberate parody of socialist fiction. She says she tried to write it as a good communist morality tale because the Russians in 1952 "were demanding in literature—greater simplicity, simple judgements of right and wrong" (*African* ix). She attempted to fill the bill:

> Well, there I was, with my years in Southern Africa behind me, a society as startlingly unjust as Dickens' England. Why, then, could I not write a story of simple good and bad, with clear-cut choices, set in Africa? The plot? Only one possible plot—that a poor black boy or girl should come from a village to the white man's rich town and . . . there he would encounter, as occurs in life, good and bad, and after much trouble and many years he would follow the path of . . . (ix, her ellipses)

In other words, she interprets socialist realism as moral allegory and turns the Dickensian orphan into a black everybody; in *Retreat to Innocence*, 1956, an idealized communist speaks of allegories as "reflections of the possible" (316). The "only one possible plot" Lessing imagines for her African story is also the plot of *Martha Quest*, 1952, her first autobiographical novel, in which progressive rationality and various corrupt conformities tempt the young white middle-class female hero.

"The Old Chief Mslanga," 1951, approaches the subject of white colonial culture, as many of her early stories do, from the viewpoint of the innocent white child who learns to operate within the privileged position of a white colonial. In this story Lessing signals her autobiographical character's lack of responsibility for the system from which she profits by describing herself as "it," "she," or "the child" as long as she is an innocent exploiter, chasing frightened black people up trees. She becomes "I" only at age fourteen, when she meets an aged black chief whose dignity shames her into respect. Didactically, the adult author applies the girl's lesson to us readers.

Although the line of "The Pig" leads to these African morality tales, most of her other early stories in the "masculine" mode are less simplistic; several explore heterosexual tensions within a racist, multiethnic, and patriarchal culture, sometimes from the viewpoint of a naive child who judges adult sexuality against the preoedipal bond between mother and child. Adolescent Katy in "Old John's Place," 1951, romanticizes her notion of the natural mother, "a plump smiling woman" who nurses in public (*African* 192), in contrast to the coldly adulterous Mrs. Lacey, a rejecting modern mother. Without the mediating child narrator, "Winter in July," 1951, encloses its analysis of a woman's identity within another heterosexual triangle, but Julia's quandary is not which man to choose but what kind of a person to be. Having decided not to have children, she asks herself, "what am I?" (*African* 251). Her crises are not just ones of female self-esteem; she is herself an agent of "evil" (260), her despair and self-hatred springing from her denial of responsibility for herself and from her fused absorption in her two men, a plight that recalls the particularly female developmental danger of inadequate individuation. Later, in "Each Other," 1963, Lessing draws a happily incestuous brother and sister whose fusion leads to moral decay. The three bitter and self-hating people in "Winter in July" may represent capitalism and white exploitation in Africa, but they provoke the author not to the easy scorns and ironies she directs at her explicitly political subjects but rather to the uncanny dis-ease of her "feminine" stories.

Lessing's stories of the early 1950s gain coherence from their focus on Africa, their realist esthetic, Marxist politics, and often their framing from the viewpoint of a naive girl. Her stories of the later 1950s continue along the same road, adding English and European settings to African ones. Although she later said she had been "unsuccessful as a dramatist" (Driver 17), in the period of the late '50s and early '60s when she was heavily involved with the London theater, she gives her short stories more dramatic structures and uses dialogue more freely than earlier. She also takes the theater as a metaphor for the roles people play in everyday life, an approach that renders her fiction more self-conscious and begins to separate it from the complacencies of "masculine" realistic representation. "The Habit of Loving," 1957, for example, dramatizes a woman's pain at feeling that she has no self inside the shell secreted by her overlapping social and theatrical roles. She appears in a nightclub act that delivers a "potted history" of the twentieth century and its wars, "a parody of a parody," as emotionless as "a corpse singing" (*Stories* 18–19) and in its sequel, an act that parodies love: "we go through all the motions. . . . If it isn't all bloody funny, what is it?" (24). As the two nightclub acts indicate, history and love both depend on a recognition of the other; without this faith in meaning and value, love evaporates, history becomes a jangle of random gestures, and individual identity disappears into posture and costume. Without empathy, based on the ability to see the other as other, history and identity vanish; the wife looks like a "twin" to her young lover dancing partner (19), and she breaks her old husband's heart by refusing to dress for the role of charming young bride. But if lack of empathy brings death, it doesn't thereby destroy art. The wife's frightingly nihilistic review gets a powerful response from her enthusiastic audiences.

Although Lessing's early story "The Trinket Box" leaves us to decipher an open but opaque symbol of women's lot, most of her stories of the 1950s follow a "masculine" and Marxist esthetic in presenting art objects simply as means to political ends. In 1957 she defended "committed" art, the "class analysis of society," and the humanism of nineteenth-century realism (*SPV* 3–6). The sympathetic young sculptor in "The Antheap," 1953, sculpts the "antheap" of a goldmine to reveal its exploitative nature; the painting of Scottish cattle in "A Home for the Highland Cattle," 1953, becomes the ersatz brideprice of an African who wants only a temporary wife; and "The Black Madonna," 1964, painted by an Italian war prisoner, exposes the sentimental racism and sexism of his Afrikaner captors.

In "The Eye of God in Paradise," 1957, two tired middle-aged British physicians visit a German doctor, director of a mental institution and also, for six months a year, its inmate. When he is cheerful and sane, Dr. Kroll paints jolly flowers. When he is demented, he fingerpaints horrible scenes of violence and mutilation. The schizophrenic pictures reflect the art of a split culture and the fragmentation of a healer who willingly carried out Hitler's "social hygiene" against "Jews, serious mental defectives, and communists" (*Stories* 154, 153). Dr. Kroll's masterpiece is a bright, primitive painting of his happy period, into which, when mad, he painted an enormous eye, the wrathful "Eye of God in Paradise." Lessing's story is also entitled "The Eye of God in Paradise," as though her judging moral vision is God's as well, the implacable judgement of a history that supersedes empathy.

The 1960s

The 1960s inaugurate a major shift in Lessing's short fiction, a shift in which "feminine" interiority supersedes "masculine" event. By this time Lessing was an established British writer linked with the "angry young men" on stage and in print. After the Russian invasion of Hungary and the revelations about Stalin, she had left the Communist Party but retained an affinity for the Left; the Suez crisis signalled the evils of Western imperialism, and Lessing marched against the hydrogen bomb. Stories like "England versus England," 1963, about a self-divided working-class Oxford student, continue her earlier "masculine" mode of realistic stories with a clear political point. Even here, however, the focus is more psychological than earlier and more self-conscious about the uses of language. At one point in *The Golden Notebook*, 1962, Anna lists eighteen story ideas for herself—almost all about the mismatched emotional dynamics between men and women. These stories are self-conscious about point of view and wary of empathy. Feeling what the other feels can be dangerous, as in the story idea about a woman who fell ill with symptoms of her lover's disease (533).

Many of Lessing's own stories of the same period have a mature, ironic, apparently autobiographical first person narrator, even stories whose political content might previously have placed them on the "masculine" line, and the division between these lines breaks down (see Butcher). The political and literary story "Homage for Isaac Babel," 1963, for instance, ironically reveres its heroic subject in a setting that indicates how diminished is Lessing's own historical period from Babel's and in a self-conscious, personal style, a style of "feminine" self-deprecation. Instead of a momentous event like the Russian Revolution, this story details a train trip that the female narrator takes with a teen-aged girl to visit a boy in boarding school. The girl borrows Babel's short stories, and the narrator, recommending "My First Goose," tells her that Babel is "a marvellous writer, brilliant, one of the very best" because of his strength, concision, and simplicity, qualities Lessing seems anxious to emulate (*Stories* 355). The girl doesn't particularly like the story, preferring a B-movie about crime that proved to her "beyond any shadow of doubt that Capital Punishment is a Wicked Thing" (357).

Lessing's story assumes a knowledge about Babel, which it does not provide the reader. A Russian Jewish revolutionary, Babel was an intellectual with independent views. Murdered in Stalin's purges, he could be seen as a socialist martyr, the embodiment of a principled but not totalitarian dedication to the people's cause and the sort of socialist hero that might well appeal to those who had left the Party without turning anti-Communist. As "My First Goose" opens, its narrator is admiring the mindless vitality of a Russian commander who billets him in a peasant's yard with a group of rough young cossacks. They ridicule him as a glasses-wearing intellectual and refuse to share their dinners with him. Desperately hungry and angry, he grabs a sword and kills the landlady's fat goose, roughly ordering her to cook it. After this display of prowess, the cossacks decide he is a good chap. Accepted into male cameraderie, he sleeps next to the warm young men, dreaming about women but feeling like a murderer.

The story thus dramatizes a chain of persecution. Even the Red Revolutionary Army persecutes a Jewish intellectual as unmmanly; he then turns against a poor old woman. When the men accept him, he dreams of women, presumably sexually, but can't enjoy this male-bonded sexual objectification because he feels guilty about exploiting the old lady. In this small incident, Babel shows how the mighty Russian revolution feels to its ordinary, unheroic participants. Racism, sexism, class solidarities and hostilities inform each individual's reactions to events. The literate narrator reads from *Pravda* to the illiterate cossacks. Triumphantly he announces that Lenin himself says there are shortages of everything, shortages that have lead to the surliness and brutality that he has just experienced.

Lessing transfers her story from the turbulent Russian Revolution to a middle-class British train trip, and her story is both an imitation and an antithesis of Babel's. The charming "pink-and-gold" schoolgirl exhibits a privileged English insularity that might be less attractive in adult readers (354). The girl questions one of Babel's similes, to which Lessing thus draws our attention. The general's legs looked "like girls sheathed to the neck in shining riding boots" (Babel 72). The safe, pretty English girl does not think she is bound like a boot, though her middle-class insularity might confine her as tightly. Lessing may have been struck by the way that Babel's image suggests that revolutionary male comradeship comes from domination, not only over others, but also over the female aspects in themselves. In the Babel story, the narrator is at length accepted by his comrades. In the Lessing story, the girl worries about whether the boy likes her well enough. Babel's text alludes to a Lenin speech; Lessing's, wryly, to Babel's own *Pravda*. Yet the narrator's desire to imitate Babel conflicts with her patronizing yet maternal desire to "protect this charming little person from Isaac Babel" (*Stories* 356). The girl declares she will "emulate" Babel "so as to learn a conscious simplicity which is the only basis for a really brilliant writing style" (357). Lessing thus parodies her own homage, as though the simple style becomes meaningless unless it has the passion of political conviction behind it. Like the boy, whose solemnity she also mocks, she does seem to think that social evils will "just go on and *on*" unless the artist can break the cycle of repetition by mobilizing the audience's response against it (355).

Issues of generation become more insistent in Lessing's stories of the 1960s, and children figure less as innocent observers of adult corruption than as stakes over whom history is fought. At the same time, these stories show a fear of corruption that may relate to Lessing's being a successful but still socialist writer; these stories do not expose evils like racism but temptations to power over others or despair within oneself, temptations to which the stories, as well as the characters, may succumb. For example, "One Off the Short List," 1963, enjoys its fantasy of humiliating a successful man. The stories of this period also evince profound uneasiness about what Lessing sees as the greedy, security-hungry generation growing up after the war, like the spoiled, ambitious working-class girl in "Notes for a Case History," 1963. Antagonism to the young, of course, produces a very different historical perspective from her earlier one of identification with the young, which implies that the corruption of the old ways can be thrown off by the coming generation. Lessing's stance in these fictions is ironic and unempathic; people's emotions are all the same; we're all a self-deluded and selfish little lot, and she praises herself most for the "toughy" assignments of writing about non-autobiographical, unsympathetic characters (*SPV* 53–54, 60). But even when such unsympathetic characters can be understood from the inside—fascists like those in the African stories, or rapists like Charlie from "One Off the Short List"—understanding seems circumscribed by wondering what makes some products of corrupt systems stay as they are, others reject the system. This question, necessary for understanding and thereby hoping to influence the attitudes that lead to political and historical change, relates to the artistic issue of the limits of empathy, especially with unsympathetic characters whom the author wants us to reject. One solution that Lessing uses especially in stories focused on the "feminine" is to place decent, empathetic characters in situations where they become incomprehensible, so that we blame the institution for the character's failures, as we do in the case of the woman driven to suicide by her lost identity within marriage and the family in "To Room Nineteen," 1963.

In "A Man and Two Women," 1963, motherhood temporarily destroys the artist in a woman and puts her adult relationships with men and women at risk, but it satisfies the mother herself. Lessing's other woman-focused stories of the early 1960s criticize marriage and motherhood more severely. These stories, written before Betty Friedan's *The Feminine Mystique* of 1963 caused the "problem without a name" to be articulated, impressed a generation of women with Lessing's prescience about women, as did her contemporaneous *The Golden Notebook*. Justly renowned for writing about female experience, Lessing throughout her career continues to understand women's experience in terms common to the 1950s, which saw men and women involved in a "sex war," a basic antagonism between the sexes, perhaps based on Freudian envies. From this perspective antagonism is natural, even inevitable; it justifies sex differences without necessarily seeing a power differential between them. Therefore, it is as legitimate for an author to present a "woman's way of looking at life" as a man's, but no more so, as Lessing says in the 1971 preface to *The Golden Notebook*, where she distances herself from her enthusiastic American feminist supporters (*SPV* 29). The concept of a "sex war" also implies an analogy to "class war." The traditional Marxist view has been that women are exploited as underpaid workers and as worker's wives, a theory that does not account for the particular listlessness of the affluent but dependent middle-class woman: "To Room Nineteen," makes effective use of this anomaly. Readers perceive the hero's despair as gender and role specific; responses like Gail Godwin's revision of this story, "A Sorrowful Woman," make this clear, even though Lessing generalizes the story's theme to liberal ennui (*SPV* 54 Gardiner "A Sorrowful Woman").

Susan Rawlings, the protagonist of "To Room Nineteen," quits her job to devote herself to rearing her four children and feels the "flatness" of the Lessing woman without a mission: "but there was no point about which either could say: 'For the sake of *this* is all the rest' " (398). Children, pleasant in themselves, are none the less not a "wellspring to live from" (398). This contradiction recurs in Lessing's work as she expands inquiries about female roles into larger, metaphysical questions about life's purpose and meaning. Insuring the continuity of humanity always seems valuable; perhaps it is the only ultimate moral justification, but any particular set of children are barely worth the effort of raising them, and simple continuity seems pointless. In her work after *The Four-Gated City*, 1969, Lessing resolves this dilemma by positing conscious evolution for coming generations who will thus achieve the otherwise discredited socialist goal of progressive improvement. Before this ideological shift, and indicating its emotional source, is the despair that drives Susan Rawlings to suicide.

The story of this period in which the "feminine" line of "The Trinket Box" flowers is "Our Friend Judith," a positive portrait of the "free" woman that also shows her limitations and susceptibilities. Unobtrusively it delineates conflicts basic to the Lessing canon, conflicts between heterosexuality and female bonding and between empathy and integrity. If "A Man and Two Women" and "To Room Nineteen" showed women damaged by marriage and motherhood, "Our Friend Judith" appears to champion a woman who is not confined by marriage or motherhood. Orphia Jane Allen, for example, heralds Judith as a modern "hero," a woman who "has found a room of her own" (73).

Published in 1960, the story questions dominant assumptions about gender roles. Its narrator introduces us to "our friend Judith," a middle-aged unmarried woman who lives alone, writes poetry, and adores cats. If these facts lead us to believe that Judith is a pitiable old maid, however, the story satirizes this deduction: "I stopped inviting Judith to meet people when a Canadian woman remarked, with the satisfied fervour of one who has at last pinned a label on a rare specimen: "She is, of course, one of your typical English spinsters" (*Stories* 327). This label-pinning, a satisfying "click" of recognition which the narrator here condemns, has been one of the special joys of Lessing's earlier short stories.

Judith is a "free" woman, to use *The Golden Notebook*'s term for a sexually active woman unattached to a man; she appears to be completely self-sufficient, content with her life as an English poet, yet still adventurous enough for a research assignment to Italy, where her sensual possibilities bloom in a love affair with an Italian barber that crosses class, national, and religious boundaries. Judith suddenly leaves her lover because he killed the unwanted kitten of a wounded mother cat. This incident reveals to her the "complete gulf in understanding" between them (340). "It's not a question of right or wrong. . . . It's a question of what one is," she says (343). But the story's question "of what one is," that is, of the nature of female identity, turns out to be less a critique of conventional female social roles than an exploration of the limits of empathy and therefore of the possibility of identifying with other people through fiction.

The title "Our Friend Judith" poses the question from which "The Trinket Box" shied away: who is this proprietary, apparently female, first person plural? As is often the case in Lessing's fiction, a "free woman" is attached to other women, even though women's loyalties to men undercut this female solidarity. In "Our Friend Judith," Judith's character rests on a baseline that connects her with her female friends, Betty, a happily married woman, and the narrator, whose own circumstances are unremarked. The narrator won't let other people meet Judith because they won't appreciate her, hoarding her like a special wine only to be shared with the discerning, who presumably include us readers.

The narrator both warns us against judgment and invites us to judge others; people are unfathomable: "one will, of course, never know" the truth of others' lives and feelings (328), though the story will corroborate one set of judgements rather than another. The narrator's impersonal "one" generalizes our ignorance about other people, and it also foreshadows Judith's style. Like Aunt Maud, Judith sometimes speaks of herself in the self-abnegating third person, saying, "one surely ought to stay in character" (329), and her few lines of dialogue thus conflate her style with that of the narrator whose own life, habits, age, and marital status are hidden from us.

The narrator treats Judith as a mysterious character she only partly understands, one whose actions friends brood over and discuss. Most of the incidents that illustrate Judith's integrity have to do with sexuality and its refusal. She refuses to wear a dress that reveals her beauty because she feels it is out of character for her. Next she refuses to geld her annoying tomcat, having it killed rather than compromising it. Then she refuses to marry a nice old professor, who has been her lover for some time, because it seems unfair to his wife, and finally she rejects her Italian suitor because he killed a kitten. It might appear that the story reinforces traditional judgements after all: Judith is not a miserable "spinster," but she maintains her autonomy only at the cost of disengagement from deep and messy human emotions. However, the story is more complicated than this.

The narrator tells some of the incidents concerning Judith and reports other incidents observed by her friend Betty. Betty, a conventional married woman, seems to be Judith's opposite, so that the narrator appears as an implied middle between the other two women, who are defined by their relationships to men. Betty reports a conversation in which Judith prefers being a mistress to being a wife but regrets not having children, and this childlessness, unlike her spinsterhood, seems to provoke contradictions both in Judith's character and in the story. Supposedly in Italy on an assignment to research the violent Borgia family of the Renaissance, she can't figure out "what made these people tick" (336) and has to abandon the project. She claims that she doesn't "understand human behaviour" and isn't "particularly interested" in doing so (340). Judith's integrity here seems defensive rather than heroic. Because she is unwilling to admit change in herself, she refuses to understand other people, and we may infer that this foreclosure of change means she can't understand history, which depends on assessing the similarities and differences between one's own culture and others. Judith's lack of interest in "human behaviour" implies that she can't empathize with other people because she is hiding from herself. She admits she doesn't understand her own reactions in the pivotal incident about the cat: "I must have had the wrong attitude to that cat," she says; "cats are supposed to be independent. . . . I blame myself very much. That's what happens when you submerge yourself in some-body else" (341). Her integrity requires the suppression of intimacy, and her yielding response to the Italian barber violated her sense of herself.

However, the cat incident is not merely an aspect of Judith's reaction to the barber, and details about cats expand disproportionately to the laconic narration of the rest of the story. A ring of sympathetic cats mysteriously surround the birthing cat, then disappear. Without children herself, Judith becomes midwife to the cat, which is too young to have kittens properly, and delivers its breach birth kitten: "the kitten was the wrong way round. It was stuck. I held the cat down with one hand and I pulled the kitten out with the other. . . . It was a nice fat black kitten. It must have hurt her. But she suddenly bit out. . . . It died. . . . She was its mother, but she killed it" (342–43). Judith phrases her participation in the kitten's birth as a manifestation of her integrity, not of her desire to nurture: "it's not a question of right or wrong. . . . It's a question of what one is" (343). This stance apparently reduces her integrity to the issue of preserving her own style, almost a literary matter, like the scientific, impersonal imagery of the poetry she writes. Moreover, this inviolability implies that she is incapable of change, withdrawing from a situation where her identity would have to reformulate rather than simply reassert itself.

At first "Our Friend Judith" seems a simple rebuttal of sexist conde-scension to unmarried women, even if it makes concessions to the stereo-type of the spinster's rigidity. However, the incidents about cats point to deeper relationships among a woman's identity, her capacity to mother, and her capacity to understand herself and others. Contemporary "moth-ering" theory emphasizes the permeability of female ego boundaries and women's difficulties with psychological individuation from mother-child symbiosis (see Chodorow, Dinnerstein, Mahler et al. 106, 213–19). The mother in "A Man and Two Women" who effaces her artistic talent and adult sexuality while psychologically fused with her infant presumably represents a benign, because temporary, exaggeration of this maternal sym-biosis. Throughout her fiction, Lessing dramatizes this polarity between fusion and autonomy; Judith, with her exaggerated need for autonomy, apparently rebels against maternal symbiosis experienced as an adult through a dangerous regression related to mothering others. This capacity of women to blur their ego boundaries appears in the odd frame of the story, not just within Judith's psyche; the narrator of the story has no character of her own but sometimes identifies with Judith and sometimes blends into Betty, who exists solely to talk about Judith to the narrator. Implausibly, both Betty and the narrator follow Judith to Italy to find out what she did there. This vague, multiple female narrative persona recalls the "we" speaker of "Aunt Maud" and contrasts with the first person child narrators of the African stories who are autonomous characters, distinct if naive centers of perception.

"Our Friend Judith" does not devalue Judith for being unmarried; rather, it shows her as an admirable new woman. However, its attitudes to motherhood are deeply ambivalent. When asked about having children, Judith replies, "one couldn't have everything," but she sounds completely satisfied with her life as it stands (333). Then the incident of the kitten exposes Judith's thwarted maternity as the essence of her character. Only in attending the birthing cat does she experience empathy and vulnerability, and only in this episode does she evoke our sympathy. But the incident closes when Judith returns to lonely integrity. The story separates this austere autonomy from both empathy and history. Presumably motherly people like the narrator, her friend Betty, and implicitly, us readers, can understand people as Judith does not because we are willing to risk the boundaries of our selves, and also because we are willing to risk speech with one another. Judith doesn't "understand why people discuss other people": "when something happens that shows one there is really a complete gulf in understanding, what is there to say?" (340). Aunt Maud frightened her nieces by understanding them too well. Judith rejects the threat to her autonomy of understanding others and so having to empathize with their needs and desires, and she rejects conversation that could lead to such understanding: she does not understand people because she does not wish to understand that they can be different from herself. She therefore cannot understand the Borgias: despite her research, she cannot understand history if she is unwilling to understand human differences. Thinking "one surely ought to stay in character" (329), Judith dooms herself to remain static, without a history, a fictional character herself rather than a motherly creator capable of empathy and therefore of change.

"Our Friend Judith," like other Lessing stories about free women, hides both a subtext of female bonding and a feminine fear of closeness. As we have seen, "The Trinket Box" uses a first person plural narrative voice that speaks for Maud's female relatives. In *The Golden Notebook*, *The Four-Gated City*, 1969, and the play "Each His Own Wilderness," 1959, pairs of women support one another in the face of their traumatic relationships with men. When they have this core solidarity with other women, "free" women can safely withdraw from entanglements with men. When they do not, like Mrs. Rawlings in "To Room Nineteen," they may lose their selves and die.

"Our Friend Judith's" ambiguity about female identity in relation to mothering surfaces in Lessing's essays in *Particularly Cats*, 1967, which tell some of the same incidents, like the story of the cat that kittened too young, as her own experiences (Gardiner "Gender" 119–20). The cat essays clarify one essential contradiction in Judith's story: maternity both defines a female's identity and separates her from her true nature. Time and time again, the autobiographical narrator judges her cats by how well they mother their kittens. Yet when her black cat "dozes off, eyes half-closed," the narrator comments that then she shows us "what she really is, her real self, when not tugged into fussy devotion by motherhood" (*Particularly Cats* 128).

In fact, the whole cat book reveals Lessing's difficult and contradictory attitudes to motherhood, beginning with reminiscences of her African childhood. Her mother loved and tended the farm cats, but it was also her job to kill the excess kittens. One year she refuses this task, and hideous, crippled cats overrun the farm. Finally her father shoots them in a sickening slaughter, a "holocaust of cats" for which the narrator angrily holds her mother responsible (19). If the mother refuses to play the goddess of nature, giving and taking life, it seems, then men are forced to extreme acts of violence. Lessing was completing her "Children of Violence" novels at this time, and the word "holocaust" must have been peculiarly charged for her.

The mother's role in the cat book extends from Lessing's mother to Lessing as mother of the next generation: she dedicated the book to the daughter she left behind in Africa when she moved to England. In this light, the book's many incidents in which the narrator faithfully feeds and nurses sick cats appear as covert proofs that she is really a good mother after all. Even in the animal kingdom, the maternal instinct seems socially acquired: she has to teach gray cat how to mother her kittens. The book thus becomes a plea for the possible coexistence of empathy and history: she can be a better mother than her mother was, and perhaps than she was as a mother to her children by her first marriage, because she has learned to understand and therefore care for the needs of others. Female life need not be merely reduplicative, and generational change, even progress, are possible.

"Our Friend Judith" cautiously criticizes Judith's fear of entangling emotions. In "How I Finally Lost My Heart," 1963, the female narrator is herself a victim of this fear in an extreme form. After counting up the men she has loved and scorning herself for wanting to attract another, she becomes heart-whole by rejecting emotion altogether, pushing her emotional overload off unto others, including us. She gives her wrapped-up heart to a woman on the subway who is enacting the gestures of "Tragedy. There was no emotion in it. She was like an actress doing Accusation, or betrayed Love, or Infidelity" (*Stories* 256). The slippery narrative voice of this story makes for uncomfortable reading. The narrator declares herself an everywoman, yet we may shrink from her self-hatred, against the apparent grain of the story, unwilling to share such self-rejection or the assessment of human nature on which it is based. She categorically rejects empathy, intimacy, and understanding, and hence rejects her readers while ostensibly appealing to us. The narrator implies that we are mechanical fools like the subway woman, deadened by our devotion to emotion for its own sake. We also resist identifying with the narrator because her self-hatred does not arise from any vice or folly we despise. We may acknowledge our capacities for evil, but this story asks us to believe that the search for love is fatuous and that a liberating indifference is the best we can hope for, perhaps something like Judith's British equanimity. This feeling that feeling itself is corrupt increases in Lessing's later prose, reaching an effectively unsettling apogee in "Not a Very Nice Story," 1972, and permeating her political discourse of the mid-1980s (*Prisons*; see Sukenick); in the late 1960s and 1970s this distrust of emotion counterpoints a distrust of reason as well, the arid everyday faculties that close people off to new mental powers.

Passing her heart to a younger woman is not progress but repetition. No saving baby provides the species' justification for emotion in "How I Finally Lost My Heart." Here as in "To Room Nineteen," the younger generation is no worthier than the current one, and the idea of history carrying on just as before seems to induce despair. Without the rationale that we build toward a better future, human emotion seems a dangerous delusion; history, a cruel joke. If love does not bind couples to build a better future together, it sinks into narcissistic self-stimulation, a perverse search for immediate sensation that menaces the future. The decent liberals and ex-leftists in Lessing's stories of the 1950s and 1960s suffer disillusionment, their Marxist faith in historical progress eroded, their reason dried to despair. After experimenting with dreams, drugs, and humanistic psychology in the late 1960s, her answer to this despair is spiritual transcendence leading to species transformation, as in the apocalyptic culmination of *The Four-Gated City*, a book that reflects the existential psychology and countercultural experimentation of the late 1960s and early 1970s.

The 1970s

Lessing's short fiction of the early 1970s exaggerates some of the tendencies of the preceding period. "Not a Very Nice Story," 1972, one of her most effectively disturbing tales in the "feminine" line, continues the diatribe against emotion of "How I Finally Lost My Heart" but directs it at the story's characters and readers rather than at the narrative itself. The story's narrative voice is not that of a character, not the naive child of the '50s or the self-satisfied or self-hating woman of the '60s. Instead, the narrative voice has grown up over the years, as its author has, into a maternal variant of traditional authorial omniscience. Without either avantgarde self-reflexivity or Brechtian distance between the fiction and what it represents, the story reflects self-consciously, chattily on its style, and seems to enjoy irritating us readers for our own good:

> This story is difficult to tell. Where to put the emphasis? Whose perspective to use? For to tell it from the point of view of the lovers (but that was certainly not their word for themselves—from the viewpoint, then, of the guilty couple) is as if a life were to be described through the eyes of some person who scarcely appears in it. . . . / To put it conventionally is simple: two marriages, both as happy as marriages are, both exemplary from society's point of view, contained a shocking flaw, a secret cancer, a hidden vice. / But this hidden horror did not rot the marriages and seemed hardly to matter at all. . . . (*Stories* 537)

The story's opening paragraph sounds like a test for young writers: decisions must be made about emphasis, perspective, point of view, and proper diction. But it is also disingenuous. Clearly, choices have already been made, the first of which is to decenter our expectations of a "short story" as a slice of life and instead to focus self-reflexively on narration itself. And the story does not answer its own question. The story is not, it seems, to be told from the point of view of its main characters, and the word "lovers" is discarded as "not their word for theselves," but neither is the offered alternative, "the guilty couple," since the most salient point about the friendly adulterers described in the story is that they do not feel guilty. The narrator pretends to adopt "society's point of view," leveling exaggerated scientific, medical, and moral judgements against its characters; "flaw," "cancer," "vice," "rot," "horror." Yet all these ills, she would have us believe, flow not from adultery but from guilt. Adultery without guilt does not function as social adultery. Scandalously, it has no ill effects. Instead, it has rather pleasant ones. Guiltless, adulterous marriage may be both "happy" and "exemplary," and we await the narrative that will justify this conclusion.

The characters of the story are two couples, the Smiths and the Joneses, named to show us that they are not distinctive personalities but types representing modern English history and culture. Their material circumstances neatly determine their ideas and emotions, conflating public issues and private results for them. Large public forces, like the postwar longing for security, explain the characters rather than anything distinctive in their backgrounds or psychologies:

> There is no need to say much about their emotions when they married. Frederick and Althea, Henry and Muriel, felt exactly as they might be expected to feel, being their sort of people—middleclass, liberal, rather literary—and in their circumstances, which emotionally consisted of hungers of all kinds, but particularly for security, affection, warmth, these hungers having been heightened beyond normal during the long war. They were all four aware of their condition, were able to see themselves with the wryly tolerant

eye of their kind. For they at all times knew to a fraction of a degree the state of their emotional pulse, and were much given to intelligent discussion of their individual psychologies" (538).

The assumption that there is "no need to say much about their emotions" implies that we readers share the same wry, weary knowledge as the narrator and the characters: we all know exactly who each other is. Awareness, self-reflection, understanding, intelligence, and sometimes even tolerance are among the cherished values of Lessing's short fiction during the late '50s and '60s; these seem to be the values the narrator expects from the reader sympathetic to the plight of postwar adolescents in "England versus England" or "Notes for a Case History" or of women left by their men, in "Between Men," 1963. In contrast, the narrator of "Not a Very Nice Story" expresses revulsion toward its characters, though the characters are not fascists, racists, or rapists, but decent liberals presumably much like us. Sometimes this distaste converts into brisk, good-humored social satire: the couples "soon established . . . that they shared views on life—tough, but rewarding; God—dead . . . society—to be cured by common sense and mild firmness but without extremes of any sort" (539). By the 1980's, Lessing is herself once again espousing moderation, "reason, sanity, and civilization" against all extremes and ideologies (*Prisons* 4). Here, the story expresses a free-floating biliousness, not directed at the wicked as it is in "The Black Madonna" but against smug decent people. Neither the characters nor their plausibility matters very much; they are only a pretext to provoke our responses in order that Lessing can prove she is "not a very nice" author, teasing, presumably, not merely for the pleasures of power and malice that a well-known, even revered author can indulge, but for our benefit.

When the two couples of the story first meet, Frederic goes home with Henry's wife Muriel and "not one word having been said . . . made love— no, that's not right, had sex, with vigour and relish and enjoyment" on the way (540). Since "the incident could not be included in their view of themselves" (540), they don't think about it. The next time they get the chance, "again, not one word having been said, they went to the bedroom and—but I think the appropriate word here is 'screwed.' Thoroughly and at length" (*Stories* 541). This is odd pornography. Lessing is at pains to interrupt the story, to open, then shut the bedroom door. Antisentimentally, she asks us to find her characters trite rather than titilating. With a self-conscious postmodern attention to representation rather than to imitation, her emphasis is not on passion but on language. Since the adulterers say "not one word" to one another, they do not feel they have committed adultery: the unspoken simply doesn't exist. Yet the narrator speaks, interrupting herself to tell us that she has found "the appropriate word"— "screwed"—implying both adolescent high spirits and rapacious dealing.

Having tarried so long, the narrator now plucks our sleeve, playing with the chronology and pace of her story as she has played with its diction and characterization. If we move on ten years within the characters' lives, we find that "these adulterous episodes . . . had no effect whatsoever on the marriages" (541). She dares us to believe it: "for surely it is absolutely outside what we all know to be psychologically possible" (542). Although fiction need not remain within the realm of "all we know to be psychologically possible," the narrator is baiting us here. She is not, as in other stories of the period, moving to the dreams, drug trips, or space fiction that allow for alternate rules of human behavior; rather she stays firmly within the kind of realistic description of event for which she is best known, but subordinates character and incident to narrative meditation. Whereas she characterized her "masculine" stories as free, bold, able to go where they chose, in fact they chose to travel relatively conventional paths, excelling in ironic incident and neat juxtapositions of character and event, and in psychological realism. In contrast, the "feminine" line of "The Trinket Box" and "Our Friend Judith" may seem "mannered" and "self-conscious" because it uses incident chiefly as a pivot for speculation about the meaning of women's lives. In "Not a Very Nice Story," the narrator exaggerates her role, emphasizing her visibility, her power to see and tell, and parading it before us, without taking a character's part in the story.

Deliberately teasing our desires for action and for involvement with the characters, she perfunctorily summarizes ten years for the two couples: "they had enjoyed a decade of profoundly emotional experience" (543). All four are happy, bringing up their children and discussing "the ghastliness of marriage as an institution" (542). At year eleven of the marriages, Althea has a brief affair with a young doctor, which she confesses to her friend. Muriel, the wise and secret adulteress, understands that "the words and tears . . . were the point" of her friend's confession, "not what was said" (544). Like the hero of "How I Finally Lost My Heart," Muriel congratulates herself on staying safely on the plane of "calm sense and pleasure, with not so much as a twinge of that yearning anguish we call being in love" (545). As she listens to her heartbroken friend, Muriel understands that people do not suffer because they have painful experiences; instead, they induce the experiences in order to achieve suffering: "the real motive for such affairs was the need to suffer the pain and yearning afterwards" (546). Perhaps an even greater need, the story implies, is the need to confess and pass a story along, not for the sake of the story, "what was said," but for the dominating role of being the teller.

Five years later Muriel resists the temptation to fall in love with her old adultering partner Frederick, who is feeling "deprived . . . of emotional experience" (547); he promptly falls in love with a dental assistant. The narrator implies that the emotions of possessiveness, modesty, shame, jealousy, and fidelity are all silly; decency and responsibilty are the best one can hope from people. To expect more is to get less. Yet sexuality is also anomalous, a sort of libidinous glue randomly sticking people together.

In much of her fiction, Lessing treats sex as an embarrassing force, though occasionally it evokes playful enjoyment or ecstatic surprise. Her fundamental moral rule is that people must take responsibility for their actions, and sex is often irresponsible. What can't be controlled must also not be repressed lest it return in darker form, and one of sex's dark forms is "that yearning anguish we call being in love" (545). In fact, love may be the primary mid-twentieth century fiction that the fiction writer feels she must expose as both dangerous and unreal.

At this point midway through her story the narrator suddenly starts lecturing us about the way television affects our lives. In 1969, Lessing called television "the biggest social change we've seen in decades," and she particularly condemned its "leveling effect" and uniform "tone of voice" for "important events" and "petty incidents" (*SPV* 64). Here such views interrupt the narrative like a public service announcement:

> Ah emotion, emotion, let us bathe in thee! For instance, the television that mirror of us all: A man has crashed his car, and his wife and three children have burned to death. "And what did you feel when this happened?" asks the bland, but humanly concerned, young interviewer. "Tell us, what did you *feel* ?" . . . And since none of us feel as much as we have been trained to believe that we ought to feel in order to prove ourselves profound and sincere people, then luckily here is the television where we can see other people feeling for us. So tell me, madam, what did you *feel* while you stood there believing that you were going to be burned to death? Meanwhile the viewers will be chanting our creed: We feel, therefore we are (*Stories* 547–48).

Ostensibly Lessing is underscoring the story's theme of Western culture's irrational, self-destructive desire for dramatic emotion. But the narrative discourse is itself emotional rather than dispassionate; it is angry, sarcastic, arrogant, even petulant, and its first person plural is as phony as a nurse's. While criticizing us modern people with our absurd emotional desires, Lessing may also be covertly inveighing against the lost power of the legitimate writer in the face of the interloping medium in which visualization provides a simulated or hothouse empathy: "we can see other people feeling for us" on television (548) and therefore appropriate their feelings as our own.

This double invective against feeling and against television interrupts the story between sensible Muriel's rejection of love and a passage on time: "But the psychologically oriented reader will be demanding, what about those children? Adolescent by now, surely? / Quite right . . . / It goes without saying too that the parents felt even more guilty and inadequate" because they worried that their "lapses . . . might have contributed to the stormy miseries of the children" (550). The narrator's real passion against feeling is frustrated anger against history, or rather, against children, against human generation for not moving history forward. The trouble with humans is that generations repeat themselves despite the appearance of conflict and diversity. The two families in the story foster adolescent children whose miseries "we all know too well to have to go through again—but what violence! what quarrels! what anguish! . . . Oh the dramas and the rebellions" (550–51). "Dramas and rebellions," art and history, are equally demeaned and trivialized here, in part, simply through Lessing's narrative distance: she does not bother to individualize the specific adolescents of the two families. Despite these tempests in teen-pots, the children will turn out well: "could they have any other future beyond being variations on the theme of their parents?" (551). Despite the pat, knowing tone, this is an anguished question for Lessing from the '70s on, the question of how to adjust large hopes for the future of humanity with the petty repetitions of parents and children. Lessing's earlier fiction imagined children could escape being their parents, with Martha Quest pointing to an optimistic future of gifted mutants in *The Children of Violence* quintet (1952–69). By 1969, Lessing was impatient with the "sentimental rubbish" of "flower power," but still said "I want to reach the young" (*SPV* 71, 65). In *The Memoirs of a Survivor*, 1974, the feral children bred by catastrophe march into a new, unimaginably better future, while Lessing's realistic fictions of the 1980s deepen their pessimism from concern about children who cannot advance civilization to fear of ones who actively retard it, the stunted, mad children in the Jane Somers books or the irresponsible hero of *The Good Terrorist*, 1985, who bombs innocent people because she is rebelling against her parents, or the mythically murderous "Neanderthal baby" in *The Fifth Child*, 1988, an "angry hostile little troll" who becomes a petty leader in the international criminal underclass (53, 56).

Meanwhile, over twenty years have passed within "Not a Very Nice Story" since its fictional onset; it is 1968 and Henry dies. Frederick, who survives, sets up an informal polygamy in their joint house with his old mistress Muriel and his wife Althea, who, in turn, fears losing her man—not to her friend, whom she does not suspect, but to death, so that the two women will be left alone together. Increasingly in her later fiction, Lessing indicates that women's future is with each other. In several of her novels in the 1970s and 1980s, women thrive better with one another than with men so that her women's needs to fuse and suffer in heterosexual relationships look like neurotic distortions of their unhealed needs for mother love. The middle-aged heroes of *The Summer Before the Dark*, 1973, *Memoirs of a Survivor*, and the Jane Somers books, 1983–84, who accept older and younger women as aspects of themselves, grow into wholeness in ways not possible for her earlier and more conflicted characters. Both Lessing's African childhood and her Marxist ideology lead her to satirize bourgeois liberalism and its hegemonic banalities—like the problems of marriage. Moreover, as her distaste for the personal increases, she redefines identity so that it has fewer and fewer components. "I've floated away from the personal," she said in 1969 (*SPV* 68). The woman in "To Room Nineteen," though burdened by her female roles, nonetheless feels that nothing is left when they are shorn from her; in "Not a Very Nice Story," people's emotions and opinions, as well as their roles, are defined as extraneous to them, and the space fiction leaves human character altogether for variations on extraterrestrial conflict and serenity. Even the return to realism in the Jane Somers novels sometimes seems perfunctory, as though old-fashioned humanistic characterization has been cryogenically interred and not wholly resuscitated.

While Lessing evolved her "feminine" woman-centered line of fiction from first person meditation to the impersonally angry narration in "Not a Very Nice Story," her more realistic and adventurous "masculine" stories become more and more dominated by similar issues, especially the meaning of mortality in relation to history and to ideology. After leaving the Communist Party in the late 1950s, Lessing remained an active leftist through the 1960s, then became disillusioned with political movements and more interested in inner change. In 1969, she felt "the writer is obligated to dramatize the political conflicts of his time" but that she was most interested in "how our minds our changing, how our ways of perceiving reality are changing" (*SPV* 70, 66). The story that dramatizes this shift is "The Temptation of Jack Orkney," 1972, a political story in the "masculine" line. It realistically describes its protagonist's escape from realism: Jack Orkney, an Old Left writer, responds to his father's death by emphasizing the spiritual life over organized politics. Despite its public and ideological focus, like "Not a Very Nice Story" this story chronicles a "shift in emphasis" that is in part a crisis of belief over the role of generational change; like Lessing's earlier "feminine" stories, its meditation on natural death throws the meaning of individuality into doubt and therefore the individual's role in history.

Greeting his relatives at his father's deathbed, Jack feels "that assault on individuality which is the worst of families: some invisible dealer had shuffled noses, hands, shoulders, hair and reassembled them to make . . . a unit that the owner would feed, maintain, wash, medicate for a lifetime, thinking of it as 'mine,' except at moments like these, when knowledge was forced home that everyone was put together out of stock" (*Stories* 582). Intellectual influences, too, are assembled from stock: Jack "in his time swallowed Keir Hardie, Marx, Freud, Morris and the rest" (569). Comparing his ideals for humanity with the atrocities of twentieth century violence, Jack feels more and more depressed: "the numbers of people grew larger, and the general helplessness augmented" (589). Jack sees his Communist comrades as consumed by egotism and frozen into postures set by World War II. Like Lessing, he casts the Left as the Cassandra of the world, always correct yet never heeded, as history itself, the roster of human inhumanity to others, gets "worse and worse" (*SPV* 76). The Old Left had been a minority; even though their radical views about race and justice became those of the dominant majority, nothing improves, and, in fact, history itself continues to run against them and their melioristic efforts: "now they forecast calamity, failed to prevent calamity, and then worked to minimise calamity" (*Stories* 597).

Like each individual life, history runs down. The generational cycle, which should be the collective comic response to individually tragic death, is also worthless, because each generation repeats the last rather than advancing to higher things. Jack is dissatisfied because his son is so exactly like himself, and the patrilineal succession he craves is intrinsically self-defeating:

> What he felt was, he knew, paradoxical: it was because his son was so much like him that he felt he had no son, no heir. What he wanted was for his son to carry on from himself . . . to be his continuation. . . . What he could not endure was that his son, all of them, would have to make the identical journey he and his contemporaries had made, to learn lessons exactly as if they had never been learned before (597–98).

Jack's disgust with repetition and generation represents a transitional stage in Lessing's work. In her early fiction, most obviously in the *Martha Quest* series, her daughter heroes fought not to become their mothers; the works satirize, disapprove, and exorcize the mother, depicting instead the daughter's escape; they break into public history by avoiding a "feminine" style, women's repetitions, and those of their own home-bound mothers in particular. Yet some of her early stories display a smug satisfaction at discovering others' repetitions—there they go, they're doing it again. For example, Lessing describes the laws of immigrant assimilation in "Home for the Highland Cattle," with a sort of triumph at their inexorability as people who can't make history succumb to it. At times her colonial perspective tends to collapse historical change into cultural difference, and thus into the eternal verities, recurrent possibilities within the same human spectrum; this perspective will lead away from determininative events, a history of Marxist progress, to the carefully demarcated spaces, the "zones" of her space fiction. In 1972 Jack's flat disgust at our inability to escape incarnation and repetition leads to a somewhat restless attempt to accept history while awaiting elevation to a new plateau, presumably via the Sufi belief in conscious evolution that Lessing has been promulgating from the late 1960s on (*Stories* 601, *SPV* 129–31, Driver 21).

Jack's socialism was egalitarian and moral: "he had not been able to stand that people submitted to being lied to, cheated, dominated by their equals" (610), and for years he organized in behalf of these ideals. Losing faith in organized politics' efficacy to achieve these goals strikes a traumatic blow to his self-concept as a rational individual in a caring community of like-minded people. When he "repudiated his past" and "abandoned socialism," he felt he was left "without comrades and allies—*without a family* " (620). His identity is so deeply implicated in his politics precisely because politics fulfills the roles for him of a family, a support group, and a validating ideology. He must fall ill and experience religion in order to accept a new set of convictions. Ironically, Jack's socialist politics alienate him from his son, a clone of his younger self now locked into antagonism against his father's power. That is, Jack felt socialism was his "family" at the same time that its recurrent oedipal dynamics estrange him from his ideology: both because he hasn't changed the world and because socialist politics haven't changed the relationship between his son and himself, Jack recants socialism for a religious view closer to that of his own dying father.

Unlike "Not a Very Nice Story," "The Temptation of Jack Orkney" positions itself in the realm of public discourse and ideological battle, not as a meditation on marriage, emotion, and women's futures, but on politics, religion, and men's futures. However, the distance between Lessing's "masculine" and "feminine" lines at this stage of her career has lessened. Jack wishes to move securely back and forth between public and private and to have beliefs that will satisfy both: he solves his anxieties about mortality and inheritance by abandoning socialism for religion. We might see this solution as responding to a problem usually posed in Lessing's work from a female perspective—what does my life mean in the cycle of generations—with terms from public, masculine discourse—what ideological system is most convincing. That is, Jack faces what in Lessing's works are usually women's problems—a parent's death, a child's defection—with apparently male solutions. But Jack's public solution turns into a private one; he gives up on public history in favor of spiritual growth. Of course, from the outside we may recuperate Jack's choice as public and historically-determined, a choice between ideologies popular in the late 1960s and early 1970s.

The one aspect of himself that Jack cannot change is his attitude to women. The Women's Liberation Movement makes Jack feel guilty "because he had never been able to cope with it. . . . He had reason to feel guilty about practically every relationship he ever had with a woman . . . but did not know how to change himself" (607). Whether or not Lessing means this as a distancing gesture on her own part, separating her from her character Jack, it is a telling point of blockage. Annoyed to be considered a feminist writer, especially by the American women's liberation movement, Lessing may be reasserting her claims to importance in the universal—that is, male—literary tradition by making her character a bit of a sexist. She may simply be trying to enhance Jack's credibility, or more accurately, her credibility as a drawer of male character and as a limner of the inner life, in perhaps the same way that she chose a male protagonist for *Briefing for a Descent to Hell*, 1971, so that his edifying madness not be minimized as the ravings of another madwoman. On the other hand, we might see Jack's sexism as Lessing's satire about the aspect of male psychology most resistant to change. In any case, ambivalence about sex roles affects Lessing's concept of history, including the grandiose future history adumbrated in her space fiction of the 1970s and 1980s.

The 1980s

In her astonishingly productive sixties, Lessing has become lionized, a popular public figure whose recent work receives mixed, often negative reviews and whose increasingly conservative political positions remain highly controversial. She has embraced the role of spokeswoman of this age and of sibyl to the future, priding herself on being ahead of, and in touch with, current opinions (see Ziegler and Bigsby 190, Bikman, Hazleton). Her work in this period addresses the meaning of individual mortality, a preoccupation since "The Trinket Box," and seeks to insure her literary immortality and sustained reputation. Recently she has pursued these goals in literary forms that once again separate the "two forks" of her earlier writings—space fiction, usually considered a man's or even a boy's realm, and woman-centered realistic fiction which alludes to the female literary ghetto of romance. She has also written numerous interviews, polemical essays, and miscellaneous prose pieces in the last decades, often either critical or autobiographical. Illustrative of her development at this most recent stage, rather than short stories, are two appendages to the two types of novels—an "Afterword" to one of the space fictions and a preface to two women's novels.

The Canopus-in-Argos space fictions are wide-ranging, rapidly-written novels about cosmic history in which the harmonious forces of Canopus battle the evil forces of Shammat for the fate of species and planets, particularly our poor little ravaged earth, called *Shikasta* in the novel of the same name, 1979. Shikasta's degraded humans have become estranged from their Canopean supply of "substance-of-we-feeling," a supraindividual, beneficent cosmic glue. The tones and genres of the volumes vary widely from the acerbic rhetorical satires in *The Sirian Experiments*, 1981, to the attractive fable about the intermingling of male and female attributes in *The Marriages Between Zones Three, Four, and Five*, 1980.

One of the shorter, yet grimmer, volumes in the Canopus series is *The Making of the Representative for Planet 8*, 1982, a novella about cosmic justice in which a planet freezes. This apparently impersonal book, its plot a device to justify necessity, meditates on the links among individual identity, mortality, and the writer's tasks. In the Afterword Lessing connects the book's writing with the slow death of a ninety-two year old friend, an event more directly echoed in the Jane Somers books but clearly associated with this book's obsession with mortality. Whereas the books that Lessing published under the pseudonym Jane Somers concern women's roles in the generational cycle, as "The Trinket Box" does, *The Making of the Representative for*

Planet 8 is unusual in avoiding sex roles altogether, as if one of the attractions of space fiction is its freedom from humanity's inevitable two sexes; its narrator Doeg, a sexless "Representative" of the planet, is not an individual but a social function, that of being the group's memory and storyteller, who speaks in the first person plural.

As an attempt to create a group or collective self that will supersede the petty limitations of individuality, the book's politics are impeccable: each person on the planet might assume the responsibilities of being a Representative, although only a few choose to do so, and it is the group soul of the Representatives that Canopus saves from extinction, like the "Stream of Life" that blows over the desert in the Sufi teaching tale (Shah 23–24). Yet the fable genre tends toward elitism: a few distinctive personalities act against the backdrop of a frightened, confused populace that is foolish, easily swayed, unenlightened, and, in the Sufi term, "asleep." As in much of her polemic and fiction, Lessing insists that she is just like us but that most of us are foolish and irrational. This ambivalence extends to the role of the writer, an immensely powerful figure, guardian of the past, potential savior of the future, and part of the collective soul that dances in the snowflakes at the end of the novel, our "Representative" since the writing will be unintelligible unless it corresponds in some measure to what we already believe. However, from the 1950s to the 1980s, we keep failing Lessing by not accepting her prevailing philosophy at each phase of her writing, the most important and continuous aspect of which, throughout her shifts from Marx to existential psychology to Sufism, may be the need for a melioristic futurology to balance a pervasive despair about contemporary corruption and collapse. Thus even though Lessing may now be getting more conservative in the traditional political spectrum of Thatcher's Britain, she has never believed that the present was good enough to save; rather that the twentieth century present has always been a time of human failure, violence, and catastrophe, and therefore that revolutionary change—even if it is at a metaphysical level—is necessary and therefore must be coming.

The problem of the future in Lessing always relates to the cycle of human generation. The Canopean agents who guide Planet 8's fate are like both God and one's parents. At first they nurture, but as icy calamity comes to the planet, the Representatives question whether Canopus is really all powerful and all-beneficent. Ultimately the Representatives achieve a heaven "where Canopus tends and guards and instructs" (121) and an eternity that attempts to solve the book's embedded doubts about children and the future: "when a species begins to think like this about its most precious, its original capacity, that of giving birth . . . then it is afflicted indeed. If we are not channels for the future, and if this future is not to be better than we are, better than the present, then what are we?" (39). Having lost belief in one optimistic ideology of history, Marxism, Lessing replaces it with another. That is, having lost belief in a "long slow progress upwards in civilisation" (5), she has lost belief in the individual identities of Western history and literature and therefore reformulated the plural, positive, sometimes posthumous voice of the novel.

Contradictions about identity and history underlying the frozen gleam of the ice fable resurface in the book's Afterword. This Afterword explains Lessing's attraction to the subject of heroic freezing and associates her Canopean tales with the British expeditions to the Antarctic led by Robert Falcon Scott between 1901 and 1913. For Lessing, these expeditions exemplify heroism and personal transcendence in the period before the World Wars, and they also exemplify class discrimination, gender discrimination, and imperialist arrogance:

> I first heard of Scott and his band of heroes thus. It was in the middle of Africa . . . on my father's farm. . . . There, most vividly in my memory, is my mother, standing head back, hands out, in a posture of dramatic identification. . . . My mother, choked with emotion, and radiant, for she enjoyed these moments, is saying, "and when I think of Captain Oates going off alone to die in the blizzards—oh, he was a most gallant gentleman!" and I then, with the raucous bray of the adolescent: "but what else could he have done? And anyway, they were all in the dying business." I regret the bray, but not the sentiment; in fact, it seems to me that I was as clear-sighted then as I have been since, and I envy the way that hard girl bulldozed her way through pieties and humbug, for there is no doubt life softens you up: tolerance makes nougat of us all (124–25).

The passage locates the young Doris in relation to places that have conflicting gender codes. "In the middle of Africa," at the warm heart of her world, she learns of Scott and his men in the Antarctic ice; on her "father's farm," she remembers her mother's words. Her mother is choked but not silenced, and thinking about death vitalizes her. Recalling with approval her adolescent "raucous bray," Lessing affirms her identity with her "clear-sighted" adolescent self, pictured as a phallic daughter, a machine in the pastoral African garden, "that hard girl" who "bulldozed her way through pieties and humbug." The narrator does not empathize with anyone in the picture, an attitude that fits the preceding novel, which seeks to limit human compassion for the suffering in favor of a wise stoicism. Lessing scorns her mother for identifying with the men who go "off alone to die in the blizzards," although exactly this "dramatic identification" inspires her own novella—a hundred pages about gallant beings who freeze to death. Instead, she envies her own adolescent intransigence, her hostility to her mother, and this hostility turns rhetorically outward to us readers, condemning our putative softness while identifying with us: "life softens you up: tolerance makes nougat of us all."

This hostility and despair continue in the Afterword as she digresses into an essay on history, denouncing us for not having heeded her prescient denunciations of southern Africa and other "criminally oppressive tyrannies" (127). "But it seems that the repetitiveness of historical, of sociological processes is not even noticed," she laments, while history consists of nothing but this blind repetition (127):

> Is it possible that we could learn not to impose on each other these sacred necessities, in the name of some dogma or other, with results that inevitably within a decade will be dismissed with: *We made mistakes.* It is only too easy to imagine The Spirit of History . . . a blowzy but complacent female, wearing the mask of the relevant ruler or satrap: "Dearie me!" she smiles, "but I have made a mistake again!" And into the dustbin go holocausts, famines, wars, and the occupants of a million prisons and torture chambers (126).

In this astonishing, even shocking passage, Lessing personifies history as the goddess Fortuna throwing people into the trash—that is, as an enormous bad mother, an exaggeration of her own mother in *Particularly Cats*, who caused a "holocaust of cats." Although women have perpetrated few of the holocausts, wars, prisons, and torture chambers of history, this sexist stereotype blames the "blowzy but complacent female," just as Lessing blames her mother for the Scott expedition's sentimental imperialism.

Blaming mother causes Lessing's despair at human endeavor here. History is like mother: if we don't understand her, we are doomed to repeat her, just as Lessing both identifies with her mother and repudiates her about the Scott expedition. In "Our Friend Judith," Lessing included history within empathy and connected both to maternal care rather than to spinsterly autonomy. *Particularly Cats* covertly argues that both empathy and history are possible for women: by understanding their mothers, women can change to become better mothers than their own mothers were. In her space fictions in the "masculine" line, Lessing often despairs of both empathy and history, despite believing that the artist's identity depends on an ability to report from within the collective and changing consciousness of humankind. The difficulty of this task appears in the rarified impersonality of the series. Like certain military strategies, Lessing comes close to destroying fiction in order to save it: saving identity only by retreating to a vague collective plural, saving empathy by cooling it to tolerance for human folly, saving history only frozen in an eternal world. But Lessing has another response as well, a response from within sublunary human life and gender, and that response is becoming the mother rather than continuing to blame her. This response returns her unabashedly to the "feminine" line of explicitly female-centered fiction.

The two pseudonymous Jane Somers book, *The Diary of a Good Neighbor*, 1983, and *If the Old Could . . .* , 1984, published together in 1984 as *The Diaries of Jane Somers* address the same issues as the Canopus series, especially *The Making of the Representative for Planet 8*, as though from the other side of a gendered looking glass. Plunging again into swampy human feelings, Lessing solves the problems of identity, history, and empathy that confront her throughout her career differently than she does in the space fiction. Here she alters identity, not by erasing gender, but by keeping gender constant and synthesizing a matrilineage upon it. Like Doeg, the keeper of stories in *The Making of the Representative for Planet 8*, the first-person narrator of the Jane Somers novels is a writer, but the editor of a popular English women's magazine rather than a cosmic chronicler. The framing of the novel disguises its author: Doris Lessing did not admit for over a year that she was "Jane Somers" (Sprague and Tiger 2).

In *The Making of a Representative for Planet 8* Lessing transposed her concern about the death of an elderly woman into the death of a planet and collapsed that planet's purported history into the novel supposedly chronicling its demise. Her *Diaries of Jane Somers* more directly describe the death of a woman in her nineties and treat a similar emotional core from a very different perspective than space fiction, that of her "feminine" line, though the characteristics previously associated with the two lines cross at this period. For example, the space fiction creates a fluid, plural narrative voice, whereas the Jane Somers books return to realistic conventions and to a fully characterized first person narrator. By writing pseudonymously, Lessing altered the frame for her book from any of her previous writing and made the issue of representation more self-conscious and explicit in it. Both in its story and in its framed and covert relationship with the reader, the *Diaries* explicitly thematize problems of empathy and identity in relation to the writing processes. In these novels, Lessing returns to the ambivalent mother-daughter dynamics of some of her earliest works, but, as in some novels of the 1970s and 1980s, especially *The Summer Before the Dark*, *Memoirs of a Survivor*, and *The Fifth Child*, from the position of the mother as well as that of the daughter.

Her explanation of the reasons for the Jane Somers hoax sheds light on her quest to solve problems incurred by writing about other people by means of manipulating empathy and identity. Claiming in a preface that she had been thinking about writing a pseudonomous novel for years, "like I am sure, most writers" (*Diaries* vii) she puts herself in the class of everyone else, but also in the class of those who know what everyone else wants, her frequent democratic but still elitist maneuver. The first attraction of pseudonymity is freedom from the "cage of associations" with her name, the chance to be young and new, "to be reviewed on merit," without "labels" (vii). Second, like a good mother, she wished "to cheer up young writers" (vii), though her method of encouragement is ambiguous: she would reassure them that publishers and reviewers are ignorant and unfair, and her third, malicious reason is just to make these self-important folk look foolish. Her other reasons speak more directly about the nature of authorial identity: a writer is bound by the characters she creates, she says, and despite critics who wish her to do so, she doesn't want to repeat *The Golden Notebook*.

Though she doesn't say so, *The Diaries of Jane Somers* do repeat, or at least recast, many of the issues of *The Golden Notebook*. Acerbic at the critics, she sounds almost desperate as well, in recognizing her most famous novel as an obstacle to her other ventures. The problem of self-repetition poses itself as a problem both of history and of identity: like history, individual identity does not produce a story and therefore does not exist unless it can tell of change, though at the same time it fears engulfment by flux. By being Jane Somers rather than Doris Lessing, Lessing says she avoids a "dryness, like a conscience" that plagues Doris (*Diaries* viii). This dryness seems connected with despair about the possibility of change. "All I know is that I see everything differently now from how I did while I was living through it," Jane Somers tells us (5), much like the narrator of *Memoirs of a Survivor*; however, Jane's conversion remains mundane and therefore intelligible. Although Lessing claims it is a "liberation" to inhabit other people (*Diaries* vii), that is, to be free from the necessary repetitions of one's own identity, this defense of negative capability is contradicted by her belief in an essential bedrock to human nature. This essential identity or soul can survive the body and exist independently. She expects "the perspicacious" to recognize her "underlying tone, or voice," which "independent of style" is "the essence of a writer . . . a groundnote" (ix). An ambivalence about interdependence runs through the opening preface and the novel as a whole. Speaking from the viewpoint of the other is a liberation from the repetitions of self-sameness; representation of the other, which is only possible after understanding the other, is also a liberation from repetition, because the fictional representation is never identical to that being repre- sented. Thus fiction, and perhaps for Lessing only fiction, can solve the dilemma of needing to stabilize an autonomous identity which remains coherent yet capable of changing itself and of empathizing with the other.

Yet Lessing's claim that it is liberating to speak from a new perspective is complicated and deepened by the particular perspective that she chooses, which is specifically that of her mother: "another influence that went to make Jane Somers was reflections about what my mother would be like if she lived now: that practical, efficient, energetic woman by temperament conservative, a little sentimental, and only with difficulty . . . able to un- derstand weakness and failure" (viii). Lessing reimagines a better version of her mother, someone who would have met her daughter's needs better than she thinks her own mother did. Thus the liberation of being the other feeds into the exhilaration of becoming one's own mother and doing it more satisfactorily than one judges one's childhood mother as having done it. This is a specially charged kind of empathy, one that empathizes with the failures and constraints of the real mother in order to triumph over them, then identifies with an idealized mother who is idealized specifically in the respect that she learns to empathize with others.

Jane Somers, a successful magazine editor and romantic novelist, can only feel love, empathy, and attachment for someone as independent, detached, angry and solitary as she herself is—Maudie, an ugly, dirty, feisty, witchlike milliner born in the Victorian era and now living in proud, abject poverty in the interstices of the welfare state. Jane describes her love for Maudie as her "secret life" (28), and her mocking reference to Victorian scandal satirically compares women's cross-class friendships in the 1980s with Victorian cross-class heterosexual liaisons, but it also hints at the hidden psychological sources that draw Jane to Maudie. With Maudie, Jane permits herself physical affection that she could not express with her mother, sister, or husband. More important, perhaps, she permits herself a regressed, unrestrained arguing with Maudie in which they shout at each other childishly, expressing their mutual anger at other people and at physical impairment. Jane can't give to anyone who is needy, except Maudie who rebels against her needs, and true love for fastidious Jane is washing excrement off the sick, incontinent old lady's bottom. For a character for whom individual autonomy is so crucial to personal identity, it is appropriate that these toilet-training issues, which psychoanalysts associate with infantile conflicts over independence and control, loom so large in the healing, regressive symbiosis between Maudie and Jane.

Too proud to ask to be hugged, the dying Maudie asks Jane to "lift" her up, an image of elevation and improvement (235). Jane does improve Maudie by writing her—writing the details of her physical struggles for our readerly empathy: "I wrote Maudie's day because I want to understand. I *do* understand a lot more about her, but is it true? I can only write what I have experienced myself, heard her say, observed" (126). Writing indicates the limits knowledge places on empathy but also itself advances that empathy: "I know that sometimes it is not possible to put oneself into the place of another" (233). Jane also writes a romantic novel placing Maudie in a sentimental heterosexual plot. This improvement over reality is a tribute to Maudie: "how I did enjoy making Maudie's relentless life something gallantly light-hearted, full of pleasant surprises" (244). Jane achieves authority over the identity of the other by writing it; she also remakes her own identity by being free to separate representation from reproduction, the simple replication of biological cycle seen both as journalistic reportage and as biological motherhood.

Early in her career, Lessing defined her esthetic choices in gendered terms, her "feminine" and implicitly "masculine" short stories marking out different ways of approaching history and working over complementary psychological issues. In the 1980s, forty years after her first stories, her esthetic choices of space fiction and romantic novels seem equally gender-polarized. However, her extraordinary productivity in the intervening period has not proceeded along neatly divided lines; rather, these polarizing tendencies in her work involve enormously fruitful and continuous renegotiations of insoluble contradictions.

Lessing came to Marxism by rejecting the unjust racial situation in southern Africa where she grew up; during World War II, she saw Nazism as a kind of racist imperialism. She was a moral Marxist first; society was unfair; it was unjust, illogical, and wrong to treat some people as better than others. She describes the reinforcing cycles of the status quo very perceptively, for example, in the white settler mentality of "Home for the Highland Cattle" or the racist exclusiveness of "The Black Madonna." But she did not turn out like her peers. She believes both that society pressures conformist ideas, especially those that sustain one group's domination over others, and conversely, that any rational person can see which institutions and ideas are unjust. At times she has concluded in despair that people don't change opinions contrary to their social conditioning and their immediate self-interest: her fifteen years of rational arguments against white African racism apparently changed no one.

But things do change, suddenly and unexpectedly. African nations won independence; the bomb alters people's minds; and travelling changes travellers' opinions. Similarly, new environments of ideas change people. The brief sketch "Spies I Have Known," (in *Temptations of Jack Orkney* 185–204; not reprinted in *Stories*) 1972, illustrates this point. After being forced to listen to hours of meetings and conversations among Communists, the spies come to understand, admire, and identify with them. A similar capacity to enthrall its audience gives fiction a privileged position in creating social change. "The function of real art," Lessing said recently, "which I don't aspire to, is to change how people see themselves" (Ziegler and Bigsby 193).

In her lectures published under the title *Prisons We Choose to Live Inside*, 1987, she describes her theme as "how often and how much we are dominated by our savage past" (3). However, she still believes that "writers are by nature more easily able to achieve this detachment from mass emotions and social conditions" which is necessary "to enable us to see ourselves as others see us" (7). If she can create new environments in fiction, Lessing can get people to experience new situations vicariously and so change their thinking, changes necessary to prevent the apocalyptic ending of human history. In *The Golden Notebook* Anna acknowledges her insistance that other people think as she does; both Lessing's late domestic and cosmic fictions, products of the evolution of her "feminine" and "masculine" narrative lines, continue to immerse us readers and await our empathic conversion.

V

THREE MASTERPIECES

The word "masterpiece" has sexist associations with male trade guilds, but it also connotes competence and artistry. Upholders of the traditional masculinist canon claim some works transcend their age and are intrinsically superior to others because of their universal appeal and esthetic perfection. Feminist critics reject such androcentric universalizing, yet we continue to make judgments. Because of its associations with demonstrating skill, we might wish to consider each writer's "masterpiece" as a text that best solves the problems she sets for herself, a work that best shows off her talent by shaping the content she has chosen into a pleasant and appropriate shape. Such a definition decenters and particularizes the category but continues to beg the question of evaluation.

The three novels discussed in this chapter—Jean Rhys's *Wide Sargasso Sea*, 1966, Christina Stead's *The Man Who Loved Children*, 1940, and Doris Lessing's *The Golden Notebook*, 1962—enjoy the highest critical reputations of each author's work. Randall Jarrell claims that *The Man Who Loved Children* is "as plainly good as *Crime and Punishment* and *The Remembrance of Things Past* and *War and Peace* are plainly great"; then he suggests that Stead's novel, too, is great rather than merely good because it makes us a part of "one family's immediate existence as no other book quite does" (*The Man Who Loved Children*, cited hereafter as *MWLC*, 493). That is, his critical judgment slides from an authoritative declaration based on undefined, absolute standards of greatness to a more particular and provisional appreciation based on the work's ability to elicit our empathy, a criterion especially appropriate for twentieth-century Western women writers, from whom many people desire and expect emotional engagement and rapport.

Although very different, these three novels share many characteristics highly valued by contemporary literary criticism. Each traces broad and rich connections between the individual and her historical period. Each reflects on the literary tradition of nineteenth-century realism and finds it inadequate to twentieth-century perceptions about women's experience. Balancing between self and other, between personal intensities and their cultural resonances, these novels help us understand the position of the other with verisimilitude, energy, and intensity.

Each of these three novels corrects imbalances that critics perceive in its author's other works. Although Rhys's four early novels are less claustro-phobically autobiographical than they have been judged, never being de-void of esthetic awareness, artistic control, and historical placement, they remain closely tied to the centered consciousness of their heroes, whereas *Wide Sargasso Sea* openly exhibits its reliance on the literary tradition and hence feels more public and accessible. In contrast, Stead, who often sur-veys society in sprawling, diffuse works, withdraws from the global pan-orama long enough to concentrate on her own childhood experience in *The Man Who Loved Children*, an experience she can contextualize within larger issues without losing emotional intensity. Whereas *Wide Sargasso Sea* is Rhys's last novel, following the others after a long hiatus, *The Man Who Loved Children* appears early in its author's career: a "masterpiece" is not necessarily its author's concluding statement. *The Golden Notebook* marks a turning point in Lessing's mid-career, an introspective and experimental text interrupting her autobiographical *Children of Violence* quintet and ques-tioning her early acceptance of Marxist historiography, Freudian psychol-ogy, and realist esthetics. Immediately recognized as an important work by some critics, though derided by others, *The Golden Notebook* has been enormously influential on readers and on other writers. The other two books, relatively successful when they first appeared, have also become canonical subjects of critical attention and American student instruction, largely to contemporary audiences encouraged by the women's movement.

The idea that there may be "masterpieces" within authors' works bears some analogy to the idea of a mature self-concept within an individual identity. Neither a "masterpiece" nor a mature self-concept exists as a thing in itself. The mature artwork may necessarily seem self-conscious, in much the same way that a person's self-concept implies not only a mature identity but also a sense of one's own identity. Defining judgements of such things are always evaluative and hence contextual, dependent on a field within which we can make comparative judgments. We may say that some literary texts give the impression of coherence, unity, and meaning, as do some people, even if we decide that there is no such thing as a unified human subject. If it is true, as feminist object relations theorists argue, that female identity among modern Western women is typically fluid, adaptable, and flexible, a lifelong process that fears engulfment and achieves autonomy only with difficulty, then women's literary works may reflect such char-acteristics. For example, the female writer may reproduce, through the role of the narrator in her fiction, the oscillation between empathy and exclusion which is a central issue of female identity formation. These three twentieth-century novels by women do thematize identity and empathy, perhaps for historical reasons connected with changes in women's roles and therefore in women's psychologies, especially disruptions in women's identification with their mothers. Canonical modernist fiction often asks the epistemo-logical riddle, "what can I know of myself and the modern world?" These three novels ask, as well, "how do I feel like the other, especially when the other is also a woman?"

All three of these novels are about "the other woman," the female miscreant traditionally denied the author's empathy, as well as about some version of the female self. *Wide Sargasso Sea* explicitly revises the female nineteenth-century literary tradition by taking the viewpoint of the other woman and by centering its narrative around this formerly marginal character. *The Man Who Loved Children* allows a twentieth-century daughter to forgive an adulteress like those in the nineteenth-century canon. In *The Golden Notebook*, the narrative self blurs into the other woman, whom it calls "the shadow of the third" (207). Formally, the three novels shift narrative focus in keeping with this theme. In *Wide Sargasso Sea*, the first person narrative voice is first Antoinette's, then Rochester's, then Antoinette's again, in contrast to its model *Jane Eyre*'s steady absorption in its main character. Thus the male antagonist who defines the "other woman" as other in *Jane Eyre* speaks to define her, and she defines herself, but no one speaks for Jane, who is absent and voiceless in the later novel. Stead writes *The Man Who Loved Children*, the earliest of the three books, more traditionally in the omniscient authorial third person; however, her focus roams among the main characters of the family romance, from father to mother to daughter, reading the minds and feelings of each. *The Golden Notebook* is different from the other novels in that in it the other is always contained within the self: we hear only Anna's versions of men and of other women.

The three novels interrogate female roles in society and in the literary tradition, particularly the role of wife. In these three novels about the other woman, marital ties are conflicted, weak, and adulterous: marriage cannot be the solution to the woman's plot. The English nineteenth-century courtship novel might end either happily, as in Austen, or tragically, as in Eliot's *The Mill on the Floss*. The Continental novel often withheld tragedy until after marriage and adultery. These three novels modify these traditional plots to produce new representations of female experience (see DuPlessis *Writing Beyond the Ending* 1–19).

The novel that aspires to describe woman's place in society must analyze the roles that mediate between the individual and her culture. Because of sexist constraints through the mid twentieth century, such conventional roles seem more damaging to female than to male identity. These three novels represent different stages in the development of one role within the traditional canon, that of the hero as artist, a role freer than others for women: only a marginalized outsider can be a kind of artist in *Wide Sargasso Sea*; the adolescent hero of *The Man Who Loved Children* aspires to be an artist; the hero of *The Golden Notebook* is a professional writer.

A mature self-concept is not a static achievement; like a "masterpiece," it is an evaluative term indicating that a process has been successfully completed, but without indicating the nature of that process or what follows it. These three novels employ very different strategies in building their unique identities. Although mother-daughter dynamics underlie female psychology, other configurations may be more salient in any given instance. With reference to the literary tradition, *Wide Sargasso Sea* is mother-identified; *The Man Who Loved Children* is father-identified; and *The Golden Notebook* constitutes itself as self-made. Unlike a person, a literary work need not develop a gender identity, and it may do so only as a reflection of the author's self-concept. Rhys accepts a female esthetic; Stead rejects it; Lessing, having divided her short fiction into feminine and masculine lines, twitches under the burden of gender identification and attempts to be both, neither, and something else.

Although working within known genres and traditions, a masterpiece may create, arouse, and fulfill its own set of reader expectations. *Wide Sargasso Sea* refers to nineteenth-century fiction by women; *The Man Who Loved Children* to canonical male realism of the nineteenth and twentieth centuries; and *The Golden Notebook* to iconoclastic postmodernism. Mastery of these traditions provides a framework within which each of these texts establishes itself as worthy to occupy a place in literary history. *Wide Sargasso Sea* rewrites a past text; *The Man Who Loved Children* revises an old literary tradition; *The Golden Notebook* questions its origins until this authorial questioning becomes much of what the novel is about, and transmission of the experience of dislocation, its accomplishment.

Wide Sargasso Sea

Rhys had long been fascinated with Rochester's mad first wife in *Jane Eyre* because of her West Indian origin, and she began a novel about this character when she was living obscurely. Her own maternal grandmother had faced a riot on her plantation in Dominica (Mellown *Jean Rhys* xxiv). Encouraged by the attention following her rediscovery in 1957, Rhys worked on the novel slowly and intermittently; it was published at last in 1966. (Athill comments that Rhys's perfectionism was such that she rewrote the novel for years and was angry at its publication because two superfluous words remained in it. *Smile* 5.) Although its West Indian setting gives Rhys a point of contact with the hero of *Wide Sargasso Sea*, it is a wholly new venture for her, a novel not primarily autobiographical, a novel that insists on its place in English literary tradition and on its right to reformulate that tradition as well as to join it, not merely adding itself to the tail of the creature but reshaping its entire anatomy.

Wide Sargasso Sea tells the story of a nineteenth-century white West Indian girl whose father was a slaveowner. He dies, leaving his young wife and two children on an isolated, decaying post-Emancipation estate, where they are cared for by a few loyal servants and jeered by the other blacks. Antoinette's childhood is wild and solitary until her mother remarries. Her stepfather tries to revive the plantation, using imported coolie labor, and the angry local blacks then burn down the house, killing her feeble little brother. Distraught at the loss of her house and her son, Antoinette's mother rejects her daughter and husband; her husband considers her mad and entrusts her to a pair of degraded housekeepers. Antoinette finds sanctuary in a convent school; when she is sixteen, her stepfather's son arranges a marriage for her with a fortune-hunting young Englishman. Briefly he finds her attractive but is repulsed by her desire for him and her strangeness, implicated with the strangeness of the island, its black people and magic. Therefore he chooses to believe rumors that she is "crazy and worse besides" like her mother (99). Unwilling to let her live alone in the islands, he brings her to England and keeps her in a locked chamber where she dreams about the fire at Coulibri Estate. Eventually she relives the dream by burning down his house.

The novel can stand on its own as a modernist text, self-enclosed and consistent in its patterns of imagery, its contrasts between lush tropical sensuality and cold English calculation, and its psychologically-convincing portrait of a woman misunderstood, rejected, and persecuted. Yet the novel does not stand on its own: its young husband is Mr. Rochester; its wife, his attic-bound madwoman; and the entire novel a prologue to and re-reading of Charlotte Bronte's *Jane Eyre*, perhaps the most influential female novel of development. *Wide Sargasso Sea* follows *Jane Eyre* by a century, but its plot precedes it. It is a novel that re-evaluates *Jane Eyre*, questioning its assumptions and revealing its origins.

The relation of *Wide Sargasso Sea* to *Jane Eyre* is a complex one, raising questions about dependence and autonomy, particularly with regard to the relations between mothers and daughters. Rhys deliberately looks to the female tradition within the English novel, seeming less anxious about in-fluence than anxious to be influenced, and validating her forebear's prior importance at the same time that she wishes to displace it: she mothers her mother text by creating its fictional antecedents. Rather than being overwhelmed by the sense that it has all been said before, she tells us what has never been said or said falsely.

Her main character, Antoinette, parallels Jane Eyre while failing and succeeding in ways that enable Jane's destiny to pick up where hers leaves off. Like Jane, Antoinette is a poor solitary waif, neglected and rejected in her childhood home. Religion attacks and solaces both girls, and both find refuge and maternal care at boarding school. As young women, both pas-sionately desire love; both retreat to nature after human cruelty; and both understand their fates and desires through dreams and apparently super-natural experiences. And, of course, both love the same man, the myste-rious, sometimes sadistic Rochester. Yet Jane has the "spunks" that the passive Antoinette lacks; by leaving Rochester when her independence demands it, she ultimately gets him on her own terms, a devoted and humbled husband.

Jane is the little engine that could, the solitary individual who triumphs over circumstances. Fate rewards her virtue with a convenient legacy, a loving husband, and the chance to lavish her son with the maternal devotion she never had. Her *alter ego* is the madwoman, her husband's wife Bertha, a bestial creature whom *Jane Eyre* describes as a vampire, a tigress, a hyena, a demon, a hereditary madwoman and drunkard. Rochester claims he was "cheated into espousing" this "bad, mad, and embruted partner" (Bronte, *Jane Eyre*, cited hereafter as *JE*, 294) who rips Jane's wedding veil in half and tries to kill Rochester. A huge, repulsive figure with red eyes and a swollen, purple face, she caricatures both aggression and desire. Bertha Mason is like an overgrown baby, crying and biting, and, as such, she resembles enraged young Jane who bit her cousin John Reed. Like the bad child Jane, too, Bertha is an undutiful daughter who fails to show her keepers a tractible and cheerful disposition. Thus the spectre can be seen as a bad baby, a vampire, sucking its mother's blood rather than her milk, and also the reverse image of these horrors, springing from childhood projections of infantile rage against the mother who is not yet separated from the child and thus becomes a raging mother, killing rather than nurturing her child and doing secret, bloody, shameful things in the dark with her husband, the child's father.

Rhys forces us to reevaluate this other woman by making her the hero of a novel that questions the judgments of *Jane Eyre* through the mind of a woman victim who cannot rise above her circumstances because her circumstances have become her character. Rhys demonstrates that a bourgeois society and its literary tradition shape the "bad, mad, embruted partner" as the obverse of its good, sane, white male master (see Gilbert and Gubar *Madwoman in the Attic* 339, 359–62). In *Jane Eyre*, Rochester calls his first wife "intemperate and unchaste"; Rhys seizes and repeats the charge, making us feel its shattering injustice as her lifelong effort to discredit the double standard of gendered morality culminates in this text (*Wide Sargasso Sea*, cited hereafter as *WSS*, 186, *JE* 309).

Jane craves a mother's love, finding partial substitutes in a kind teacher, two friendly cousins, a protective husband, and the ghostly voice of her mother in the moon. Antoinette, too, craves her mother's love, but she is threatened by her culture's insistence that she can have no fate but to become her mother, that is, either a pretty, protected narcissist, glancing in her glass, or a mad, ravaged female body, mindless and dependent. She cannot make her mother love her; she does succeed, within her imprisonment, in keeping her spirit and making her own fate.

But we should not judge *Wide Sargasso Sea* strictly in terms of its individual characters and their pathologies. The novel seeks and invents origins; its project is not just to understand the other woman, but to seek the sources of modern representations of women in the nineteenth century. *Wide Sargasso Sea* searches for origins, not just the primal scene that Bronte's madwoman represents, but a scene of primary social and literary repression from which Antoinette suffers but which the novel about her can repair. Like those films of the 1940s in which a nervous woman suspects that her husband wishes to murder her, *Wide Sargasso Sea* returns to the gothic house of *Jane Eyre* and there breaks down its ballustrades of heterosexual romance (see Waldman).

In her earlier novels, Rhys attacked patriarchal values, including the double standard, hypocritical religion, and imperialism, and she also alluded to the masculinist literary tradition of her mentor Ford Madox Ford and of modernist masters like James Joyce so as to disable their views of women (see Gardiner "Rhys Recalls Ford" and *"Good Morning, Midnight"* 247–49). Her relation to the tradition of women writers is different— at once apologetic, grateful, and critical—as though she sees nineteenth-century fiction by women as a rejecting mother to her own needs. Absent, hidden, deemed mad or inferior or useless, the literary foremothers need to be recreated and their wrongs revenged by daughters who can pardon their misogyny because they have outlasted its social ubiquity.

Issues of dependence and autonomy are central to this novel, not just to the psychology of its characters; these issues arise in relation to the mothering tradition as well as to mothering figures within the text. *Wide Sargasso Sea* plunges us into a fated universe, whose overdetermination increases because we already know the story's end. In most books, the author knows more of what is to come than the audience. In this sort of historical remake, we join the author in moving toward the inevitable, so that the entire novel is in the position of a foreknown flashback from the other text. Even though Rhys undermines our assurance about what the diagnosis of madness means when applied to a woman, we know that the hero is fated to madness and death. As in a Greek tragedy, our foreknowledge increases our pity and terror: the characters cannot escape, and Rhys locks us into a universe that saps our confidence in the ability of individual effort to triumph over social circumstance. Instead, the novel existentially suggests that choosing one's own death becomes the only possible act of real initiative. *Wide Sargasso Sea* questions the concepts of choice and freedom implied in *Jane Eyre*, as it does those of dependence and autonomy. Jane calls her cousin John Reed a slave driver but thinks complacently of Rochester as a genuine "master." In *Wide Sargasso Sea*, the former slave owners are not wickedly tyrannical people, but those who claim to be masters over others deserve our scepticism. From this perspective, Antoinette's suicide becomes a fulfillment of her destiny, completing her dream, revenging herself on her oppressor, and returning her both to the most traumatic event of her childhood and to primitive and exciting fantasies of losing oneself in the other. The fire that cripples Rochester and destroys Thornfield enables Jane her happy ending in a scene repeatedly described but never seen, receding like the dream of an origin from both books. However, the novel of origins simultaneously reverses its own sense of fatality: if endings are known, beginnings become mys-

terious. The novel is open-ended in that the causes of anything, which this
novel explores, recede further and further from view.

Between the two novels, the mother grows into her daughter so that
Antoinette is reborn not as mad Bertha, her oppressed shadow, but as
powerful Jane. One way out of the mother-daughter cycle is to jump to
another text. *Wide Sargasso Sea* replaces Jane's absent mother, typical of the
nineteenth-century novel, with the more common twentieth-century figure
of the rejecting mother whom the daughter fears becoming. Even though
she is confined, as her mother was, Antoinette betters her by keeping her
anger and vengeance ready to blossom. From the perspective of *Wide Sargasso Sea*, *Jane Eyre*'s hero is naive to accept Rochester's dismissal of other
women, mercenary Blanche and crazy Bertha. Instead, *Wide Sargasso Sea*
deconstructs the erotic mystery of the other and reverses the fields of choice
and victimage between Rochester and his wife. Rochester's secret, his sorrows, are not fated but the results of his willful choices; he drinks and
adulters, but calls his wife intemperate and unchaste. His choices preclude
hers.

The opening paragraphs of the novel highlight the interplay among dependence, autonomy, and authorial independence in the text.

> They say when trouble comes close ranks, and so the white people did. But
> we were not in their ranks. The Jamaican ladies had never approved of my
> mother, 'because she pretty like pretty self' Christophine said. She was my
> father's second wife, far too young for him they thought, and, worse still,
> a Martinique girl. When I asked her why so few people came to see us, she
> told me that the road from Spanish Town to Coulibri Estate where we lived
> was very bad and that road repairing was now a thing of the past. (My father,
> visitors, horses, feeling safe in bed—all belonged to the past.) (17)

Wide Sargasso Sea opens as a maze of gates and barriers, of exclusions
and distinctions through which we readers must thread our way. The
opaque, anonymous, and authoritative voice of society speaks first; "they
say." "When trouble comes close ranks": their advice implies that trouble
is always coming and one must prepare for it through military solidarity.
The shape of a Rhys novel is the shape of trouble coming: the first section
of this novel leads from the death of Antoinette's father to the ex-slaves
burning the estate; the second section leads from Antoinette's marriage to
its breakdown in Rochester's vengeful hatred; and the third, to the fore-
known and troubled end of Antoinette's suicide in the flames of Thornfield.
Although white, the narrator is not in the "ranks" of "the white people"
and so left rankless and raceless between society's defensive rows and lines.
"They" exclude the narrator in multiple ways, based on their exclusion of
her mother. A young second wife, her mother seems self-sufficiently beautiful, as though the presumption of self-sufficiency, "she pretty like pretty
self," automatically leads to others' exclusion and envy. After "they," ap-

parently the white Jamaicans speak, Christophine judges. We do not yet know who Christophine is or what her connection is with the narrator's mother. The narrator's focus begins with exclusion, moves to her mother, then blurs her mother into the as yet undefined Christophine, who will more actively mother Antoinette than her mother does. In fact, Christophine is clearly outside all the categories that blame Antoinette's mother. She is unequivocally black, non-Jamaican, not a lady, not a wife, not a beauty, but both motherly and self-sufficient through powers of intimidation and magic. Speaking a childish staccato patois, the narrator represents herself as innocent of the social rules that exclude her. When she says that "we were not in their ranks," she turns the horizontal barrier of whites against blacks into a vertical distinction of social class, in which age, ethnicity, and personal beauty all tell against the speaker and her mother.

The book's first conversation between mother and daughter is one of their few exchanges in the novel. Here the mother protectively lies to her daughter; later she ignores her. The daughter's first question to her mother is not how she got where she is but why no one else is there. The mother blames their social isolation on the bad road, not human ill will, but the narrator generalizes this excuse into an elegy for her young, lost life, seeing "now" the present, diminished and vanished into the better past; as so often happens in Rhys's novels, things irreparably run down to decay and disaster. Conversation and comfort are still possible between mother and daughter when the novel begins, but the father is already gone. Never a human presence, he is instead a memory of society, law, and authority: "my father, visitors, horses, feeling safe in bed—all belonged to the past." Antoinette's childhood is orphaned and innocent, alone at the beginning of the world: "our garden was large and beautiful as that garden in the Bible—the tree of life grew there. But it had gone wild. . . . / All Coulibri Estate had gone wild like the garden. . . . No more slavery—why should *anybody* work?" (19).

The past is ambiguous; the present, more so. "Emancipation" has occurred without "compensation" to the owners, and, on the other hand, for women, blacks, or anyone else, promises of freedom are illusory without the cash to buy it. The mother's only friend, a planter, commits suicide, making the sad young widow who sticks it out on her estate seem relatively tough in comparison. The mother rides until the ex-slaves poison her horse and "maroon" her on her impoverished estate (see Emery 426). The mother keeps up her spirits, however, until a doctor diagnoses her little son as incurably feeble; this blow changes the mother "suddenly, not gradually. She grew thin and silent, and at last she refused to leave the house at all" (19). By focusing on her abandoned mother, the narrator identifies with her and reveals one source of her insecurity. Yet revealing this cause removes the blame from her mother and sets it back on the mother's persecutors.

Young, isolated, rejected, Antoinette attempts to maintain her love for her pretty mother and for the pretty, equally indifferent landscape. She refuses a providential Christian view, finding nature neither malevolent nor helpful but indifferent to human affairs, independently beautiful. From her solitary childhood paradise she falls not into sin but into engagement with the human world. Antoinette sees herself in her black friend Tia, in reflections in the glass and the pool, and in the scents, hair, and gestures of her mother. Her identity is always being created and always at risk in the novel, by the engulfing octopus orchid, the wild woods, the ocean, death and sex as well as by happiness, fear, or dependence on others. But the most salient merger in the book is not infantile regression; instead it is the superimposition of Antoinette on both the other women of the prior book, Jane and Bertha. Within *Wide Sargasso Sea*, the old black nurse Christophine is the enabling mother who has the powers of the body and nature, of things and not of words; she assumes maternal responsibility for Antoinette and tries to get Rochester to fulfill his marital obligations to her. Christophine and Antoinette's widowed Aunt Cora are independent women and speakers of truth, yet in a patriarchal and racist society, they cannot protect Antoinette. The title of the novel indicates its ambivalence about entrapment and opportunity, dependence and autonomy: the wide Sargasso Sea promises land but traps the traveler in seaweed; in "Portrait d'Une Femme" Ezra Pound called a woman's confused mind "our Sargasso Sea."

First heard after his marriage to Antoinette, whom he calls Bertha, Rochester is a greedy, shallow young man, angry, self-deceptive, and self-pitying:

> So it was all over, the advance and retreat, the doubts and hesitations. Everything finished, for better or for worse. There we were, sheltering from the heavy rain under a large mango tree, myself, my wife Antoinette and a little half-caste servant who was called Amelie. Under a neighbouring tree I could see our luggage covered with sacking, the two porters and a boy holding fresh horses, hired to carry us up 2,000 feet to the waiting honeymoon house. (65)

Rochester begins in the past as Antoinette does: "it was all over." His war imagery does not suggest ranks of comrades but instead a battle that advances and retreats, though "for better or worse" reveals the battle's source in the marriage service that will mean "everything finished" for Antoinette. The wedding party appears as a primeval family under the tree of life, though already they are a triangle, with the child not theirs but the serpent's: Rochester will commit adultery with little Amelie. The recurrent images of horses on a bad road, the tree, and the sheltering house recall both *Wide Sargasso Sea's* opening and *Jane Eyre's* Thornfield where Antoinette will end her life.

By entering Rochester's consciousness, the text seems to empathize with him. Unlike Antoinette, for whom the deaths of her father and brother are disasters, Rochester profits handsomely from the deaths of his relatives, happily stepping into their financial places and home. Although the novel allows him to express his estrangement on the island, it does not forgive him for hating a woman because she desires him. Rochester disappears from *Wide Sargasso Sea* at the point where he decides to break Antoinette, to keep her as his property and not as a companion. From her locked room, she dreams of him as "the man who hated me" (190). We never see him with Jane, either, and he cannot be passionate, mysterious, or suffering to us as he seems to her in the earlier novel.

Male law makes Antoinette subsidiary to her money; early nineteenth-century capitalism simply does not recognize female identity: man and wife are one, and that one is the husband. In *Wide Sargasso Sea*, Antoinette develops her identity within the context of her own West Indian culture, learning from her frail white mother and her strong black nurse Christophine. To protect his name and honor, Rochester suppresses her by exaggerating his lawful rights as patriarchal husband: he renames her, refuses sexual relations with her, takes her money, transports her to his country, and imprisons her in his house. Because he does not want people to talk about him, he silences her.

Between Rochester the master and Antoinette the victim, both of whose minds we enter, stands the opaque and impersonal voice of the other—black, maternal Christophine. Rochester has the force of patriarchal law; Antoinette the appeal of sympathy; and Christophine the temperate and mediating powers of her magic arts, which can foment lust, intoxication, and temporary dependence but not create love, peace, or autonomy. Christophine the illiterate witch writes with things, like dripping blood, not with words, though she can rise to denounce Rochester's cruelty and greed. This cathartic moment replaces the conventional recognition scene of a character's self-knowledge with the audience's vicarious triumph in seeing through the self-deluded male narrator.

The last section of the novel restores Antoinette's voice, which again dwells on origins and female identity. She wonders "why I have been brought here" and "what is it that I must do?" (179). Like an abused child, she doubts her purpose in the world, feeling lost, trapped, and confused. She sees herself in a mirror as "the ghost. The woman with streaming hair," her lost mother and lost self (189). Despite this self-deprecation, Antoinette achieves her identity through her dream, a web of personal memory, the wall of fire of mythic initiation and the symbol of her passion and her culture. She fulfills herself through this dream, although it involves death and loss as well as merger with the past, her mother, and an ideal of truth and passion.

Deciding "at last I know why I was brought here and what I have to do," she shields the flickering candle that lights her "along the dark passage" (190). Her avenging purpose lights her along the dark passages of women's subordination and also along the dark passages of literary texts, which can be illumined by reopening their pages and firing their stories.

As a search for origins, two causes determine Antoinette's fate, causes behind which stretch the implacable deserts of patriarchy. The first is her mother's preference for her son. After his death, her mother cannot focus her attention on her daughter because she cannot imagine her as a source of protection. Years later, when Antoinette is confined to Thornfield, she visualizes her mother in a tapestry, "dressed in an evening gown but with bare feet. She looked away from me, over my head just as she used to do" (180). Midnight comes and Cinderella's prince won't help her; instead, Cinderella will burn the castle to ashes. Rhys draws a psychologically convincing portrait of a narcissistic, rejecting mother and her consequently neurotic and narcissistic daughter, but she also motivates the mother's preference for her son in her isolation as a young widow and in the unequal laws that favor male possession of land and money.

Thus patriarchy operates on Antoinette from within, from the first sources of her personality and self-esteem, but also from without, in the simple and absolute law that gives her husband exclusive control of her patrimony. The law also prevents Christophine from helping Antoinette by threatening to jail the black woman as a witch, and Rochester refuses the nurse's plea for Antoinette's freedom, not only out of greed but also out of a love of domination. He will possess Antoinette and her money without letting her touch the money or him. Economic interests wall Antoinette in. At Coulibri the black people refused to consider Antoinette and her mother as white people because real white people have money; poor ones are only "cockroaches" (23). Later Antoinette realizes that "gold is the idol" that the English people worship (188). In comparison to Rhys's earlier works, *Wide Sargasso Sea* connects capitalism, colonialism, and patriarchal domination more explicitly; she shows that they constitute a unified ideology against which a woman cannot win except by rewriting the script, perhaps by burning the literary passages that block her way.

Wide Sargasso Sea was written before the second wave of the women's movement but long enough after the successive tides of modernism and postmodernism had washed across the literary scene so that nineteenth-century realism no longer seemed intimidating to the twentieth-century writer. Perhaps the women's novel never did. Rhys can expose the contradictions of her predecessor's novel without satirizing the earlier work, validating its broad outline while questioning its ideology. She can emphasize contradictions among patriarchy, colonialism, and capitalism in Bronte's text because dominant ideologies have shifted since Bronte's time, permitting her to dissociate God's will from women's roles and from sexuality as Bronte could not. Brought up at a time when the double standard, ideas about women's inferiority and sinful sexuality still held sway, Rhys argues against them in *Wide Sargasso Sea* with passionate bitterness, but also from the distance of old age and a changing culture.

Rhys raises the issue of dependence not only in relation to her hero's personality but also to the literary tradition as a whole. No child is self-made, yet many men claim their accomplishments as exclusively their own. No novel is self made, and each author's accomplishments spring from her language, her tradition, and her culture as well as from her individual talent. Rhys forces us to think about the enabling origins of a text because her text, pretending to stand alone, never mentioning *Jane Eyre*, is so clearly a work of homage and rebellion to a preexistent tradition. Virginia Woolf, only eight years older than Rhys, thought Bronte too angry, too self-concerned in her hero's injuries (76). Bronte's anger at patriarchal injustice was too like her own, yet too tactlessly expressed. Writing forty years after Woolf's *A Room of One's Own*, Rhys keeps her cool distance yet stirs a rage both at the outrages Bronte suffered and at those she perpetrated, like her placid acceptance of British superiority over heathen savages.

Rhys does not kill Bronte's mother text in an oedipal rivalry but instead treats it with gratitude and ambivalence. *Wide Sargasso Sea* becomes an independent life that admits it was formed on the identity of its mother. It does not replace but reinserts itself into and behind an earlier novel, surrounds and reoriginates it, just as Antoinette's proleptic dream provides guidance to her and hence a new understanding to her foreknown end.

The Man Who Loved Children

Whereas Rhys looked away from the personal core of her four earlier novels to center her last, most deliberately representative work around a marginal woman from a canonical woman's text, Stead after four volumes of fiction surveying many stories in many cultures, opened her next novel to the enormous emotional power of her childhood memories. She set the autobiographical story of her adolescence not in Sydney where she grew up but near Washington, D.C., in her husband's country, because, she said, it would be "too naked" to tell the story undisguised (Whitehead 242).

The Man Who Loved Children focuses on a few years in the life of a family from prosperity to partial dissolution. It begins as the father, Samuel Clemens Pollit, a naturalist working for the government fisheries, learns that he is to go on a prestigious expedition to Malaya; he is happy in his six children and many home projects, though estranged from his bitter second wife, Henrietta. Brought up as an heiress, she resents her marital poverty and hard work; she has a casual lover. Meanwhile, Louisa, Sam's eleven-year-old daughter from a brief first marriage, escapes from family drudgery by reading and daydreaming. The novel immerses us in its family's conflicts, rituals, and daily work. When Sam returns from Malaya, enemies in his department cause his dismissal and persuade him that his seventh child, born shortly after his return, is not his. His once rich father-in-law dies in

debt, and Sam's ruined family moves to a poorer district where Sam cheerfully organizes family activities while Henny pays for their food by bor-
rowing money at usurious rates. In this seedy area Louie blossoms,
attending a new school where she makes friends, develops a crush on a
teacher, and begins to write. As her parents' warfare becomes intolerable
to her, she decides to kill them; she doses a cup of tea with cyanide, and
Henny drinks it, exonerating her step-daughter as she falls.

The story of Louisa's growth as a potential artist slowly emerges from
the sticky bed of family interconnections and takes its place as the novel's
subject. *The Man Who Loved Children* resolves the ambivalence about being
a woman in a culture that devalues women by projecting this devaluation
onto the hero's stepmother. When Louisa herself internalizes self-doubt,
it can be excused as typical adolescent insecurity. In *The Man Who Loved
Children*, the daughter's identity is made and the mother's broken by male
rules and texts. Stead clearly connects patriarchy, misogyny, and imperialism with the denigration of women. She allows Louisa a way out of her
parents' impasse, but not a sustained vision of female success in male
culture. The father's identity in *The Man Who Loved Children* is that of his
culture—patriarchal, imperialist, and racist. He is a comic and idiosyncratic
figure, yet entirely representative, so that Louie resists the culture's misogyny in resisting him. However, the novel stops with her vision of herself
as androgynous adolescent genius. Unlike the other two novels considered
in this chapter and unlike Stead's later novels of development, *The Man
Who Loved Children* does not force its hero to deal with her sexuality. Louie
ends her novel immersed in the euphoric myth of a walk around the world.
Her new cultural tradition combines male rebel heroes like Shelley, wom-
en's bedtime stories and superstitious lore, and her own myths of self-
origin: "I'm my own mother," she claims, although at other times she
acknowledges her stepmother Henny as her mother (309).

Unlike Sam, who is oblivious to his real power position in his family,
Henny understands her situation but has inadequate resources to fight it.
Ultimately she succumbs to death, beaten by male texts which not only
fail to imagine a happy ending for her but which also reward her with a
tragic destiny if only she will die like Madame Bovary. Through her, Stead
shows that a mother can achieve an identity in death and literature that is
not permitted her alive. Male texts control Henny's life, from the rules of
marriage to the anonymous letter that reveals her adultery. Her own sig-
nature, scrawled on notes of indebtedness, creates her only independence
from her husband, her passionate, fearful, secret life; however, the notes
belong not to her but to the usurer, the outside capitalist rather than her
home employer. In rewriting *Madame Bovary*, *The Man Who Loved Children*
controls the tragic woman's fate by relocating its causes not in her individual folly or the literary tradition of women's romantic novels, but rather
in her cultural situation and in the male literary tradition that predestines
women to failure (see Gardiner "Christina Stead" 69, Apstein).

The novel's title implies a family without a mother. At first Sam, a wonderful comic character, dominates the novel. Gradually we realize, as Louisa does, that her jolly father oppresses her and that there is something to be said on the side of her apparently witchlike stepmother. Although Louie is the book's hero, its title is not deceptive: it is her father with whom Louisa is locked in battle; it is he who threatens her identity; it is his "love" for children and hatred for women she must overcome. Moreover, she revises canonical "father" texts to write herself a new script, one in which she identifies her father with the oppressing culture even though she acquires some of its protective narcissism.

In order to celebrate Sam's fortieth birthday, Louie writes a play that dramatizes her conflict with her father (see Lidoff 49). She calls it, in a pseudo-classical gibberish of her own invention, "Tragos. Herpes. Rom," which translates as "the *Tragedy of the Snakeman, or Father* " (375, 377). The daughter in this performance claims that her father daily "ravish[es]" her "peace of mind" and that he is trying to steal her breath (377). Writhing and hissing like a snake, he demands a kiss from her. She dies calling, "Mother, father is strangling me. Murderer!" (378). Not surprisingly, Sam fails to understand this remarkable drama, in which Louie adumbrates her desires for autonomy and artistic maturity while indicating her incestuous attraction toward her father and her fear of his stifling engulfment. The mother in this drama remains offstage, not as her daughter's rival but as her impotent supporter.

The play's murderous plot reflects the familial violence that structures the novel, and its theme reveals the novel's psychological dynamics. The Snakeman play represents Sam's incestuous and hostile attitudes to his daughter and also projects her hostility and adolescent sexual desires onto him. In order to mature, Louie must reject this romantic tradition of stifling incestuous love, that is, of women "ravished" into perpetual daughterhood, and in so doing she revises both oedipal and electral models of female development.

Louisa is right in thinking Sam does not want her to grow up. He loves little girls but fears mature female sexuality, wanting "a slim, recessive girl whose sex was ashamed" (309) rather than his fat, developed daughter. He intrudes into all aspects of her life, trying to possess and control both her mind and her body, poking, prying, and ridiculing her secret poems. He wants Louie to relate to others only through him: "It is the father who should be the key to the adult world, for his daughters, for boys can find it out for themselves" (355). When high school gives her the first inkling of a world broader than her own family, Sam resents it. He says he will take her out of school until she recovers her docility: "I am going to watch every book you read, every thought you have," he warns (488). His repressed fascination with her sexuality is so strong that he wants to defend a father accused of incest, "on top of the sorrow he must be feeling at finding his daughter in trouble, a little girl with a baby to come" (356).

Sam sees his children as extensions of himself, believing he understands them intuitively. When he was widowed, he "had to be mother and father, too, to little Looloo. . . . We were very close then . . . and communicated by thought alone" (58). This relationship with his oldest daughter shares the intensity and ambivalence usually associated with the mother-daughter bond, and her growth depends on escaping his incestuous engulfment. In one particularly grotesque scene, he tries to spit chewed-up banana into her mouth like a mother bird, saying that he did so when she was a baby. He treats knowledge in the same way, forcefeeding his children with information: "already he was beginning to slop over, drown them with his new knowledge, bubbling, gurgling as he poured into them as quickly as possible all he had learned" (277). Like Adam in the garden, Sam names and nicknames everything he owns, including his children. He claims that after he was widowed, his "first true joy" was teaching baby Louisa; "as a reward, he one day heard her say his name, 'Tamma, Tamma!' " (116). Baby Louie thus returned the "childnamer" his name, gratifying his pride and ownership of children and of language, although as a baby she innocently did what she later does willfully; that is, she distorts Sam's names for her own uses.

Sam makes up his own comic dialect and insists the rest of the family speak it. Louie too invents a new language, and the Snakeman play also shows her ability to wrest the patriarchal literary canon to her subversive, antipaternal purposes. She takes her theme of father-daughter incest and her imagery of vipers and devils from Milton's *Paradise Lost*, from Shakespeare's *King Lear*, and from Shelley's *Cenci*. In *Paradise Lost*, Satan copulates with his daughter Sin to produce Death and then slides into a snake to seduce God's daughter Eve, for which crime God dooms him to a hissing, humiliating serpentine metamorphosis. Daringly, Louisa's daughter-character champions Western literature's wickedest daughters, the ungrateful vipers Goneril and Regan, threatening her father: "if I could, I would hunt you out like the daughters of King Lear" (377). Shelley's *Cenci* portrays a more sympathetic daughter who murders her father. Louisa wants to marry a man like Shelley, and she memorizes passages from the play to apply to herself: "so my lot was ordered, that a father / First turned the moments of awakening life / To drops, each poisoning youth's sweet hope" (358, qtg *Cenci* 5.2). Louie reveals the extremity of her feelings about Sam, then, in believing that, "eliminating the gloomy and gorgeous scene," Shelley's Beatrice, daughter of an incestuous profligate, "was in a case like hers" (358). Thus Louisa fights her father's power over her by ranging against him the most powerful patricidal texts of the patriarchal canon.

Stead makes clear that Sam is more than a psychologically threatening father; he also embodies patriarchal political power. Even though Pollit father and mother are deadlocked in reciprocal warfare, their forces are not equal. Society sanctions the father's power and joins him in inhibiting his daughter's independence. Stead connects Sam's arrogance with patriarchy in the sense of adult male rule over women and children, and also more generally with an ideology of male superiority over women; of "masculine" technology, science, and reason over "feminine" nature, religion, and emotion; and of capitalist United States imperialism over the "childlike" rest of the world.

Like Dickens, Stead paints psychological narcissists who are also socially representative types. She does not claim that only men are such egotists, but she does show how society reinforces male narcissism and how male narcissism fuels patriarchal sexual and political attitudes. Sam's egotism overwhelms everyone around him. Henny calls him the "great I-Am" and "that Big-Me" (88). Like other male narcissists, he both envies and hates women and holds a highly-polarized male supremacist view of the sexes, believing that men can do everything women do better than women can. Thus he claims that "all the improvements in household technique have been made by men, becaze women got no brains" (349). In fact he requires his wife, sister, and daughters to serve him and tend his whims as unpaid, exploited laborers. He confines his women to the house and therefore excludes them from public life as unworthy citizens: "En if I had my way no crazy shemales would so much as git the vote! Becaze why? . . . Becaze they know nuffin!" (108).

The Pollit children understand the political structure of their difficult household; "their father was the tables of the law, but their mother was natural law; Sam was household czar by divine right, but Henny was the czar's everlasting adversary, household anarchist by divine right" (36). The roles in the Pollit family also have their class connotations. To self-made, bourgeois Sam, Henny is a fallen aristocrat, a "worthless, degenerate society girl" expecting to live on inherited money (37). To married Henny, Sam is a slave master. Sam is a boss; his wife and children, his workers. "I wish I had a hundred sons and daughters," he muses; "then I wouldn't have a stroke of work to do, see. All you kids could work for me. I'd have a CCC camp for the boys and an SSS, spick-and-span settlement for the girls" (49).

Sam is the family boss and also its high priest, preaching his religion of science and technology. An atheist who poses as a scientific Christ, Sam says there is "no sich animal" as God, and he thinks when he walks by a brook that "nature was licking at his feet like a slave, like a woman, that he had read of somewhere, that washed the feet of the man she loved and dried them with her hair (443). He believes scientists like himself should rule society and that they already rule nature: "I make it rain, don't I kids" (262). In his fantasies, "a council of scientists" run the world, and if he were "autocrat of all nations," he "might arrange the killing off of nine-tenths of mankind in order to make room for the fit" by gassing them in eugenic concentration camps (349). He muses, "what it must be, though, to taste supreme power!" (20). With marvellous zest, Stead shows how Sam's egotistical hypocrisies parallel the bourgeois myths necessary to those who self-righteously dominate other races and nations and the other sex. "He talks about human equality, the rights of man, nothing but that," Henny rails, "How about the rights of woman, I'd like to scream at him. It's fine to be a great democrat when you've a slave to rub your boots on" (89).

Sam's trip to Malaya indicates the extent to which his domestic patriarchy parallels Western imperialism in the third world. Throughout the expedition, Sam claims scientific objectivity while he treats the residents of other nations as he does the residents of his own household; they are all his children, whom he misunderstands, bullies, patronizes, and says he loves, imagining he is their great white father. Just as Sam's idea of the family is to make his children extensions of himself in the name of love, so his idea of the world is to remake it as the United States in the name of interracial and international concord; he looks forward to "the United States of Mankind" (202). Henny says her husband thinks he lives at the White House; Sam sings patriotic songs and rhapsodizes on the beauties of the United States. After he loses his government job, he takes on a new project, doing a radio show. He promises that his show will talk of "our forefathers" and praise "the freedom we have" in America, in comparison to "poor bonded Europe" (483). His officemates call him "Softsoap Sam" because of his verbal lather, and, as Samuel Clemens Pollitt, he is named for American humorist Mark Twain. However, he achieves his finest, most powerful public hour under another, more famous name that conflates his domestic and political roles: he becomes the nation's uncle with his radio "Uncle Sam Hour" (483). Stead said she didn't think that Sam is a "totalitarian" but agreed that he is "Mr. America" (Raskin 73, 77), and Jose Yglesias describes the novel as a "profoundly political work," "the story of the bourgeois family in America of Roosevelt's second term" (369). Sam's fascism, big brotherism, radio personality, and his rise, depression, and further rise suggest that he is in tune with the history of Western culture between the wars.

Louie's chief conflict is with her father, who behaves both as a father and as a mother to her. But she is not a motherless child, telling her father "Mother is my mother (meaning Henny)" (MWLC 309), and one of the wonderful things about the novel is its ability to show her rejecting Henny's self-hatred and demeaning social roles while growing more sympathetic to her plight. Psychologically Henny both nurtures and endangers Louisa, but less than Sam does. Step-mother and child never bonded in infancy, and Henny respects Louie's differences from herself even though she scorns their common lot as women. By playing a fairy-tale stepmother or wicked witch, Henny embodies all the negative aspects of maternal personality and womanly role that Louie must kill in order to become her mature self. In one of the opening scenes of the novel, Henny pretends to strangle her step-daughter. "Louisa looked up into her stepmother's face, squirming, but not trying to get away, questioning her silently, needing to understand, in an affinity of misfortune" (23). As she approaches puberty, she begins to shift her loyalties from her bombastic father to her miserable stepmother. Louie engages in "an entirely original train of thought which was, in part, that Henny was perhaps not completely guilty towards Sam, that perhaps there was something to say on Henny's side" (37). Moreover, "Henny's treasures, physical and mental, the sensual, familiar house life she led, her kindness in sickness, her queer tags of folklore, boarding-school graces, and femininity had gained on Louie" (35). Louie empathizes with her stepmother, seeing her as a creature like herself who "was guilty, rebellious, and got chastised" (37). Henny, "one of those women who secretly sympathize with all women against all men," hates both her stepdaughter and herself (38): Louie "had not been wrong in seeing a distorted sympathy for her in Henny's pretense of strangling her" (39).

Like her husband, Henny despises traditional female roles, although she sees no possible alternatives to them: "about the girls she only thought of marriage, and about marriage she thought as an ignorant, dissatisfied, but helpless slave did of slavery" (426). She believes "a woman's children are all she has of her body and breath" (463) but thinks that is still little compensation for her hard life. She considers her daughter Eve, a "nice, obedient, pretty girl, as cursed from birth: 'some man will break her or bend her' " though she credits Louie with being able to to fight back: "I'm sorry for the man *she* marries" (426). Just once, looking at her wedding ring, does she feel marriage as positive, and then only in terms of mutual enslavement: "if this plain ugly link meant an eyeless eternity of work and poverty and an early old age, it also meant that to her alone this potent breadwinner owed his money, name, and fidelity, to her, his kitchen-maid and body servant. For a moment, after years of scamping, she felt the dread power of wifehood" (139). Her attempts at autonomy are weak. "Somewhere between all these hustlers," she "made herself a little life. But she had the children, . . . she had no money, and she had to live with a man who fancied himself a public character and a moralist of a very saintly type. . . . She belonged to the great race of human beings who regard life as a series of piracies of all powers." (16). Although her acts of rebellion are futile, she teaches Louie resistance, "a brackish well of hate to drink from . . . something that put iron in her soul and made her strong to resist the depraved healthiness and idle jollity of the Pollit clan" (243).

If Sam treats Louie as a mother might, psychologically devouring her, Louie sometimes joins with her stepmother in an even odder alliance, an unholy parthenogenesis in which they bear a strange, new Frankensteinian monster child: "against [Sam], the intuitions of stepmother and stepdaughter came together and procreated, began to put on carnality, feel blood and form bone, and a heart and brain were coming to the offspring. This creature that was forming against the gay-hearted, generous, eloquent, good-fellow was bristly, foul, a hyena, hate of woman the house-jailed and child-chained against the keycarrier, childnamer, and riot-haver" (38).

To be free, Louie must reject the confining traditional roles of dutiful daughter and of prospective wife and mother. When she strikes out on her own, she wavers: "I suppose, if I had any decency . . . I'd think of my little sister and brothers" (490), then decides to let others care for them. Thus Louie's way out of the family is the way of the rebel, even of the revolutionary. Paradoxically, rejecting her stepmother is also rejecting her father's sentimental sexism, a necessary step in her growth as a creative woman, and sympathizing with her stepmother is part of her seeing through her father's mystifications.

The Man Who Loved Children superimposes the plot of a *bildungsroman* upon that of a novel of adultery. Like Emma Bovary, Henrietta Pollit is brought up to a conception of femininity that includes nice clothes and dainty ways but not housework, childbearing, or childcare. Emma, too, sides with women and likes novels about "persecuted women fainting in solitary little houses" (*Madame Bovary* 57). "Nurtured in the idea that she was to be a great lady," Henny learned water-color painting, embroidery, and the playing of Chopin, and she married "with no more sense of married life or of social life than a harem-reared woman, being a gentle, neurotic creature, wearing silk next to the skin and expecting to have a good time at White House receptions" (*MWLC* 60, 85). Like Emma, she finds married life a terrible disillusionment, and she loathes her husband and hopes for romance. Like Emma she connects material wealth with happiness, and like her, foolishly indebts herself to an unscrupulous moneylender. Both women hide their lovers and their debts, and both are incompetent house-keepers and negligent mothers. Both disparage daughters and want sons. Unlike her novel-reading predecessor, Henny gives up on such diversion, asking "why don't they write about deadbeats like me—only it wouldn't sell" (414).

Like Emma, she asks her lover for money, and he rejects her. After her father dies in debt, her creditors close in. In a haze of despair like Emma's, she runs a last round of efforts to get loans. Throughout her decline, she sees her wedding ring chaining her at every step, when she is "drinking cocktails with Bert and when signing away her every cent on some scrap of paper at the moneylender's" (138–39). In killing Emma, Flaubert inex-orably concludes her foolish aspirations in a demeaning milieu. In killing Henny, Stead endows her with some of the dignity of Flaubert's novel, even though both deaths are physically ignominious. Unlike Flaubert, Stead does not satirize her adulteress's romantic delusions but rather the grim consequences of her social roles as financially dependent wife and mother. Whereas Emma Bovary ends her life delirious, Henny apparently chooses death with a clear head, and her end conflates the naturalistic novel of adultery with the fairy tale felling of the wicked stepmother.

One indication that *The Man Who Loved Children* condemns women's social roles more than their literary delusions is the way it condenses two other key figures of *Madame Bovary*. Sam Pollit resembles both Emma's deceived husband Charles Bovary and the smug, self-satisfied pharmacist Homais. Like Homais, Sam is a simplistic freethinker who ridicules religion. Both believe in science and progress and name their children after great figures of the past. Homais has a slovenly wife and many children whom he organizes into family projects; he is ambitious and thinks of no one except himself. Through Homais Flaubert satirizes the rationalist liberal pretensions of provincial nineteenth-century French society, but the pharmacist has no direct effect on Emma's fate. By making him into the equivalent of Emma's husband, Stead packs the antagonistic follies of men and women into one marriage and one household so that men's naive and self-satisifed rationalism, misogyny, and egotism confront women's dependence and self hatred and we understand both sexes' partial and warring personalities as the sad effects of restrictive bourgeois gender roles.

Stead puts all the tensions of bourgeois marriage into one couple, but she also creates the child who can withstand those pressures. Louisa resists her father and understands, then kills, her step-mother. She grows beyond her parents, and Stead transforms the legacy of the *bildungsroman* to portray the artist as a young woman who is empowered rather than destroyed by the "monstrous tempers and egotisms" of adults (464). Louisa decides that the only way to free herself and to "save the children" from "those two selfish passionate people, terrible as gods in their eternal married hate" is to kill their parents: "the only thing is, I don't want to go to jail," and "all this quarreling and crying is just ruining my face" (468, 467). When she admits the murder, no one believes her: fate acts as a kind mother to protect her, just as Henny had done in exonerating her from blame: "fate itself had not only justified her but saved her from consequences" (482).

Louie's maturity is a psychological achievement with significant political dimensions, involving her rejection of paternal seduction and her refusal of traditional female social roles. It is also a literary achievement. She appropriates patriarchal language and literary tradition as Stead refashions the female novel of development. Louie learns to ignore Sam's pronouncements on women and identify instead with the male heroes whose words Sam makes her memorize. She also imagines her life in terms of saving myths and fairy tales: she "knew she was the ugly duckling. But when a swan she would never come sailing back into their village pond; she would be somewhere away, unheard of, on the lily-rimmed oceans of the world" (59–60). Her most powerful and consoling fantasy is that she is a genius.

When she starts her new school, she suddenly discovers "dazzling aptitudes" (315). Like her parents, she is astonishingly fluent; she begins to write comic prose and rhapsodic poetry in reams. Moreoover, she is encouraged by models of rebellion that her stepmother lacks. Her friend Clare is a Wobbly, and Louie's mother's family at Harper's Ferry remind her of

John Brown and the American revolt against slavery. Louie becomes an artist and achieves autonomy by rejecting the polarized and stereotyped female roles of passive wife and of stepmother witch. She also refuses her father's patriarchal views. She kills the mother she fears to become and escapes the father, sustaining herself with the narcissistic, androgynous vision of herself as rebel genius.

Although rejecting both father and mother, she learns from them her mastery of language, a mastery that renders her fantasies of artistic eminence plausible. In many ways she resists patriarchal domination in language and the literary canon. She learns Henny's language in opposition to Sam, and she turns off her father's platitudinous gurgles by ceasing to listen to him. Her parents speak two separate languages: "he called a spade the predecessor of modern agriculture, she called it a muck dig: they had no words between them intelligible" (132), but Louie understands them both.

Before she leaves home, Louie tries her skill at another kind of art, the superstitious surreal lore of women and children. In the Snakeman play, she makes up her own language. Finally, like the artist of her novel, she revises the canon to serve her own purposes. The snakeman tragedy alludes to Shakespeare, Shelley, and Milton. Stead alludes to another key literary text in order to show Louisa's growth diverging from the pattern that might be expected, based on the traditional male novel of development. Stead claimed that *Great Expectations* was part of her family's private myth and that reading it had encouraged her grandfather Samuel to emigrate from England to Australia. *Great Expectations* powerfully documents the way adult obsessions destroy children. Jilted Miss Havisham brings up her ward Estella to break men's hearts, and criminal Magwitch raises Pip as a gentleman so that he can flaunt his wealth to vindicate Magwitch's past. Great expectations wither Estella's heart and make Pip a debt-ridden snob. Only their collapse brings maturity, mellowing Estella and returning Pip to honest labor and incidentally to imperialism, as a British clerk working in Cairo. *Great Expectations* softens its exposition of adult hypocrisy with its allegiance to the kind heart, the good woman, the happy hearth, the noble tear, and the redeeming empire. Stead is much less sentimental. Where Dickens centripetally reassembles severed families, Stead flings her characters centrifugally out of them. Henny plays solitaire with herself, always loses, and sighs, "anything rather than lose my expectations!" (132). When her father dies, her financial expectations die with him. Louisa takes the novel's title to herself with more enthusiasm and optimism, though more ignorance: "there was a book called *Great Expectations*, which she had never read: she supposed, though, that it referred to something like her own great expectations, which were that at a certain moment, like a giant Fourth of July rocket, she would rise and obscure all other constellations with hers" (395).

The Golden Notebook

As we have seen, *Wide Sargasso Sea* looks back to the "mother" tradition of the nineteenth-century woman's novel and *The Man Who Loved Children* to the "father" tradition of nineteenth-century male realism. Born after the advent of modernism, Lessing sets her fiction in opposition to both modernism and realism; she works in the new tradition of the self-referential child, and the literary texts to which she most frequently refers are her own. *The Golden Notebook*'s main character, Anna Freeman Wulf, is a divorced woman with a young daughter. During World War II she joins left-wing political group made up of English airmen and local white activists in southern Africa. She marries the group's leader, a cold and doctrinaire German refugee, divorcing him after the war and emigrating to England. There she writes a successful novel, *Frontiers of War*, which like Lessing's first novel, concerns race relations and forbidden love in an African setting. Anna has a long affair with a married man and a consoling friendship with Molly, another activist single mother. Anna campaigns for the Communist Party, and she spends two years in psychoanalysis. She is plagued by "writer's block" and by feelings of dryness and despair.

This synopsis misrepresents the experience of *The Golden Notebook*, since it reduces the novel's multiplicities into a single story line (see Draine 69–88, Schweickert "Reading a Wordless Statement"). The novel contains many sections: a five-part novel within the novel, called "Free Women," about Anna, Molly, and their relations to their children, men, work, and politics; and Anna's notebooks in which she records various aspects of her life: the black notebook about the African sources of her writing; the red notebook about her involvement in left politics; the yellow notebook of story ideas, often focusing on heterosexual relations and their psychology; and the blue notebook, ostensibly Anna's diary entries about daily life. The four notebooks, she thinks, represent the divided aspects of her personality (475). Before completing the last section of "Free Women," she replaces the four colored notebooks with a single, golden notebook. Writing the golden notebook enables her to write a new novel, "Free Women," which we have been reading as we read the notebooks.

The Golden Notebook has a careful and symmetrical structure. In keeping with its first slogan, "the point is, that as far as I can see, everything's cracking up" (3), this careful structure elegantly cracks up as the book progresses. The book starts out as a novel about "free women," which breaks up into five sections interspersed with notebook entries supposedly written by Anna, the main character of the novel, so that *Free Women* both does and does not include the rest of *The Golden Notebook*, which in turn includes it. Anna claims that everything in the notebooks is "chaos" (41) and that is why they must not be shown to anyone, except, of course,

us readers. When she writes about the notebooks, she assumes a passive voice, the voice of an authorial narrator superior to Anna's consciousness: "it seemed that order had not immediately imposed itself," "as if
Anna had, almost automatically, divided herself into four" (55). Yet this
self-division is not just under Lessing's artistic control, but also, it seems,
Anna's, since she sees the notebooks spread before her like "armies" of
which she is the "general" (55).

Book one, the longest, sets up the key incidents and characters for the
rest of the novel. The first black notebook summarizes Anna's successful
novel and the events she says underlay its fictions: a series of confrontations
among members of her leftist political group, the local racist whites, and
a few black servants, staged during their first and last weekends at the
Mashopi Hotel during World War II. The red notebook focuses on Anna's
decisions to join, then to leave, the Communist Party in postwar London.
The yellow notebook, supposedly Anna's fictional jottings, narrates the
exciting start and sad decline of Ella's affair with married physician Paul.
Diary-like, the blue notebook records the beginning and end of Anna's
psychoanalysis. The pattern set in the first section, then, is circular and
all-inclusive: beginnings imply endings; hopeful starts lead to disillusioned
finishes—and such disillusionment seems inevitable in the downward
slope from idealistic youth to cynical middle age. The second section fills
in the middle events of the first stories; whereas in book three, efforts at
reform fail, and despair must be fought. These failures terminate three of
the notebooks: in section four, the blue, journal-like entries stand alone.
There Anna accomplishes a breakdown of her identity that permits her to
reconsolidate her forces, writing the fifth, golden notebook.

The Golden Notebook's title promises an alchemical transformation of the
base metals culled from notebook, diary, short story, parody, pastiche, and
financial receipts. The novel purports to be the history of an effort to understand history and the fiction of the effort to understand fiction. It dramatizes an author's inability to tell a coherent story and to find a coherent
identity while postulating, and delivering, a new kind of story and a new
understanding of female identity in the context of twentieth-century history.

At this point Lessing thinks history is getting worse—a chaos of violence,
war, and death—instead of better, as Marxism promised. Given such a
world, *The Golden Notebook* asks whether a thinking woman now can pos-
sibly have an integrated identity and answers that she can not. This question stands prologue to the more powerful question of how one can write
honestly when one is such a divided creature, especially how one can write
honestly about female experience. The book answers that the self must
recognize the splits and alienations through which it is constituted and
also that it must create such splits through which the truth may emerge.
Anna understands personal alienation, the alienation of the writer, in Marxist political terms: capitalist consumer culture tries to steal and profit from

her intellectual labor, to get something for nothing, just as her married lovers benefit from her sexual favors and emotional support without reciprocal attachment. However, these issues imply by their terms another, and contradictory, set of assumptions. Even though the self is fragmented and the subject in doubt, truth and reality exist.

The Golden Notebook brings the issue of authorial identification to its surface. The novel empathically merges and individuates its author, readers, and characters, playing with our assumptions about the autobiographical nature of women's fiction by representing a woman novelist like her author who writes autobiographical fiction. The author dares us to sort out Anna from Ella from Doris Lessing. The boundaries of character overlap, even as the main characters fragment. Anna undergoes a beneficial breakdown, she thinks, whereas the two versions of her friend's son Tommy—blinded in a suicide attempt or normal young man—reflect one another like funhouse mirrors, with Anna's emotional projections and fictional desires unacknowledged sources of the evident distortions. That is, Lessing may wish to invent two alternate forms of the confused young man of the 1950s, but her containing story—that Anna writes everything in the book—insists that one version of Tommy is a modification of the other, not of infinite fictional space, and so it is with the other characters.

Thus *The Golden Notebook* always contains the other within the self. Anna reads other's minds, not doubting her accuracy, and reads the words behind Molly's words: "Anna held herself quiet, with effort. What Molly had said was pure spite: she was saying, I'm glad that you're going to be subjected to the pressures the rest of us have to face. Anna thought, I wish I hadn't become so conscious of everything, every little nuance" (43). Men argue with women in the novel but never speak to one another without a woman present except in distanced, romanticized, or parodied sample writings supposedly written by men, like Saul's Algerian novel or the parody American buddy novel or the fake communist novel by Comrade Ted. We only know what a man thinks in the novel when his mind speaks through Anna's: everyone else's thought or speech passes through her consciousness before we hear it.

In *The Golden Notebook*, the daughter's identity remakes and breaks itself and its culture, internalizing rather than projecting its ambivalence toward sex roles and holding itself responsible for facing cultural conflict by absorbing and hence containing it within the self. Thus Anna resolves to sort the chaos of modern life by experiencing it all, denying herself the defenses of evasion. But she does not digest all this experience raw: it comes to her partially precooked in the ideological wrappings of the age. Anna internalizes these ideologies like parental identifications, personifying her dominant ideologies as mother Jung and father Marx and bravely trying to connect the personal and the political: "if marxism means anything, it means that a little novel about the emotions should reflect 'what's real' since the emotions are a function and a product of society" (42). Yet her representations of the two realms tend to slide apart; she associates the personal, emotional, and psychological with the feminine and with both the positive and negative aspects of motherhood. Although Freud smiles down from his portraits as a bearded patriarch, the novel's representative of psychoanalysis is a female Jungian analyst, Mrs. Marks or "Mother Sugar." Her therapy involves her successful remothering and empathic support, and Anna's fundamental conflicts are those associated specifically with female psychology, even when she works these out in the wild analysis of breakdown rather than in her official sessions. Anna criticizes her analyst for thinking herself too important in Anna's life and for taking too much credit for Anna's progress when Anna wants to think she's done everything for herself. Mrs. Marks is "a most intelligent wise old woman" but also a "pillar of reaction" (236, 237). Anna thinks that psychoanalysis lies and is regressive, whereas the neurotic is in tune with her historical period. Anna angrily resists being "ordered to dream" and thinks her analyst always wins against her (238). She feels the analyst robs her of her diary just by mentioning it, yet she dreams of her as a "large maternal witch" to whom she will be able to turn for help after the anlysis is over (253).

In contrast, the public political world is run by men. Pompous Richard may be a failure in his personal life, but he is a mogul of British industry, a capitalist of power and importance. Uncle Joe Stalin failed his devoted children by purging rather than by nurturing them, and Marx's ideas about history don't always work, yet when Lessing imagines war, revolution, prison, or parliament, the characters are male.

Lessing personifies psychoanalysis as like a mother, but a mother culpably complicit with the laws of the father, an agent of bourgeois stability: "what is this security and balance that's supposed to be so good?" Anna asks (9). Anna similarly blames women for "not thinking when it suits us" and thus for complacently accepting conservative views (435). In contrast, the male ideology she champions is that of the rebellious son, an unfettered Marxism attacking the cultural fathers. Her natal name "Freeman" indicates this male posssibility; her married name "Wulf," man's more predatory relations as well as her most famous feminist modernist forebear. Although the men in the African political group compete uselessly with one another and some of them aspire only to become dictatorial fathers themselves (as her ex-husband Wulf will become an East German bureaucrat), the Communist Party does contain men Anna reveres, men who truly desire social change, love humanity, and try to tell the truth.

In comparison with *Wide Sargasso Sea* and *The Man Who Loved Children*, the main characters of *The Golden Notebook*, like its literary referents, are self-made. Anna's mother died early; her father is obscure. Molly's disastrous parents vanish from the book after a few paragraphs that make them representatives of the century's fads. Anna fights with paternal and maternal ideologies within herself, but not with real human parents. This move to ideological autobiography and away from personal character makes *The Golden Notebook* very different from the more conventional autobiographical novels of the Martha Quest series.

The question of Anna's identity is largely a question of her literary voice, which we find by reading it. Anna claims, "I am incapable of writing the only kind of novel that interests me: a book powered with an intellectual or moral passion strong enough to create order" (61), though this plaint seems designed to elicit the reader's response that the novel being read fulfills this aim. But if the text is all one can know of a literary figure, it nonetheless misses something essential about them. Anna discovers that what you read of a person represents them badly. In writing, one discovers truths not previously known: "having written that, I am astounded" (70), Anna comments, yet merely writing something down creates "a wrong emphasis" like her transcription of menstrual smells (340). None the less she only finds herself in the confrontation with her own written texts. Anna recognizes irony and negativity in her past self and finds truth by recognizing the space between memory and text, a gap between presymbolic female space and male-dominated cultural space in which fall the warring words of commercials, parodies, and popular fiction.

Writing creates the female self through strong emotion and memory, the needs to fight pain, to analyze the self and world, pattern them, and reassure oneself that the external world is still there by naming it. But under these are questions of how one becomes a woman writer at all, and *The Golden Notebook* is a giant anxiety dream about the erasure of a writing self: what if this power were taken away from me, the writer asks herself; who would remain? This doubt about a writing self leads to an especially female anxiety about agency, so that Ella's version of the existential question of why not commit suicide is transformed into a novel about not knowing that one has already decided to kill oneself.

The paradox of Anna's writing is also the paradox of her identity. She can only be known through her text, which will never fully or adequately represent her; at the same time, anything which solidifies or pins her down diminishes her. The advantage she has over the bourgeois others is that she is not rigidly defined. Tommy says Molly and Anna "aren't what they *do*. . . . they could change and be something different. . . . they haven't set into a mould" (36). Paradoxically, then, intregrity is defined in terms of potential change and of the risks of change. Molly's "source of self-respect" is that "she had not—as she put it—given up and crawled into safety somewhere. Into a safe marriage" (17). Milt sees himself and Anna as part of the "team" that "haven't given in" (642). This saving flexibility, then, defines the integrity of identity of the self not through but in contrast to social roles and group identifications. It is by avoiding a defining job and marriage that they stay themselves. The ambition of the novel, too, is to avoid being set, instead to be a continuous book, one always in process but not completed, one which is not molded into a final form. Lessing brilliantly achieves this effect through her paradoxical self-enfolding structure, in which, as in female personality structure, it is difficult to tell what is inside and what is outside the boundaries of the self, and the reader must continue to travel the Moebius strip of the narrative's surface.

Anna rejects being confined, pinned down, by a man or a job, but the role of mother is riskier and inescapable for her. Her friend Molly acts in motherly ways toward Anna that she resists. Molly is older than Anna and physically bigger, and Anna used to live in Molly's house. At the start of their friendship, Molly "had frankly domineered Anna," but with the help of Mother Sugar, Anna has "learned to stand up for herself" (9–10): "Anna could remember her mother very little; she had died so early," but with Molly Anna "was able to form for herself the image of somebody strong and dominating, whom Anna had had to fight" (42). Molly tries to live vicariously through Anna's talent, telling Anna, "it's always meant so much to me that you should produce something, even if I didn't," and Anna reasonably replies, "but I'm not an extension of you" (41–42). In stories about other minor characters in the book, the villain is often a mother. For example, one of the socialists in Anna's African group is a sweet young woman who incestuously loved her brother in rebellion against their "impossible, bullying, embarrassing mother" (103). Similarly, in a synopsis of Anna's novel *Frontiers of War*, racist society separates a noble English airman from his black beloved; however, the immediate enemy is not some police official but a white mother jealous of the affair and of her daughter's attraction for the airman.

As a daughter in relation to motherly women, Anna's goal of autonomy is clear, but as a mother in relation to her own daughter Janet or her friend's son Tommy, her values are profoundly ambiguous. Responsibility is the prime maternal virtue and also the universal touchstone of morality: Anna said "the socialists had ceased to be a moral force . . . because they wouldn't take moral responsibility" (40). Although the "control and discipline of being a mother came so hard" to Anna (334), it founds her sanity, her stability, her definition of self: "I can't be ill . . . because of Janet," she thinks (389). "Anna understood . . . she had depended on the discipline" of being a mother (647); and the world would never get itself understood, be ordered by words, unless "Janet's mother remained a woman who was able to be responsible" (651). Though maternal responsibility anchors the mother in reality, it need not benefit her children. By using Janet as her anchor, Anna may sink Janet's possibilities for individual development, and Anna encourages Janet's dull conventionality, saying "she is my normality" (543). Anna thinks "how war could explode, chaos would follow. I was cold and sweating with fear, and then I thought of Janet, the delightful rather conventional little girl . . . and I was angry, so angry that anyone anywhere could harm her, that I stood upright, able to fight off the terror" (589). Janet seems better off at boarding school than with her mother, and Anna and Molly accept the 1950s anti-mommism that blames maternal over-involvement for children's failures. Molly says she doesn't want her son Tommy "to grow up one of these damned mother-ridden Englishmen. I wanted him to break free of me" (17).

Although Anna is quite open about her need to "break free" of maternal influences, she denies her desire to free herself from her children, that is, to reject them, even though "only alone, in the big room," not with a man or with her daughter, is she truly "herself" (54). Anna claims unequivocal love for her daughter, but the novel rejects both Tommy and Janet. Janet is a conventional bore, and Tommy—the other woman's child about whom one may say such things—is repulsive. In "Free Women" he decamps with his father's second wife, a simpering alcoholic, having paid in advance for such semi-incest by blinding himself. In the blue notebook, he is merely dull. Anna reveals her repressed guilt at being a rejecting mother in a dream in which "plump and glossy" Janet drinks all the milk from her breasts, so that she starves Tommy, who withers "in a tiny coil of pale bony staring flesh" (651–52).

As a daughter Anna wants autonomy; as mother she claims to take responsibility and wants freedom. In heterosexual relationships, echoes of maternal roles cause doubt and confusion. As a mistress to married men, Ella futilely competes with the men's wives, the mothers of their children. She fantasizes that the wives are what she wants to become, "serene, calm . . . self-sufficient, yet always ready to give happiness" (207). One husband who is undergoing psychoanalysis tells his wife, "yeah, you're my mom. . . . Well it's O.K. to hate your mom, it's in the book" (491). Anna feels the most disgusting nadir of heterosexual relations is mothering a lover. Although Anna and Saul spend days in symbiotic role playing, when she "cradled him in" her arms and he clings to her, saying "Ise a good boy," she responds with shame and horror: "we can't either of us ever go lower than that," they agree, though this lowpoint marks the beginning of their return to adult sanity (640–41).

Thus contradictory assumptions and values underlie *The Golden Notebook*: the theories of psychoanalysis are reactionary sugar water, yet they help unfreeze the blocked secret sources of the self; a mother needs maternal responsibility to hold her world together; her child fights to be free, though often headed to self-destruction, like the suicidal Tommy. Fathers matter much less, though they may be powerbrokers of the nation like Tommy's father Richard, a cynical opportunist. Similarly, father Marx disappointed his children, who are left with only a vague disillusioned nostalgia for their former beliefs. Mary Rose says, "we believed that the world was going to change and everything was going to be beautiful and now we know it won't" (131). For Anna, Marx doesn't seem to have much to do with class conflict—as he does, for example, for Paul, but rather with love of humanity versus despair and with the truth versus lies. When political leaders lie, "one small lie could spread into a marsh of lies and poison everything" (39) and "few people really care" about the truth (567). Nihilism, self-hatred, and lying nostalgia cause war, and "an inability or a refusal to fit conflicting things together to make a whole" causes "death or impoverishment of the individual" (65). In contrast, utopian attitudes, even when they are unrealistic, are necessary to the future. Despite her despair at the cycle of history, Anna sees change: this era brings new consciousness about Africa's racist practices, the universal desire for authorship, the condition of unmarried women, and sex. The most persistent claim for the new is the situation of the "free women," who are free only ambiguously—liberated, able to follow their own bent, waiting to be tagged. Both Molly and Anna think they are "living the kind of life women never lived before" (472), but when Anna asks Molly, "if we lead what is known as free lives, that is, lives like men, why shouldn't we use the same language," Molly counters, "because we aren't the same" (44).

Although heralded for her proto-feminist perceptions and condemned for negative portraits of men, Lessing frequently denies feminist sympathies, and this denial is accurate, too (SPV 79). Unlike Rhys and Stead, she does not believe that men are the obvious beneficiaries of modern culture. She is unequivocal in condemning the double standard and the evils of marriage, but she is ambivalent about blaming men. A women's self-hating text tends to be an anti-female text, too, and Lessing's women are often treacherous, complicit, and cowardly; "every conversation" seems to Anna "like crossing a mined field; and why can't I accept that one's closest friends at moments stick a knife in, deep, between the ribs" (43). Anna feels the comfort of joining women to condemn men but defines it as false, wrong: Ella derides the "bitter spinster" tone of her talks with Julia (452). Anna does not want to be classed with women, though her writing and behavior provoke an outraged backlash in men. The only revolution is that of women against men, says a man reading her novel, and he jokes viciously about ice on the ovaries and parthenogenesis. Anna herself condemns "a new note" of "being betrayed" in women's writings (596). She describes heterosexuality as innate and natural, and the heterosexual woman's body insists on its own truth, the vaginal orgasm. If the bodies are attuned, the relationship is "true"; "real women" feel, "it's terrible to pretend you don't need love" (257). Men need other men; women need men. Women's strongest need is being with a man, being in love, although marriage destroys love, and couples' only happy times occur in the beginnings of illicit affairs.

Although Lessing shows common male attitudes that oppress women, she thinks of the solidarity between women as a nasty collusion against men. The breakdown of gender roles is wrong, and the war between men and women distinguishes our times. Ella, who dislikes her "sensitive and feminine" stories, as Lessing does hers, decides to live chaste unless she is in love and not to speak to women (170). That is, she withholds her body from men and her talk from women, as though that is what each values most about her, and this equates sexlessness with self-sufficiency. Thus to be a writer is not to be a woman, to talk to women is a danger and a trap, and female identity is a precarious and endless process.

Despite her fragmented, unfinished qualities, Anna represents herself as having an essential core: In comparison to her friend Molly, who rejoices in trying on different roles, Anna is "too self-conscious ever to become somebody else" (4). In these roles, Molly loses her sense of herself, "it's as if I were really different" (9). In contrast, Anna defines being an artist as making the other into the self, reversing maternal empathy: Anna feels "this awful need to make other people see things as I do. It's childish. . . . I'm scared of being alone in what I feel" (10). When Anna does take on the other person's perceptions instead of the other way round, she disparages her empathy: for example, she claims, "I shrink, in affection, to Janet's size, and become Janet" (334–35).

Yet as the book progresses, Anna finds seeing from the other person's perspective and feeling as they do essential to her mental health and to her fiction. Sometimes she uses empathic emotions to control others: she calms Tommy and Marion by getting "all hysterical just like they are" and crying (527). Sometimes she involuntarily finds herself possessed by the other, as when she finds herself in Saul Green's anxiety state. At other times she attempts empathic identifications as an aid to understanding history and as an aid to writing: "I saw an Algerian soldier stretched on a torture bed; and I was also him, wondering how long I could hold out" (596). But there are limits to this sort of imaginative identification. Anna says she tried to imagine herself as "a black man in a white-occupied territory" but "failed totally" (597).

Ella, having written a novel about an unconscious suicide, associates choice and change—Marxist variables, the ability to imagine alternative possibilities—with role change and empathic fictional identifications. She tells her father, who confuses her with her friend, "next time I'll try to write about that—people who deliberately try to be something else, try to break their own form" (466). A very different kind of identification is that based on her overlapping versions of herself in which empathy for the other is not at issue. Thus Anna overlaps with Ella, with Anna of "Free Women," and with the author: "I, Anna, see Ella. Who is, of course, Anna. But that is the point, for she is not" (459).

This meditation on the partial autonomy of the literary creation recalls Ella's view of the novel she wishes to write as entirely within herself and waiting to come out, like a baby: Ella "searches herself for the book which is already written inside her. . . . She spends a great deal of time alone, waiting to discern the outlines of this book inside her" (459). Once again, inside and outside boundaries blur: Ella awaits the book inside her, like Anna, who has written the notebooks inside her and this whole book, *The Golden Notebook*, "outside" her, in which Ella, then seems to be writing.

This leads her to reengagement with the project of imagining herself as the other, identifying with others without merely labeling them: "then Anna's brain went out like a candle flame. I was the Algerian"; this threatens Anna with the "terror" of "total disintegration" (601). She dreams she flies over the world, the perfect omniscient author, filled with "the joy of freedom" as she enters the body of a Chinese peasant woman. She imagines that this experience means she "woke a person who had been changed by the experience of being other people. I did not care about Anna, I did not like being her. It was with a weary sense of duty I became Anna, like putting on a soiled dress" (602). Identifying with the other here, unlike empathy, destroys both the self and the self-referential text and becomes self consuming—a terror or exhilarating possibility of freedom.

The self-referential text, then, does try to establish its relations in the world, including the origins of that world, what it calls truth, and its wholeness or lack thereof. It also must determine its relation to the world in terms of origin, truth, and wholeness. *The Golden Notebook* gives many points of origin in the world and in the text. At times individual identity seems to be a subset of history, and the historical conditions create the writer and the text in a fairly simple Marxist fashion. Ironically, this is most obviously true of the hack prose produced by party faithfuls, their texts produced by their common ideology, not by their individual experiences, which they deny for the common good. Yet when Anna hears their identical novels, she wonders "what stereotype am I? What anonymous whole am I part of?" (49), and she wishes she understood the "relations between society and the talent it creates, between art and the tensions that feed it" (60). In order to be true to the experience of the times, to fragmentation and confusion, the self must be fragmented and so must the text: "the novel has become a function of the fragmented society" (61). Each person reflects and contains, microcosmically, all the forces in the world around it, and like the text, is only untrue when it rules out the chaos or seals the breaches. Yet Anna longs for the "intellectual or moral passion strong enough to create order" and overcome fragmentation (61).

If the traditional masterpiece places man in society, a woman's "masterpiece" should articulate women's various experiences in the world. It is not surprising, therefore, that these three disparate novels parallel one another in their search for female identity, a crisis felt by many Western women in the mid-twentieth century. These three novels, all published before the second wave of the women's movement was widely felt, describe how female identity is made or broken in patriarchal societies. This is a broad theme, certainly, but not an inevitable one, and it differentiates these three novels from other of their author's best works, like Stead's novel about banking, *House of All Nations*.

The novels' main issues are those most germane to twentieth-century female personality development, especially the two conflictual areas of autonomy, which is seen as the daughter's goal, and responsibility, the mother's task. The author may see her fiction as though it is a daughter she must free or as a mother that she may forgive. All three novels blame, then forgive, their heroes' mothers. At the end of the books, their heroes are empowered to initiate their own quests, and their texts, like daughters, can stand up for themselves in the literary tradition.

These women's masterpieces thematize empathy and represent it structurally through the manipulation of narrative point of view. The mature work succeeds in engaging the reader's and author's empathy with its characters yet retains our ability to judge the characters independently. As Elizabeth Abel says of female friends, these works teach us to know as the other woman knows ("(E)Merging Identities" 415–18).

The danger to the female text or character from the father tradition is that of annihilation; the outside force tries to kill the upstart so that all is other, none is self, from the perspective of the destroyed female self. The mother tradition, instead, poses the dangers of engulfment or fusion, obliterating the distinction between self and other. The mother tradition seeks to merge with the female self so that no distinctions between them are possible. The danger of the self-referential tradition, however, is that the self will destroy the other, finding itself alone in a depleted and empty universe. The danger posed by the self-referential text, then, is self-hatred. Thus in *The Man Who Loved Children* Louie fears that she will be nothing; her father, everything. The achievement opposite to this danger is triumph: Louisa kills her mother and deserts her father. In *Wide Sargasso Sea*, Antoinette fears that she must become her mother and thereby lose her own identity. The possible achievement of this tradition is empathy; she and her text fuse with *Jane Eyre* to understand it from the inside. In *The Golden Notebook* Anna and her multiple texts suffer from despair as everything turns into fragmenting self reflections, but the possible achievement is autonomy, the text that can stand on its own.

These three books appeared in 1940, 1962, and 1966 respectively, with the influential reissue of *The Man Who Loved Children* with a favorable introduction by Randall Jarrell in 1965. Thus all three books about women, female novels of development and quests for identity, were written after the heyday of literary modernism and after the first wave of feminism but before the popularization of the second. *The Golden Notebook*, in fact, may be considered, with Betty Friedan's *The Feminine Mystique* of 1963 as one of the inspiring texts for second wave feminists, especially in the United States. By selecting these three books as "masterpieces," I wish to acknowledge a very specific and historical evaluation, not an allegedly timeless one; these are books I, along with many other (American academic) feminists, value, books that speak profoundly to questions of female identity in ways accessible to me, fitting my values—of integrating gender oppression with other inequalities like race and class, for example, in ways that seem original.

These are books that have taught us to read them, and they also appeal to my values as a feminist: they are focused on experiences of women, realistic enough for identification and my readerly empathy, but also elegantly and adequately artful in ways acceptable to academic postmodernist reading styles—rich with contradictions and vivid imagery, surreal as well as realistic. All three are self-reflexive, self-conscious works in which language and respresentation are at issue. Each of the three works places itself with respect to the literary tradition and to language. For Rhys, the text is more powerful than the spoken word; for Stead, speech overwhelms text. Lessing opposes silence to both. For Rhys, the word may be magic, a barrier or a way through one. For Stead, the word is a tool of control. For Lessing, the word is often a lie.

On the other hand, giving these books kudos means an interpretative community with a new set of values—at the very simplest, one that does not object to novels whose portrait of men is considerably shallower or more negative than their portraits of women, a disability felt by some original reviewers of *The Golden Notebook*, for example. The question of women's values raises the issue of ideologies and their limitations for women. At times Lessing adheres to the ideologies of Marx, Freud, Jung, Laing, and the Sufis, and Stead to Marx. Yet both writers also criticize these influential ideologies. Rhys, Stead, and Lessing claim an identification with the oppressed as their primary ideological commitment, yet all three reject explicit identification with feminism. That is, the three understand their own ideological commitments morally, esteeming what might be called a politics of empathy. Despite specific disclaimers about (bourgeois) feminism, the three writers modify their political ideology in the light of female experience; for example, they all recognize that imperialist nations treat subject ones as men treat women. These writers' colonial origins encourage them to equate imperialism and domestic patriarchy, though each starts with a different paradigmatic inequality: gender for Rhys; class for Stead; race for Lessing.

Written between active phases of the women's liberation movement, these books have a certain daring and bravado. Each writer feels herself an emboldened original, unsure of her enterprise. Without consciously writing to or for an existing women's movement, she writes from the perspective of an outsider for whom self-creation is necessary, as is an active search for literary precursors that will find nothing exactly to hand, everything needing to be modified for the modern woman's story. From a position of outsider each becomes a commentator, moving toward self creation: all three books are woman-centered, matricidal texts: *The Man Who Loved Children* most obviously kills the hero's stepmother to enable her full development; in *Wide Sargasso Sea* the hero both repeats and transcends her mother's ignominious death. *The Golden Notebook*, in contrast, imitates nineteenth-century novels in reducing the hero's mother to insignificance: unlike the very present Mrs. Quest of the Martha Quest series,

Anna's dead mother is only a remote memory, and the matricidal impulse is projected, instead, as the hero's ambivalence about her own motherhood, her filiacidal fantasies about Tommy and ambivalent sending away of her daughter Janet.

The most important mothering relationships of the three texts, however, involve us as readers. Precursor texts for our generation, especially for white, middle-class anglophone feminists coming to maturity in the 1960s and thereafter, these texts "mother" us as they teach us how to read them.

VI

TEXTUAL SELF SERVICE
TOWARD A FEMINIST
SELF-PSYCHOLOGICAL MODEL
OF LITERARY PROCESSES

It has become fashionable to speak of the pleasures of the text and to refer to reading and writing in erotic terms. "The text you write must prove to me that it desires me," writes Roland Barthes provocatively, and he defines the writer as "someone who plays with his mother's body." This textual erotics requires replacing a Freudian cultural story with another as yet undefined: "Today we dismiss Oedipus and narrative at one and the same time," says Barthes; "we no longer love, we no longer fear, we no longer narrate." Instead, we respond to literature as split subjects who enjoy "the consistency of [our] selfhood (that is [our] pleasure) and seek its loss (that is [our] bliss)" (6,37,47,14).

These textual erotics are tantalizingly metaphoric and implicitly sexist; the male critic sits fondling text bodies that we had not previously seen as sexual and labeling them, along with other objects of male attention and domination, as female. Suggestive as such discussion is, we need a way of talking about our literary pleasures that is not constrained to follow the man's inevitable path to or even beyond the Oedipal crossroad, one that can, instead, speak succinctly about the engagement between our selves—mobilized as writers and readers—and written words. Having looked in some detail at the work of three twentieth-century women writers, I now wish to return to one of my original questions, the question of what—if anything—characterizes twentieth-century writing by English-speaking women, reading by women, and the whole range of women's relationships to literary texts and to offer some speculative answers informed by the prior investigation.

The first answer that a skeptical reader might give to the question of what characterizes writing by women is that nothing does: there are no differences between writing by men and writing by women, only the individual characteristics of each writer. If the question is posed in a simplistic enough way, this has to be its answer. Clearly all writing by women is not pink and frilly, all writing by men blue and macho. Students often cannot tell the sex of the writer when given sample passages to read. The same thing is true of whole novels, since many of them were misattributed when they first appeared. Yet once the sex of a woman author is known, her work is judged by that fact. Mary Ellmann wittily complains, "books by women are treated as though they themselves were women, and criticism embarks, at its happiest, upon an intellectual measuring of busts and hips" (29).

Alicia Ostriker responds to those who doubt the existence of gender-specific literature: "most critics and professors of literature deny that women's poetry, as distinct from poetry by individual women, exists, yet we do not hesitate to use the term 'American poetry' . . . on the grounds that American . . . poets are diverse. . . . The belief that true poetry is genderless—which is a disguised form of believing that true poetry is masculine—fails to recognize that writers necessarily articulate gendered experience just as they necessarily articulate the spirit of a nationality, an age, a language" (28). One might accept this reasoning for writing by women more generally or attempt to localize it to mid-twentieth-century American women's poetry.

Another proponent of the view that literature is genderless might agree that women's literary forms do exist, as distinct from men's, but only at the lower levels of literary quality. Clearly *True Romance* fiction differs from that in *Playboy*. In the job market today, men's and women's occupations remain sex-segregated, with the masses of women secretaries and nurses distinct from the male truckers and plumbers, despite the increasing minority of women in high prestige occupations like law and medicine. Similarly, one might argue, the literary world is divided by gender only in its lower classes, so that popular fiction for women and men is widely distinct whereas great literature is a single incandescent glow. As with the prestige occupations, the assumption that great literature is genderless validates the traditional and institutionally dominant viewpoint that defines "greatness" as precisely that which excludes distracting female markings.

A related approach is to claim that texts may be either masculine or feminine but that these distinctions have no relation to the anatomical sex of the author, who may assume either a male or female "subject position." Thus, for example some French feminists define avant garde literature by men as "feminine" because it is nonlinear, antirational, and hence supposedly subversive of the dominant "phallogocentric" culture. This approach risks conflating one set of distinctions—between the semiotic and symbolic orders—with another—between femininity and masculinity, the attributes of gender into which we are socialized; so it renders the literary relationships of actual men and women invisible.

Thus the simplest answer to the question of what characterizes women's writing is that nothing does. The next simplest, perhaps, goes to the opposite extreme to find difference inevitably springing from the fact of female embodiment, sometimes through analogies between women's writing and fluidity, maternal milk, internal spaces, and the like (see Cixous). No one believes that women write only with their bodies, but some people feel that women's writing is influenced by body consciousness, and some contemporary French writers self-consciously produce "feminine writing" lavish with such imagery. Philosopher Sandra Bartky claims that today women are defined more and more exclusively by having feminine faces, gestures, and bodies shaped by conventions aimed at pleasing men, rather than by traditional roles of wife or mother. As women are perceived to have more options in occupations and lifestyles than these traditional roles, the pressure to keep up a "feminine" appearance—whether one is a fast-food carhop or a dress-for-success executive—increases. This "femininity is an artifice, an achievement, a certain 'style of the flesh' "; it produces "a body on which an inferior status has been inscribed" (4, 15). Such persistent self-creation may affect women's writing, as we can see in Rhys's constant references to mirrors and cosmetics. If to be a woman means continually to make up one's appearance, gender-specific attitudes implicating self with feminine body may well surface in writing. One possible effect might be women's pleasure in writing's invisibility, with its concomitant freedom *not* to be conventionally feminine, and its separation of self-presentation in print from the traces of one's fleshy form.

Perhaps the most readily acceptable answer to what characterizes writing by women is that women's writings reflect women's experiences, so that references to pregnancy, shopping, cooking, and so on will appear in writing by women because such activities fill women's lives and become symbolically weighted. Thus Rhys's description of a botched abortion in *Voyage in the Dark*, Stead's dinner menus in *I'm Dying Laughing*, and Lessing's famous reference to menstruation in *The Golden Notebook* appeal directly and wryly to typically female experiences. The idea that women's writing reflects women's experience appeals to common sense, but anti-humanist critics challenge this common sense "expressive realism" and its preconception that literature transparently expresses real life (see Belsey 46–47, Moi 46–49).

A common variant of the idea that women's writing reflects women's experience is the specific notion that the distinguishing experience of women is that of oppression or marginalization within a male-dominant culture. Susan Gubar and Sandra Gilbert speak of the nineteenth-century woman writer's anxiety about authorship in a culture that defines wielding a pen as a kind of phallic power (*Madwoman in the Attic* 3–7). Elaine Showalter adapts an anthropological model originally applied to colonized countries to contrast the overlapping circles of a dominant and a muted culture. Outside the dominant culture lies a "wild zone" of "muted" female activities that have been silenced and repressed; it includes women's writings for and about other women, especially in noncanonical forms like diaries and letters, forms that Lessing most obviously, but also Rhys and Stead reproduce in their fiction (Showalter "Feminist Criticism" 262). The advantage of this theory is that it allies women's position with that of other oppressed groups, and this is also its disadvantage, since it does not differentiate gender oppression from other oppressions. Moreover, as we have seen by looking at these three colonial women writers who try to identify with the colonized, such oppressions are complex and interactive in their effects.

A further variation on the concept of women as an oppressed group is the notion that "Woman" in patriarchal culture is defined exclusively as man's Other. Since this definition is purely oppositional, proceeding from men's needs for selfhood, it provides no substantive definition for what women are, and hence women are represented only through absence, silence, the gaps and contradictions of the dominant discourse. If one concedes that all symbolic discourse, including language itself, is under the sway of "phallogocentrism" or male cultural and linguistic power, women face the difficult choice of either writing as men—as Stead sometimes tries to do—or heroically attempting subversion from within, a tactic employed especially by Rhys and Lessing.

Focusing on readers rather than writers, feminist reader response critics study the strategies women do and should use as readers, although these literary relationships overlap. In their book on *Gender and Reading*, Elizabeth Flynn and Patrocinio Schweickart say, "to know what it means to read as a woman, one must also know what it means to read women's writing and to write for women" (xix). Those theorists who see literature as predominantly based on male values consider women's relation to literature as oppositional. Judith Fetterly suggests that the woman reader should resist identifying with the viewpoint of the misogynist text, as we have seen Rhys's and Lessing's characters do. For example, the hero of Rhys's *Voyage in the Dark*, who becomes a prostitute, reads Zola's *Nana*, and her woman friend objects, "I bet you a man writing a book about a tart tells a lot of lies one way and another" (8). Jean Kennard's proposed lesbian reading strategy reminds us that women readers are not a uniform group but are divided in interests and power. She advises the lesbian reader to learn a new way of reading in order to avoid domination by heterosexual texts, "leaning into" them, as in some of the softer martial arts like Aikido, in order to feel her own difference the more securely as a result (654). The differences remain. Barbara Christian suggests writing and reading participate in "our attempts to define and express our totality rather than being defined by others" (159).

Feminist strategies for reading culturally male-dominant texts recall the controversy among film critics about how the female spectator does and should respond to film. According to Laura Mulvey, women watching a Hollywood film are unable to identify as subjects because the camera's "gaze" is male-defined, subordinating its object. In contrast, Linda Williams sees a less pessimistic prospect: especially when watching a so-called women's film, she believes, the woman spectator oscillates between the position of male-identified viewer and a female position that is suggested by the gaze and dialogue between female characters on screen, often mothers and daughters. "The female spectator tends to identify with contradiction itself," Williams claims. Women's films, like soap operas, encourage reader identification with multiple points of view, making the viewer like a good mother who understands all her children even when she can help none of them. The female spectator is a "dialectician," and the woman's film "constructs the female spectator in a female subject position locked into a primary identification with another female subject" (17, 22).

This idea of dialogue or oscillation occurs in other feminist reader response theories as well. Schweickert upholds a dialogic model of the interaction between woman reader and text. When a woman reads a man's text, according to Schweickert, she engages in a "dialectic of emancipatory struggle"; when a woman reads a woman's text, on the other hand, the dialectic is one of intimate conversation (31). Showalter's model of dominant and muted cultures also applies to women's reading. "Women's fiction," she says, "can be read as a double-voiced discourse, containing a dominant and a muted story." This process is like those object/field problems "in which we must keep two alternative oscillating texts simultaneously in view" ("Feminist Criticism" 263). For Showalter it is the texts that oscillate; others see this oscillation taking place within the reader.

In *The Implied Reader*, Wolfgang Iser says that the reader "oscillates between involvement in and observation of the illusions" in the text (286). He speaks for generic male readers in his description of the reading process reproducing within the reader the subject/object division between self and other. He sees literary identification as a stratagem through which authors stimulate attitudes in their readers, but his model assumes authorial control over these strategies, and it excludes traditional women's literature. "Texts which offer nothing but a harmonious world . . . we generally do not like to classify as literary," he says, citing "women's magazines" as one example (286). Thus Iser does not recognize women's typically close identifications with texts like soap operas and romances as one valid form of literary response; instead, he separates non-literary women readers from implicitly male competent "implied" readers.

Although the ideas of dialogue or oscillation are promising, I would like to shift our focus from the idea of two polarized positions to the process of negotiating between them, especially in the case of the contemporary woman who is reading a woman's text, that is, in the case where the woman reader is shifting between female subject positions rather than moving back and forth between dominant male and resisting female positions.

Theorist Toril Moi is hostile to the whole issue of gender difference in writing. "The pursuit of sex difference in language is not only a theoretical impossibility, but a political error," she says (153). Nonetheless, she suggests that proper contextualizing can clarify some confusions. She quotes studies showing that although people could not tell by reading a literary work whether its author was female or male, once they learned the identity of the author, they responded differently to the text. Similarly, students perceive scholarly articles signed with women's names as less authoritative than the same articles when attributed to male authors (Crittenden). According to feminist linguists, "no matter what women do, their behavior may be taken to symbolize inferiority" (Thorne and Henley 28, qtd in Moi 153). These conclusions resemble those in which people declare that the same baby is either cute or strong depending on whether they see the child dressed in pink or in blue.

To take this idea of contextualization a bit further, I suggest that women's relationships to literature may now be more distinctive than the literature itself, as in the cartoon of the little girl who cradles her truck while her brother vroom vrooms a doll around the floor. Among English-speaking women readers and writers, empathic relationships with texts may now be more typical than among men. Yet I do not wish to imply that there is a single key to gender differences in these relationships, nor that they are natural, inevitable, or transhistorical. If, as the cognitive psychologists believe, gender schema are pervasive but various throughout our culture, we will see evidence of gender difference in many ways at this cultural moment as individual men and women relate differently to texts by men and by women, and these differences will be matters of tendency or frequency, not absolutes (Crawford and Chaffin; Bem). To structure the multiple possibilities of twentieth-century women's relationships to modern texts, I find psychoanalytic analogies useful, especially those based on the theoretical structures of "self psychology," which I modify to render gender specific. I hope these analogies prove suggestive even for those critical of psychoanalytic readings of literary texts or those specifically hostile to Kohut's therapeutic techniques or broad philosophical claims.

Self psychologists Heinz Kohut and his followers believe that their theories allow them to "examine works of art more broadly than has been possible up to now" (Kohut "Psychoanalysis"; also see Kohut *Analysis* and *Restoration*). Although Kohut, who died in 1981, meditated frequently about literature and creativity, he did not develop a coherent model of literary processes, and he usually assumed that the artist and the self were male. Because of self psychology's preoedipal focus and non-masculinist values, it adapts well to feminist uses; moreover, it solves several problems posed by object-relations theory, including "mothering" theory (see Gardiner "Self Psychology"). Unlike some object relations theories, self psychology's model of maturity is not a unilinear striving for autonomy. Instead, it places interdependence as one of many adult developmental goals, along with love, empathy, and creativity. Unlike autonomy, these goals are not conventionally linked to masculinity. In addition, because self psychology detaches the formation of self-esteem from the choice of sexual partners, its model for healthy development is not necessarily heterosexual. Perhaps most important, self psychology conceives of psychological development in a historically-changing context, and its concept of "selfobjects" explains the means through which cultural and historical forces can shape the individual psyche. "Now . . . it is up to the historian," Kohut writes, "to undertake a comparative study of the attitude of adults toward children at different periods in history, in order to throw some further light on the conditions that Freud tried to explain biologically" ("Self in History" 777). Thus this is a theory that fits late twentieth-century values and explains twentieth-century psychologies.

Originally an orthodox Freudian psychoanalyst influenced by object relations theory, Kohut developed self psychology in response to clinical experience with people who manifested what he defined as "narcissistic personality disorders" stemming from difficulties in their preoedipal infancy that caused defects in their "nuclear selves." This self is a construct or fiction; it is not the ego of ego psychology, and it should not be reified. Basch's definition of the self as "conferring a sense of cohesion and continuity on the disparate experiences of that individual throughout . . . life" does not insist that unified selves exist but that the concept is a useful "symbolic abstraction" (Basch 53). According to Kohut, the components of the self include each person's goals, ambitions, values, ideals, and talents: he departs from Freudian orthodoxy in believing that these components develop on a separate course from its loves and hates for other people, which are based on the libidinal conflicts of childhood. This separate course is shaped by the child's early self/selfobject relationships, Kohut's name for the child's way of treating others in the caretaking environment in terms of functions performed for the self as though by a part of the self rather than in terms of emotional response to a person perceived as an independent agent. On the way to adulthood, the child progresses through three main types of these self/selfobject relationships, and they remain important ways of relating to others throughout adult life.

Psychoanalytic transferences are interpersonal relationships created through dialogue. In analysis, analysands who have developed relatively coherent selves will form traditional transferences with their analysts, projecting upon their doctors dramas of fear, guilt, competition, and desire originally experienced in conflicts with their parents. Freud first described such transferences, which became the chief means of effecting psychoanalytic therapy for patients afflicted with the so-called classical neuroses. Although such neurotics still exist, self psychologists believe that they are rarer than in Freud's time. Instead, today's patients are likely to have fragmented, alienated, defective selves; these defects are not inevitable results of the human condition or of the entry into language, but instead the result of specific childrearing practices. In analysis with an empathic analyst these patients will form therapeutic "selfobject (narcissistic) transferences" (Kohut *How Does Analysis Cure* 4). When represented in literature, such narcissistic personalities may appear like depressed Antoinette in *Wide Sargasso Sea*, or grandiose Louisa in *The Man Who Loved Children*, or self-absorbed Anna in *The Golden Notebook*.

Some literary critics use analogies to the psychoanalytic transference to explain aspects of literary processes, particularly to explain reader responses. Beginning from the premise that "literature is communication," Arthur Marotti compares the analyst's countertransference to the critic's response to a work of art and locates art and cultural experience in the "potential space" that D. W. Winnicott has defined as "an intermediate area . . . between primary creativity and objective perception based on reality testing" (Marotti 476, 479; Winnicott 51). This concept of a "potential" or "transitional" space is a slippery one. Meredith Skura questions the idea that a work of art "is equivalent to the transference in a psychoanalytic session or to the child's transitional object" because adult esthetic "play spaces" are self-conscious in ways childrens' and patients' are not (189). The self psychological concept of the self/selfobject relationship, though awkwardly named, offers advantages over the Winnicottian notion of a transitional space "between" self and other. It does not merely rename or relocate the problem being investigated, as the "transitional space" may do, but instead focuses attention on the variable nature of the negotiations between self and other and on the ability of the self to treat other people as though they are functioning parts of the self. Self psychologist Ernest Wolf defines literature "as a created selfobject" in this sense. He claims that its selfobject function can be shared and that "lasting, reliable, fulfilling, and yet humanly alive empathic resonances can be established with it" (404–405).

Marshall W. Alcorn, Jr., and Mark Bracher argue that literature edifies and changes its readers in the same way that the classical psychoanalytic transference alters the deep structure of the analysand's "internal world": "the process of altering a person's introjective configuration and consequently re-forming the self culminates—in psychoanalysis and also in reading, it would seem—with the provision of a model of a more effective, fulfilled, conflict-free self (345, 348). Their theory, which is largely based on ego psychology, avoids mythologizing a "transitional space," but it tends to sentimentalize psychoanalysis as perfectly therapeutic and hence to produce a utopian and moralistic theory of reader response. I believe that we can achieve greater clarity and specificity about the multitude of literary processes by dropping the concept of the transitional space in favor of that of the self/selfobject relationship and by comparing literary processes not only with the classical transference as a unitary phenomenon in which the analysand desires and competes with the analyst, but also with the three narcissistic transferences and the distinct subject positions, especially parent/child and male/female, available within them. This allows us to look at a multiplicity of gender and power positions, and to avoid the binary critical polarity subversion/complicity, without claiming that this model or its categories are fixed, all-inclusive, or transhistorical.

Most accounts of the transference, like Alcorn and Bracher's, idealize the role of the analyst and see all aspects of psychoanalysis positively; however, as analysts describe their patients' projections onto them of materials from their childhoods, one glimpses the possibilities that the positions of both parent and child, repeated in those of analyst and analysand, may be occupied in destructive or harmful ways. These developmentally negative experiences may have analogies in literature as well, where of course the representation of "bad" experience does not make for bad literature. To explore the analogies between literary processes and psychoanalytic transferences, we must be alert to unwarranted assumptions about gender typical of psychoanalytic discourse: for example, that the doctor and the patient's self are male and that the mirroring selfobject is the child's mother. Instead of accepting these stereotypes, we can raise the issue of the difference it makes to each position within a transference whether it is assumed by a person of either gender. In addition to the classical transference, there are three kinds of narcissistic transference based on the three main self/selfobject relationships of childhood: the mirroring, idealizing, and twinship transferences. The positions of the two people involved in each are not symmetrical, since the theory assumes that the parent or analyst is better able to treat the other person as an independent being, while the child or analysand more frequently treats the parent or analyst as an extension of the self. Moreover, the positions of parent and child, analyst and patient imply differences of power as well as psychological differences. In looking at literary relationships in these terms, I sometimes treat persons' relationships with texts, sometimes with other people. The concept of the selfobject reminds us that psychologically we do blur these categories at times; however, we also need to remember the mediating status that the written word performs in our dealings with texts and language's relative autonomy. A writer may love or compete with another writer, but readers or writers only metaphorically "desire" a text, whereas the "self/selfobject relationship" may accurately, if awkwardly, designate the relationship they establish with their own or another person's words on a page. The examples of these relationships that follow draw particularly on the three authors considered in this study, but obviously others might be adduced. Such examples can not prove a theory, though they may illustrate it and render it plausible; instead, the theory should advance discussions of female specificity regarding these and other writers.

I will focus disproportionately on the first, or mirroring transference, because I think it is most typical of twentieth-century English-speaking women's relationships with literature. Optimally the parent both empathically mirrors the child's proud self-display and also nontraumatically deflates her or his archaic illusions of grandiose power, thus helping the child achieve positive self-esteem and realistic goals and ambitions. Kohut privileges the empathic mirroring role as the essence of the self psychological method.

The self psychological definition of empathy as "vicarious introspection" is based on Freud's contention that "a path leads from identification by way of imitation to empathy, that is, to the comprehension of the mechanism by means of which we are enabled to take up any attitude at all towards another mental life" (Freud "Group Psychology" 110; Kohut "Introspection" 222). Self psychology sees empathy as an adult process in which a mature person takes on the position of the other person. From this perspective, empathy is not the same as but opposite to the position in which a person sees the other as an extension of oneself, and this self psychological view of empathy entails no merging, blurring, or loss of self for the adult. Psychoanalyst Hyman Muslin distinguishes empathic readers, who can put themselves in the position of dramatic characters, from projecting readers, whose own psychological situations prevent them from perceiving those of the characters; on the other hand, Norman Holland believes we are always projecting readers in the sense that our reading is inevitably shaped by our expectations, fantasies, and defenses in order to conform to our individual "identity themes."

In contrast to Barthes' writer who "plays with his mother's body," we may see the writer or reader taking an empathetic "maternal" attitude to the text, as Rhys does in her late stories like "On Not Shooting Sitting Birds" and "Fishy Waters." This position comes closest to fulfilling my original metaphor that the hero is her author's daughter. Marotti claims that the "artist must . . . do for himself what the infant's emotionally nurturing mother does for him . . . freely accept the material of the unconscious in its rawest (often most aggressive) form," a quality we have seen in Stead's symbolic late tales and ranting characters (483). Kohut suggested, then dropped, the analogy between artist and mother: "the creative person's relationship to his work has less in common with the expanded narcissism of motherhood than with the still unrestricted narcissism of early childhood," he says, adding that "the personality of many unusually creative individuals is more childlike than maternal" (*Self Psychology* 112). Since Kohut's creative exemplars are male, his judgement may indicate an area where the genders differ: I surmise that maternal empathy rather than childlike narcissism may be more characteristic of female than male writers. Nancy Chodorow claims that girls, hence women, have "a basis for 'empathy' built into their primary definition of self in a way that boys do not" (167). Unlike self psychology, feminist mothering theories like Chodorow's attribute empathy more pervasively to women than to men and consider empathy as an entirely positive trait. Such views run the risk of simply reversing traditional evaluations of the sexes, seeing women as more empathic, intimate, and nurturant than individualistic and competitive men, that is, as generally nicer. In psychological studies of empathy, both women and men believe that women are much more empathic than men; women see themselves as empathetic and men do not (Eisenberg and Lennon). Attempts to test empathic behavior in laboratory situations have not succeeded in validating these self reports, but reading and writing are more likely to be affected by one's self image than by one's testable behavior.

Expanding on Chodorow's theory, I speculate that empathy is a characteristic that is more "marked" for women than for men in our culture. Also, women's self-image and self-esteem typically form differently from men's—again, not because of women's essential nature but because of specific child rearing practices that vary by time, race, class, and other factors. According to self psychologist Joan Lang, women disavow from their self-concept aspects of themselves that are socially proscribed for women, especially aggression. Rhys's early narrators lash out at their readers, then censor themselves; Lessing's late narrators moralize and disguise attacks on their audience. As the women writers considered in this study age, their works turn from daughterly concerns about autonomy to maternal ones about responsibility, and their narrative strategies also become more maternal and sometimes empathetic; at times the authors even seem to become their heroes' mothers. Thus Marotti's comment on the aggression-accepting artist might apply more frequently to men, while women writers instead deploy strategies of indirection in creating aggressive surrogates for themselves.

I see twentieth-century English-speaking women writers and readers as typically relating to texts through empathy, as the self psychologists define that term, that is, as a mature process that is both affective and cognitive. Female literary identifications are a process, and the specific nature of that process is often empathizing. What is typical of contemporary women's relationships to literature, I speculate, is having to negotiate one's way, not just between dominant and muted cultures, but between and among a variety of relational networks or webs inscribed in texts and in our experience.

To believe that empathy plays a central role in women's literary relationships is not necessarily to romanticize it. If empathy is "marked" as especially important for women, a woman writer may play the role of the unempathic or rejecting mother rather than that of the maternal nurturer to reader or text. Because of cultural attitudes expecting nurturance from women, this position is particularly powerful. Doris Lessing, for example, provokes vehement and polarized responses to novels like *The Good Terrorist* by rejecting her main character as an "impossible daughter" and by appearing to disdain and reject her readers as well.

To go from women writers to women readers, I think that a typically female reading mode currrently involves negotiating one's way through empathic attunement. Rachel Brownstein claims that women form more personal identifications with literary characters than men do, so that the identities of writer, reader, and character become entangled. Brownstein believes that the woman reader joins the novel in what she calls the "fantasy" of "becoming a heroine"(xix). Her notion of women's more personal relationship to literature is corroborated by some empirical studies. Elizabeth Flynn's women students were more interactive and empathic readers than her male students, whereas the men's responses polarized around domination or submission to the text (276). Similarly, David Bleich claims that his male students read novels for a chain of information, whereas his female students seek to define a pervasive atmosphere in the text (255–56). Anti-humanist critics decry reader identification with characters and texts as reactionary, implicating the reader in bourgeois myths of individualism, authority, and the unified self. Their criticism becomes moralistic on this issue; they do not deny that readers identify with texts but condemn them for doing so, as elite critics have traditionally condemned women readers of romances, for example (see Belsey 127, Moi 7). Instead of simply praising or condemning this sort of reader identification, in contrast, I wish to understand its operations, especially for women.

My stress on empathizing as a typical female literary response is connected with the view that twentieth-century English-speaking women may typically have a different relationship to both empathy and language than men do. Literature depends on language, and language need not be seen exclusively as a realm of alienation or of phallic primacy. "The growth of empathy belongs to the same maturational process" as the growth of language, argues Henry Edelheit; both spring from the child's need to "restore and in some ways improve upon the surrendered maternal connection" (55). That is, both empathy and language arise at the same time from the same situation, as an expansion rather than a rupture or replacement of the child's ties to the mother. As Michael Basch says, the mother-infant unity is never ended but expanded and transformed through language, an expansion that Stead describes in her childhood relationship, after her mother died, with her father who overwhelmed her with his "ocean of story"(50). Self psychologists see the mother/infant relationship as reciprocal and transactional from the beginning, yet feminist theorists remind us that this reciprocity is asymmetrical for the two genders. According to observational studies, mothers respond to their daughters more intensely than to their sons, making girls more adaptable to verbal and social reinforcement (Notman 40–41). Thus women's exclusion from certain forms of discourse may depend less on their intrinsic relation to the symbolic order and more to specific historical factors.

So far I have discussed the mother's position in the mirroring transference; the child's position is that of seeking approval by showing off one's body or accomplishments. Clearly, exhibitionist display may be rewarded when suitably channeled into art. Virginia Woolf thought men's writing was shadowed by an omnipresent phallic "I," and Patricia Meyer Spacks sees typical female narcissism in women's writing, indicating that complementary narcissistic modes—arrogance and vanity, to simplify things—

may be typical of the artistic stances of the two sexes (Spacks 406; Woolf 35). Rhys's heroes are mirror-checking narcissists whose attention to their looks hides deep doubts about their self-worth, whereas Stead's narcissists include grandiose men like Sam in *The Man Who Loved Children* and conflicted, yet dangerously self-centered women like Nellie in *Dark Places of the Heart*. To pick a more positive example, perhaps contemporary women's literature, especially lesbian love poetry, can now display overt enthusiasm for the female body in a way that was previously prohibited to women writers: Ostriker asserts that "women's poetry now is generating an enriched stock of tropes for bodily experience" (29). Despite enthusiasm for the pleasures of female sexuality, the three authors considered here all exhibit an ambivalence about the female body that may be waning in more recent writers.

The unmirrored child becomes the typical twentieth-century fragmented, alienated adult. Kohut says that modern writers treat "the falling apart of the self and of the world and the task of reconstituting the self and the world." Fragmentation is not merely the writer's subject in this view, but an aspect of the author that writing may cure: "the broken self is mended via the creation of the cohesive artistic product," Kohut explains. Similarly, he believes Proust wrote "his total life history . . . to reestablish a continuity within himself" (*Self-Psychology* 169, 235). Although Kohut prefers to recuperate and contain the unsettling aspects of modernism, his theories allow us to describe anxieties about self-loss and fragmentation in literary themes and style. Much reader difficulty with Rhys may spring from the narcissistic threat of identifying with her devalued characters. When reading her fiction, we oscillate between transient empathetic identifications with her characters and defenses against them, defining ourselves through them. In *The Golden Notebook*, Lessing imitates such a process, showing us Anna identifying with and separating from her multiple memories and fictions, and the novel imitates this process through its repetitive, overlapping style. Moreover, male and female expressions of fears about fragmentation may differ. For example, many women write about fears of self-loss through immersion in the roles of marriage or motherhood. Such fears characterize the heroes of Stead's *Puzzle-headed Girl* and Lessing's *A Proper Marriage* and are symbolically dramatized by the heroes' annihilation in Rhys's *Wide Sargasso Sea* and Lessing's "To Room Nineteen." In contrast, male fears of self-loss are usually expressed in imagery that is more abstract and less role specific, though not therefore more universal. This may be one reason that most of the writers of the *avant garde*, heralded by some French theorists as subversively "feminine," are male. At a popular, more superficial level, a man may seek confirmation that his sexual body is still intact by viewing pornography, whereas a woman may be more likely to seek affirmation, reassurance, and advice through the gender-specialized but less overtly sexual gloss of the women's fashion magazine. Lessing's

Jane Somers, as her sense of her self-worth increases, graduates from women's magazine writing to romantic fiction and women's studies sociology.

The very different feelings we have about reading different writers may depend to a considerable degree on the different, transference-like relationships that they establish with us. In Rhys, not being understood feels to the characters like isolation and abandonment, whereas the narrative voice solicits our understanding and empathy. For Stead, to understand is not necessarily to forgive and empathy may be dangerous; hence her fiction often assaults us with a rush of verbiage so that we will harden our selves in resistance to it. In Lessing, being understood often feels like being dominated, and her fiction therefore seeks to understand and dominate us, rather than to let us fully understand it. Readers accept or reject Rhys's work; they feel overwhelmed by Stead or intimate with her characters; they argue with Lessing or identify with her.

The second narcissistic transference is called the idealizing transference. In it, the child looks up to the parent as a source of strength and value. While remaining available for such idealization, the good-enough parent will also realistically disillusion the child's fantasies. The position of the idealized parent or analyst is perhaps analogous to the relationship some established authors take to younger writers. Recently some women writers have begun to foster such relationships, although women have traditionally been uncomfortable when idealized; the woman writer often appears as a public figure in retreat from being a public figure, like each of the three writers in this study, disclaiming that she is a feminist, or a leader, or a spokeswoman in an interview that the interviewer tells us was difficult to arrange.

The child who forms an idealizing transference seeks to merge with an idealized, powerful figure in order to participate in the parent's strengths and ideals. Religious literature encourages such desires for merger with an all powerful being. Recently women have forged new mythologies in order to imagine uniting with a goddess untrammeled by conventionally patriarchal religious ideologies. Lessing's Sufi-influenced space fiction may be seen in a similar light. Another possibility is the rebellious reaction against idealization that remains locked into shape by the ideals rebelled against. Stead at times idealizes Marxist idealists, at times rages against pseudo-idealistic hypocrites. Kohut compares the biographer who falls "in love with his subject" to those analysts who have a "firmly established identification" with Freud as "an idealized figure (or, in reaction formation, of rebelliousness against this identification)" (*Self Psychology* 172, 174).

Women biographers, according to Susan Merrill Squier, alternate between "absorbing enmeshment" and "affectionate separation" from their female subjects, "testing and redefining the boundaries of the essential self" and continually asking, "Where does she end, and where do I begin?" (406). All three of our writers sort their fiction into "autobiographical" and "not autobiographical" categories as though trying to preserve the boundaries of the self from the imaginative encroachments of their own fiction. Male and female writers and readers may well relate to the idealized, male-dominated canon differently; for example, women readers may try to appropriate a writer like Shakespeare as "one of us," a subversive demystifier of male anxieties, or, on the other hand, to reject Milton's supposed anti-authoritarianism as woefully patriarchal. Rhys repeatedly condemns the misogyny of male writers and parodies Joyce's yes-saying earthmother at the end of *Good Morning, Midnight*, and Lessing parodies the American male buddy novel in *The Golden Notebook*.

Readers who need to idealize may include romance and fantasy readers, and men and women may differ in the sorts of power with which they can usually imagine being merged—political or scientific authority for men, natural or magic forces for women. Currently popular women writers portray idyllic feminist societies set in the primitive past or the postnuclear future, or, as in Lessing's *Marriages of Zones Three, Four, and Five*, in a mythical alternative space. Some of the appeal of a book like Alice Walker's *The Color Purple*, 1982, may spring from its ability to mythologize while retaining a recognizable social and historical context, so that the fiction first creates the perfect victim—a girl at the bottom of age, class, race, and gender hierarchies—and then empowers her in a myth that unites her with her African heritage, the sisterhood of all women, and even the American entrepreneurial dream. On the other hand, rebellion against the male canon produces antiromantic feminist poetry and novels debunking marriage and romance, like those by our three authors, and "resisting readers" of male texts (Fetterley).

Third and last of the narcissistic transferences is the twinship transference, which Kohut in his final years detached from the mirroring transference, deciding that the need to be sustained by others like the self differed from the need for empathic understanding. Developmentally, this desire for the reassurance of similarity occurs first as the infant's need for a human environment, then in latency as confirmation that other people are like oneself. Without such reassurance, a person may feel isolated, anomalous, and alone in the world. Kohut speaks of the fear of finding oneself in a nonhuman environment, the most "dreadful fear of our time, to be shot off into space and to be all alone": "that is why Kafka . . . is the literary representative of our time. Over and over again he describes the vacuum that surrounds Mr. K, the everyman of our times." (*Self Psychology* 222). Similarly, Rhys's heroes suffer agonies of loneliness and isolation in cities that appear empty and cruel. According to one study, women associate violence with stories of isolation, whereas men associate violence with stories of intimacy. (Gilligan "On *In a Different Voice*" 331). Lessing combines the two attitudes in "Leopard George," in which a native woman is eaten by a leopard after her white lover forces her to leave his farm in the middle of the night. Lessing parodies this tendency within *The Golden*

Notebook by describing Saul Green's novel in which an Algerian soldier and
a French student he has tortured intimately discuss their beliefs and are
then both shot for their camaraderie. Another suggestive study finds that
women grow fonder of people the more self-disclosure is involved in the
relationship, whereas there is no such correlation for men (Greeno and
Maccoby 314). This result supports the idea that women typically create
and enjoy more personal relationships with literary texts than men do,
especially in such intimacy-dependent forms as confessional poetry and
autobiographical fiction. Rhys, Stead, and Lessing all write confessional
and autobiographical fiction, and the reader tends to develop an identifying
affection for many of their women who pour out their intimate hopes and
complaints to us. This intimacy holds as well for feminist critics and scholars
working on women writers. Domna Stanton muses, "it is almost as
if . . . the feminist scholar's own identity depended upon the referential
reality of the woman in the text, as if that woman was the same and different
other through whom [the feminist scholar] needed to construct herself"
(18 qtd in Squier 408).

In the twinship transference, the positions are reciprocal rather than
parental or childlike. Similarly, writers or readers may use a text to create
alter egos, autobiographical twins, whose sex role specific conflicts may
sustain them simply by echoing their own experiences. This may be of
especial importance to women writers who do not have a clear, publicly-
recognized reference group, women whose socially unscripted experience
feels anomalous to themselves. This must have been the case for many
years for Rhys, Stead, and Lessing, the former two especially writing largely
in obscurity without public support. Both writers and readers may seek
confirmation of their selfhood through reflection, for instance in novels
about solitary old women like Rhys's, or secretaries deciding to write novels
like Stead's, or frustrated housewives like Lessing's, or lesbians coming
out.

This model of literary processes involving the complex politics of empathy is more sophisticated than the metaphor that the hero is her author's
daughter, but it expands from the metaphor to imply that bonds between
women currently structure the deepest layers of female personality and
establish the patterns to which literary identifications are analogous. It also
insists that the relations between literature and life must always be politically and historically situated in terms of ideologies as well as of events.
Clearly this is a model of literary processes, and especially of the place that
empathy occupies in them, that has only begun to achieve articulation,
and it is a model congruent with my values as an American materialist
feminist. According to Barthes, "the writer is someone who plays with his
mother's body," that is, the mother tongue, "in order to glorify it, to em-
bellish it or in order to dismember it" (31). A historically-grounded self
psychological literary criticism allows us to look at such fantasies of idealization, exhibitionism, and fragmentation, not in terms of the male self's

metaphorical mastery over a prostrate maternal body, but in terms of the manifold dialogues we establish with literary texts and with each other. Such dialogues do not end; history will continue to contextualize empathy; empathy, to understand history, in the continuing politics of twentieth-century women's reading and writing strategies.

BIBLIOGRAPHY

Abel, Elizabeth. "(E)Merging Identities: The Dynamics of Female Friendship in Contemporary Fiction by Women," *Signs* 6.3 (1981), 413–35.

———. "Women and Schizophrenia: The Fiction of Jean Rhys," *Contemporary Literature* 20 (1979), 155–77.

———. ed. *Writing and Sexual Difference*. Chicago: University of Chicago Press, 1982.

Abel, Elizabeth; Hirsch, Marianne; and Langland, Elizabeth. *The Voyage In*. Hanover and London: University Press of New England, 1983.

Alcorn, Marshall W., Jr., and Bracher, Mark. "Literature, Psychoanalysis, and the Re-Formation of the Self: A New Direction for Reader-Response Theory," *PMLA* 100.3 (May 1985), 342–54.

Allen, Orphia Jane. "Structure and Motif in Doris Lessing's 'A Man and Two Women,' " *Modern Fiction Studies* 26 (Spring 1980), 63–74.

Angier, Carole. *Jean Rhys*. Harmondsworth: Penguin, 1985.

Apstein, Barbara. "*Madame Bovary* and *The Man Who Loved Children*," *International Fiction Review* 7 (1980), 127–29.

Arnow, Harriet. *The Dollmaker*. New York: Avon, 1972.

Athill, Diane. Foreword to *Smile Please*, by Jean Rhys. New York: Harper and Row, 1979. 3–9.

Babel, Isaac. "My First Goose." in *The Collected Stories*. Ed. and trans. Walter Morison. New York: Criterion Books, 1955. 72–77.

Baer, Barbara. "Castaways of History," *Nation* 26 April 1975, 501–503.

Bamber, Linda. "Jean Rhys," *Partisan Review* 49.1 (1982), 92–100.

Barthes, Roland. *The Pleasure of the Text*. Trans. Richard Miller. New York: Hill and Wang, 1975.

Bartky, Sandra. "The Feminine Body." Unpublished paper. Department of Philosophy, University of Illinois at Chicago, 1986.

Basch, M. F. "The Concept of Self: An Operational Definition," in *Developmental Approaches to the Self*. Ed. Benjamin Lee and Gil G. Noam. New York and London: Plenum Press, 1983. 7–58.

Bawer, Bruce. "Doris Lessing: On the Road to "The Good Terrorist." *The New Criterion* 4.1 (September 1985), 4–17.

Belsey, Catherine. *Critical Practice*. London and New York: Methuen, 1980.

Bem, Sandra Lipsitz. "Gender Schema Theory and Its Implications for Child Development: Raising Gender-Aschematic Children in a Gender-Schematic Society," *Signs* 8.4 (1983), 598–616.

Bertelson, Eve, ed. *Doris Lessing*. Johannesburg: McGraw Hill, 1985.

Beston, John B. "A Brief Biography of Christina Stead," *World Literature Written in English*. 15.1 (April 1976), 79–86.

———. "An Interview with Christina Stead," *World Literature Written in English*, 15.1 (April 1976), 87–95.

Bikman, Minda. "A Talk with Doris Lessing," *The New York Review of Books*, 30 March 1980, 1, 24–26.

Blake, William James [Blech]. *Elements of Marxian Economic Theory and Its Criticism*. New York: Cordon, 1939.

Bleich, David. "Gender Interests in Reading and Language," in Flynn and Schweickart, 234–66.

Bowen, Stella. *Drawn from Life*. Maidstone, Eng.: George Mann, 1974.

Bronte, Charlotte. *Jane Eyre*. New York: New American Library, 1960.

Brownstein, Rachel. *Becoming a Heroine: Reading about Women in Novels*. New York: Viking, 1982.

Butcher, Margaret. " 'Two Forks of a Road': Divergence and Convergence in the Short Stories of Doris Lessing." *Modern Fiction Studies* 26 (Spring 1980), 55–61.

Caws, Mary Ann. "The Conception of Engendering: The Erotics of Editing," in *The Poetics of Gender*. Ed. Nancy K. Miller. New York: Columbia University Press, 1986. 42–62.

Chodorow, Nancy. *The Reproduction of Mothering: Psychoanalysis and the Sociology of Gender*. Berkeley: University of California Press, 1978.

Christian, Barbara. *Black Feminist Criticism: Perspectives on Black Women Writers*. New York: Pergamon Press, 1985.

Cixous, Hélène. "The Laugh of the Medusa." Trans. Keith Cohen and Paula Cohen. *Signs* 1.4 (Summer 1976), 875–93.

Crawford, Mary and Chaffin, Roger. "The Reader's Construction of Meaning: Cognitive Research on Gender and Comprehension" in Flynn and Schweickart, 3–30.

Crittenden, Kathleen. Unpublished communication. Department of Sociology, University of Illinois at Chicago, 1986.

Cummins, Marsha. "Point of View in the Novels of Jean Rhys: The Effect of a Double Focus," *World Literature Written in English* 24.2 (1984), 359–73.

Dickens, Charles. *Great Expectations*. New York: Holt, Rinehart, Winston, 1962.

Dinnerstein, Dorothy. *The Mermaid and the Minotaur: Sexual Arrangements and Human Malaise*. New York: Harper and Row, 1976.

Drabble, Margaret. "Doris Lessing: Cassandra in a World Under Siege," *Ramparts* 10 (1972), 50–54.

Draine, Betsy. *Substance under Pressure: Artistic Coherence and Evolving Form in the Novels of Doris Lessing*. Madison: University of Wisconsin Press, 1983.

Driver, C. J. "Doris Lessing—A Profile," *The New Review* 1.8 (Nov 1974), 17–23.

DuPlessis, Rachel Blau. "For the Etruscans," in *The New Feminist Criticism: Essays on Women, Literature & Theory*. Ed. Elaine Showalter. New York: Pantheon, 1985. 271–91.

———. *Writing Beyond the Ending: Narrative Strategies of Twentieth-Century Women Writers*. Bloomington: Indiana University Press, 1985.

Edelheit, Henry. "On the Biology of Language," in *Psychoanalysis and Language*. Ed. Joseph H. Smith. New Haven and London: Yale University Press, 1978. 45–74.

Eisenberg, Nancy, and Lennon, Roger. "Sex Differences in Empathy and Related Capacities," *Psychological Bulletin* 94.1 (1983), 100–31.

Ellmann, Mary. *Thinking about Women*. New York: Harcourt, 1968.

Emery, Mary Lou. "The Politics of Form: Jean Rhys's Social Vision in *Voyage in the Dark* and *Wide Sargasso Sea*," *Twentieth Century Literature* 28.4 (Winter 1982), 418–30.

Erikson, Erik. *Childhood and Society*. New York: Norton, 1950.

———. *Identity and the Life Cycle*. New York: Norton, 1959.

———. *Identity: Youth and Crisis*. New York: Norton, 1968.

Fagan, Robert. "Christina Stead," *Partisan Review* 46.2 (1979), 262–770.

Fetterley, Judith. *The Resisting Reader: A Feminist Approach to American Fiction*. Bloomington: Indiana University Press, 1978.

Fishburn, Katherine. *Transforming the World: The Art of Doris Lessing's Science Fiction*. Westport, Conn.: Greenwood, 1983.

Flaubert, Gustave. *Madame Bovary*. New York: New American Library, 1964.

Flynn, Elizabeth. "Gender and Reading," in Flynn and Schweickart, 267–88.

Flynn, Elizabeth, and Schweickart, Patrocinio. *Gender and Reading: Essays on Readers,*

Texts, and Contexts. Baltimore and London: John Hopkins University Press, 1986.

Ford, Ford Madox. Preface to *The Left Bank and Other Stories*, by Jean Rhys. 7–27.

Freud, Sigmund. "Female Sexuality" (1930) in *The Standard Edition of the Complete Psychological Works of Sigmund Freud*. Trans. and ed. James Strachey. London: The Hogarth Press, 1973. 22:3–182.

——. "Group Psychology and the Analysis of the Ego" (1921) in *Standard Edition*. 18:67–143.

——. "On Narcissism: An Introduction" (1914) in *Standard Edition*. 14:69–102.

——. "Some Psychical Consequences of the Anatomical Distinction Between the Sexes," (1925) in *Standard Edition*. 19:243–58.

——. "A Special Type of Choice of Object Made by Men" (1910) in *Standard Edition*. 11:163–76.

Friedan, Betty. *The Feminine Mystique*. New York: Dell, 1963.

Fromm, Gloria. "Making Up Jean Rhys," *The New Criterion* Dec 1985, pp. 47–50.

Gardiner, Judith Kegan. "Christina Stead: Dark Places of the Heart," *North American Review* 262 (1977), 67–71.

——. "Gender, Values, and Doris Lessing's Cats," in *Current Issues in Feminist Scholarship*. Ed. Shari Benstock. Indiana University Press, 1987.

——. "*Good Morning, Midnight*: Good Night, Modernism," *Boundary 2* 11.1&2 (1983), 233–51.

——. " 'The Grave,' 'On Not Shooting Sitting Birds,' and the Female Esthetic," *Studies in Short Fiction* 20.4 (Fall 1983), 265–70.

——. "The Heroine as Her Author's Daughter," in *Feminist Criticism*. Ed. Cheryl Brown and Karen Olson. Metuchen, N.J. & London: Scarecrow, 1978, 244–53.

——. Introduction to *The People with the Dogs* by Christina Stead. London: Virago, 1981, i-iv.

——. "Male Narcissism, Capitalism, and the Daughter of *The Man Who Loved Children*," in *Daughters and Fathers*. Ed. Lynda Boose and Betty Sue Flowers. Baltimore: Johns Hopkins, 1988.

——. "On Female Identity and Writing by Women," in *Writing and Sexual Difference*. Ed. Elizabeth Abel. Chicago: University of Chicago Press, 1982. Reprinted from *Critical Inquiry*, 8.2 (1981), 347–61.

——. "Rhys Recalls Ford: *Quartet* and *The Good Soldier*," *Tulsa Studies in Women's Literature*, 1.1 (1982), 67–81.

——. "Self Psychology as Feminist Theory," *Signs* 12 (1987), 761–80.

——. " 'A Sorrowful Woman': Godwin's Feminist Parable," *Studies in Short Fiction* 12 (Summer 1975) 286–90.

——. "A Wake for Mother: The Maternal Deathbed in Women's Fiction," *Feminist Studies* 4.2 (1978), 146–65.

Garner, Shirly Nelson; Kahane, Claire; and Sprengnether, Madelon, eds. *The (M)other Tongue: Essays in Feminist Psychoanalytic Interpretation*. Ithaca, NY: Cornell University Press, 1985.

Gilbert, Sandra, and Gubar, Susan. *The Madwoman in the Attic: The Woman Writer and the Nineteenth-Century Imagination*. New Haven: Yale University Press, 1979.

——. *No Man's Land: The Place of the Woman Writer in the Twentieth Century*. Vol. 1, *The War of the Words*. New Haven and London: Yale University Press, 1988.

——. eds. *The Norton Anthology of Literature by Women: The Tradition in English*. New York: Norton, 1985.

Gilligan, Carol. *In a Different Voice: Psychological Theory and Women's Development*. Cambridge: Harvard University Press, 1982.

———. "On *In a Different Voice*: An Interdisciplinary Forum," *Signs* 11.2 (1986), 304–33.

Godwin, Gail, "A Sorrowful Woman," in *Scenes from American Life: Contemporary Short Fiction*. Ed. Joyce Carol Oates. New York: Random House, 1973.

Gornick, Vivian. "Quiet Desperation," review of *The Complete Novels of Jean Rhys*, *Women's Review of Books* 3.9 (June 1986), 9.

Greene, Gayle. "Women and Men in Doris Lessing's *Golden Notebook*: Divided Selves" in Garner, 280–305.

Greeno, Catherine, and Maccoby, Eleanor. "How Different is the 'Different Voice?' " *Signs* 11.2 (1986), 310–16.

Hanson, Clare. "Woman Writer as Exile: Gender and Possession in the African Stories of Lessing" in Sprague and Tiger, 107–14.

Hardin, Nancy. "The Sufi Teaching Story and Doris Lessing," *Twentieth Century Literature* 23.3 (1977), 314–26.

Hazleton, Lesley. "Doris Lessing on Feminism, Communism, and 'Space Fiction,' " *The New York Times Magazine*, July 25, 1982, 20–29.

Heilbrun, Carolyn. *Reinventing Womanhood*. New York: Norton, 1979.

Hellman, Lillian. *Scoundrel Time*. Boston: Little, Brown, 1976.

Herman, Judith Lewis with Hirschman, Lisa. *Father-Daughter Incest*. Cambridge, Mass. and London: Harvard University Press, 1981.

Hirsch, Marianne. "Mothers and Daughters: Review Essay," *Signs* 7 (1981), 200–22.

Holland, Norman. "Human Identity," *Critical Inquiry* 5.3 (1978), 451–69.

Horney, Karen. *Feminine Psychology*. New York: Norton, 1967.

Iser, Wolfgang. *The Implied Reader: Patterns of Communication in Prose Fiction from Bunyan to Beckett*. Baltimore: John Hopkins University Press, 1974.

James, Louis. *Jean Rhys*. London: Longman, 1978.

Jameson, Fredric. *The Political Unconscious: Narrative as a Socially Symbolic Act*. Ithaca: Cornell University Press, 1981.

Jarrell, Randall. Afterword to *The Man Who Loved Children* by Christina Stead. New York: Avon, 1966, 492–504.

Jung, Carl. *The Basic Writings of C. G. Jung*. Ed. Violet Staub de Laszlo. New York: Modern Library, 1959.

Kappers-den Hollander, Martien. "Jean Rhys and the Dutch Connection," *Journal of Modern Literature* 11.1 (March 1984), 159–73.

Kennard, Jean. "Ourself Behind Ourself: A Theory for Lesbian Readers," *Signs* 9.4 (Summer 1984), 647–62.

King, Bruce. *West Indian Literature*. London: MacMillan, 1979.

Kloepfer, Deborah Kelley. "*Voyage in the Dark*: Jean Rhys's Masquerade for the Mother," *Contemporary Literature* 26.4 (Winter 1985), 443–59.

Knapp, Mona. *Doris Lessing*. New York: Ungar, 1984.

Kohut, Heinz. *The Analysis of the Self: A Systematic Approach to Psychoanalytic Treatment of Narcissistic Personality Disorders*. New York: International Universities Press, 1971.

———. *How Does Analysis Cure*. Ed. Arnold Goldberg with the collaboration of Paul E. Stepansky. Chicago and London: University of Chicago Press, 1984.

———. "Introspection, Empathy, and Psychoanalysis: An Examination of the Relationship between Mode of Observation and Theory" (1959) in *The Search for the Self: Selected Writings of Heinz Kohut: 1950–78*. Ed. Paul H. Ornstein. New York: International Universities Press, 1978. 1:205–32.

———. "Psychoanalysis and the Interpretation of Literature: A Correspondence with Erich Heller," *Critical Inquiry* 4.3 (Spring 1978), 433–450.

———. *The Restoration of the Self*. New York: International Universities Press, 1977.

———. "The Self in History" (1974) in Kohut, *The Search for the Self* 2.771–82.

————. *Self Psychology and the Humanities: Reflections on a New Psychoanalytic Approach.* Ed. Charles B. Strozier. New York and London: W.W. Norton, 1985.

Kohut, Heinz, and Wolf, Ernest. "The Disorders of the Self and Their Treatment: An Outline," *International Journal of Psychoanalysis* 59.4 (1978), 413–25.

Laing, R. D. *The Divided Self.* London: Penguin, 1965.

Lang, Joan. "Notes Toward a Psychology of the Feminine Self," in *Kohut's Legacy: Contributions to Self Psychology.* Ed. Paul E. Stepansky and Arnold Goldberg. Hillsdale, N.J.: The Analytic Press, 1984. 51–69.

Lessing, Doris. *African Stories.* New York: Popular Library, 1965.

————. *Briefing For a Descent Into Hell.* New York: Bantam, 1980.

————. *The Diaries of Jane Somers.* New York: Random House, 1984.

————. *Documents Relating to the Sentimental Agents in the Volyen Empire.* New York: Knopf, 1983.

————. *Each His Own Wilderness* in *New English Dramatists: Three Plays.* Ed. E. Martin Browne. Harmondsworth: Penguin, 1959.

————. *The Fifth Child.* New York: Knopf, 1988.

————. *The Four-Gated City.* New York: Bantam, 1970.

————. *Going Home.* New York: Fawcett Popular Library, 1968.

————. *The Golden Notebook.* New York: Bantam, 1973.

————. *The Good Terrorist.* New York: Knopf, 1985.

————. *The Grass Is Singing.* New York: Popular Library, 1976.

————. "Impertinent Daughters," *Granta* 14 (1984), 51–68.

————. *In Pursuit of the English.* New York: Popular Library, 1960.

————. *Landlocked.* New York: New American Library, 1966.

————. *The Making of the Representative for Planet 8.* New York: Knopf, 1982.

————. *The Marriages Between Zones Three, Four, and Five.* New York: Knopf, 1980.

————. *Martha Quest.* New York: New American Library, 1964.

————. *The Memoirs of a Survivor.* New York: Bantam, 1976.

————. "My Mother's Life," *Granta* 17 (1985), 227–38.

————. *Particularly Cats.* New York: Simon and Schuster, 1978.

————. *Play with a Tiger.* London: Joseph, 1962.

————. *Prisons We Choose to Live Inside.* New York: Harper and Row, 1987.

————. *A Proper Marriage.* New York: New American Library, 1964.

————. *Re: Colonised Planet 5: Shikasta.* New York: Knopf, 1979.

————. "A Reporter at Large: The Catastrophe," *The New Yorker*, March 16, 1987, 74–93.

————. *Retreat to Innocence.* London: Joseph, 1956.

————. *A Ripple from the Storm.* New York: New American Library, 1966.

————. *The Sirian Experiments.* New York: Random House, 1982.

————. *A Small Personal Voice.* Ed. Paul Schleuter. New York: Random House, 1974.

————. *Stories.* New York: Vintage Books, 1980.

————. *The Summer Before the Dark.* New York: Knopf, 1973.

————. *The Temptation of Jack Orkney and Other Stories.* New York: Bantam, 1974.

Lidoff, Joan. *Christina Stead.* New York: Frederick Ungar, 1982.

Mahler, Margaret; Pine, Fred; and Bergman, Anni. *The Psychological Birth of the Human Infant: Symbiosis and Individuation.* New York: Basic Books, 1975.

Marcus, Jane. "Art and Anger," *Feminist Studies* 4 (1978), 69–98.

Marotti, Arthur. "Countertransference, the Communication Process, and the Dimensions of Psychoanalytic Criticism," *Critical Inquiry* 4.3 (Spring 1978), 471–490.

Mellown, Elgin. "Character and Themes in the Novels of Jean Rhys," *Contemporary Literature* 13.4 (1972), 458–74.

————. *Jean Rhys: A Descriptive and Annotated Bibliography of Works and Criticism.* New York: Garland, 1984.

Miles, Rosaline. *The Fiction of Sex*. London: Vision Press, 1974.

Miller, Nancy K. "Changing the Subject: Authorship, Writing, and the Reader," in *Feminist Studies/ Critical Studies*. Ed. Teresa de Lauretis. Bloomington: Indiana University Press, 1986.

Modleski, Tania. *Loving with a Vengeance: Mass-Produced Fantasies for Women*. Hamden, Conn.: Archon, 1982.

Moi, Toril. *Sexual/Textual Politics: Feminist Literary Theory*. London and New York: Methuen, 1985.

Morrell, A. C. "The World of Jean Rhys's Short Stories," *World Literature Written in English* 18 (1980), 235–44.

Mulvey, Laura. "Visual Pleasure and Narrative Cinema," *Screen* 16 (1975), 6–27.

Nebeker, Helen. *Jean Rhys: Woman in Passage*. Montreal: Women's Publications, 1981.

Newton, Judith and Rosenfelt, Deborah. Introduction to *Feminist Criticism and Social Change: Sex, Class and Race in Literature and Culture*. Ed. Newton and Rosenfelt. New York and London: Methuen, 1985.

Notman, Malkah. "The Psychology of Women: A Contemporary Appraisal," in *Psychoanalysis: Critical Explorations in Contemporary Theory and Practice*. Ed. Alan M. Jacobson and Dean X. Parmelee. New York: Brunner/Mazel, 1982. 29–55.

Oates, Joyce Carol. "A Visit with Doris Lessing," *The Southern Review* 9 (1973), 873–82.

Olsen, Tillie. *Yonnondio: From the Thirties*. New York: Dell, 1975.

O'Rourke, Rebecca. "Doris Lessing: Exile and Exception" in Taylor, 206–26.

Ostriker, Alicia. "American Poetry, Now Shaped by Women," *The New York Times Book Review*, March 9, 1986, 28.

Plante, David. *Difficult Women*. London: Victor Gollancz, 1983.

Pound, Ezra. *Collected Shorter Poems*. 2nd ed. London: Faber and Faber, 1968.

Pratt, Annis, and Dembo, L. S., eds. *Doris Lessing: Critical Studies*. Madison: University of Wisconsin Press, 1974.

Raskin, Jonah. "Christina Stead in Washington Square," *London Magazine* 9.11 (Feb. 1970), 70–77.

Reynolds, R. C. and Murray, B. J. "A Bibliography of Jean Rhys," *Bulletin of Bibliography* 36.4 (1980), 177–86.

Rhys, Jean. *After Leaving Mr Mackenzie*. New York: Random House, 1974.

———. "Fishy Waters." McFarlin Library, University of Tulsa. Dated 1960s or 1970s.

———. *Good Morning, Midnight*. New York: Random House, 1974.

———. "I Spy a Stranger" and "Temps Perdi" in *Penguin Modern Stories I*. Ed. Judith Burnley. London: Penguin, 1969. 53–88.

———. *The Left Bank and Other Stories*. Preface by Ford Madox Ford. New York and London: Harper and Brothers, [1927].

———. *The Letters of Jean Rhys*. Ed. Francis Wyndham and Diana Melly. New York: Viking, 1984.

———. "On Not Shooting Sitting Birds." McFarlin Library, University of Tulsa. Dated Oct. 20, 1974.

———. *Quartet*. New York: Random House, 1974.

———. *Sleep It Off, Lady*. New York: Popular Library, 1976.

———. *Smile Please*. Foreward by Diana Athill. New York: Harper and Row, 1979.

———. *Tigers Are Better-Looking*. New York: Popular Library, 1976.

———. "Vienne," *Transatlantic Review* 2 (Dec 1924), 639–45.

———. *Voyage in the Dark*. New York: Popular Library, n.d.

———. "Voyage in the Dark." McFarlin Library, University of Tulsa.

———. *Wide Sargasso Sea*. New York: Popular Library, c. 1966.

————. Black, Green, Red unpublished notebooks. McFarlin Library, University of Tulsa. Used with permission.

Rich, Adrienne. *Of Woman Born*. New York: Norton, 1976.

Rubenstein, Roberta. *The Novelistic Vision of Doris Lessing: Breaking the Forms of Consciousness*. Urbana: University of Illinois Press, 1979.

Ruddick, Sara. "Maternal Thinking," *Feminist Studies* 6.2 (1980), 342–67.

Sage, Lorna. *Doris Lessing*. London: Methuen, 1983.

Scharfman, Ronnie. "Mirroring and Mothering in Simone Schwartz-Bart's *Pluie et Vent sur Télumée Miracle* and Jean Rhys's *Wide Sargasso Sea*," *Yale French Studies* 62 (1981), 88–106.

Schlueter, Paul, ed. *The Fiction of Doris Lessing*. Evansville: University of Evansville, 1971.

Schweickart, Patrocinio. "Reading Ourselves: Toward a Feminist Theory of Reading," in Flynn and Schweickart. 31–62.

————. "Reading a Wordless Statement: The Structure of Doris Lessing's *The Golden Notebook*," *Modern Fiction Studies* 31.2 (Summer 1985), 263–79.

Seligman, Dee. *Doris Lessing: An Annotated Bibliography of Criticism*. Westport: Greenwood, 1981.

Shah, Idries. "The Tale of the Sands," in *Tales of the Dervishes*. New York: Dutton, 1970. 23–24.

Showalter, Elaine. "Feminist Criticism in the Wilderness," in *The New Feminist Criticism: Essays on Women, Literature and Theory*. Ed. Elaine Showalter. New York: Pantheon Books, 1985. 243–70.

————. *A Literature of their Own: British Women Novelists from Bronte to Lessing*. Princeton: Princeton, 1977.

Skura, Meredith Ann. *The Literary Use of the Psychoanalytic Process*. New Haven and London: Yale University Press, 1981.

Spacks, Patricia Meyer. *The Female Imagination*. New York: Knopf, 1975.

Spafford, Roswell. "The Politics of Pronouns: The Changing Nature of 'I' and 'We' in Doris Lessing's Work," in Bertelson, 178–86.

Sprague, Claire and Tiger, Virginia, eds. *Critical Essays on Doris Lessing*. Boston: G. K. Hall, 1986.

Squier, Susan Merrill. "Book Reviews," *Signs* 11.2 (Winter 1986), 405–409.

Staley, Thomas. *Jean Rhys: A Critical Study*. Austin: University of Texas Press, 1979.

Stanton, Domna. "Difference on Trial: A Critique of the Maternal Metaphor in Cixous, Irigaray, and Kristeva," in *The Poetics of Gender*. Ed. Nancy K. Miller. New York: Columbia University Press, 1986. 157–82.

Stead, Christina. *The Beauties and Furies*. New York: Appleton-Century, 1936.

————. *Cotter's England*. London: Virago, 1980. American title *Dark Places of the Heart*.

————. *For Love Alone*. New York and London: Harvest/HBJ, c. 1972.

————. *House of All Nations*. New York: Avon, 1966.

————. *I'm Dying Laughing: The Humourist*. Ed. and preface by R. G. Geering. New York: Henry Holt, 1987.

————. "The Impartial Young Man," review of *Inhale and Exhale* by William Saroyan, *New Masses* 18 (17 March 1936), 25–26.

————. Letter to author, 1977.

————. Letters to E. F. Patterson of Davidson, N.C., May 16, 1975 and June 19, 1975. Used with permission of Mr. Patterson.

————. *The Little Hotel*. New York: Avon, 1980.

————. *A Little Tea, A Little Chat*. New York: Harcourt Brace, 1948.

————. *The Man Who Loved Children*. New York: Avon, 1966. Afterword by Randall Jarrell.

————. *Miss Herbert (The Suburban Wife)*. New York: Random House, 1976.

————. *Letty Fox, Her Luck.* New York: Harcourt Brace, 1946.

————. *Ocean of Story.* Ed R.G. Geering. New York: Viking, 1985.

————. *The People with the Dogs.* London: Virago, 1981.

————. "On The Women's Movement," *Partisan Review* 46.2 (1979), 271-74.

————. *The Puzzleheaded Girl: Four Novellas.* New York: Holt, Rinehart & Winston, c. 1967.

————. *The Salzburg Tales.* New York and London: Appleton-Century, 1934.

————. *Seven Poor Men of Sydney.* New York and London: Appleton-Century, 1935.

————. "Some Deep Spell: A View of Stanley Burnshaw," *Agenda* 21.4 (1983–84), 125–39.

————. "What Goal in Mind," in *We Took Their Orders and Are Dead: An Anti-War Anthology.* Ed. Shirley Cass, Ros Cheney, David Malouf, and Michael Wilding. Sydney: Ure Smith, 1971. 119–30.

————. "The Writers Take Sides," *Left Review* 1.11 (August 1935), 453–62.

Stead, Christina, and Blake, William, eds. *Modern Women in Love: Sixty Twentieth-Century Masterpieces of Fiction.* New York: Dryden Press, 1945.

Stern, Frederick. "The Changing Voice of Lessing's Characters: From Politics to Sci Fi," *World Literature Written in English,* 21.3 (1982), 456–67.

Sturm, Terry. "Christina Stead's New Realism: *The Man Who Loved Children* and *Cotter's England,*" in *Cunning Exiles: Studies of Modern Prose Writers.* Ed. Don Anderson and Stephen Knight. Sydney: Angus and Robertson, 1974.

Sukenick, Lynn. "Feeling and Reason in Doris Lessing's Fiction," *Contemporary Literature* 14 (1973), 515–35.

Taylor, Jenny, ed. *Notebooks/Memoirs/Archives: Reading and Rereading Doris Lessing.* Boston and London: Routledge and Kegan Paul, 1982.

Thorne, Barrie and Henley, Nancy. "Difference and Dominance: an Overview of Language, Gender, and Society," in *Language and Sex: Difference and Dominance.* Rowley, Mass.: Newbury House, 1975. 5–42.

Thorpe, Michael. *Doris Lessing's Africa.* London: Evanson, 1978.

Vreeland, Elizabeth. "Jean Rhys: The Art of Fiction," *Paris Review* No. 76 (1979), 218–37.

Waldman, Diane. " 'At Last I Can Tell It to Someone!': Feminine Point of View and Subjectivity in the Gothic Romance Film of the 1940s," *Cinema Journal* 23.2 (Winter 1983), 29–40.

Walker, Alice. *The Color Purple.* New York and London: Harcourt Brace Jovanovich, 1982.

Wetherell, Rodney. "Christina Stead Talks to Rodney Wetherell," *Overland,* 93 (1983), 17–29.

White, Edmund. "The Woman Who Loved Memory," review of *Ocean of Story, New York Times Book Review,* May 25, 1986, 7.

Whitehead, Ann. "Christina Stead: An Interview," *Australian Literary Studies,* 6.3 (May 1974), 230–48.

Williams, Linda. " 'Something Else Besides a Mother': *Stella Dallas* and the Maternal Melodrama," *Cinema Journal,* 24.1 (Fall 1984), 2–27.

Winnicott, D. W. *Playing and Reality.* New York: Basic Books, 1971.

Wolf, Ernest S. "Empathy and Countertransference" and "Concluding Statement" in *The Future of Psychoanalysis: Essays in Honor of Heinz Kohut.* Ed. Arnold Goldberg. New York: International Universities Press, 1983. 309–26, 495–505.

Wolfe, Peter. *Jean Rhys.* Boston: G K Hall, Twayne Publishers, 1980.

Woolf, Virginia. *A Room of One's Own.* New York and London: Harcourt Brace Jovanovich, 1957.

Wyndham, Francis. Introduction to *The Letters of Jean Rhys.* Ed. Francis Wyndham and Diana Melly. New York: Viking, 1984. 9–12.

Yglesias, Jose. "Marx as Muse," *Nation* 5 April 1965. 368–70.

Young-Eisendrath, Polly and Hall, James A. Introduction to *The Book of the Self: Person, Pretext, and Process*. Ed. Polly Young-Eisendrath and James A. Hall. New York and London: New York University Press, 1988. 1–10.

Ziegler, Heide and Bigsby, Christopher, eds. *The Radical Imagination and the Liberal Tradition: Interviews with English and American Novelists*. London: Junction Books, 1982.

INDEX

**Help us preserve
our collection.
Report damage at
Circulation Desk.**

**You are
responsible for
materials borrowed
on your card.**